Adobe
Photoshop CS2
A–Z

Picture credits

Author's dedication

Always for Kassy-Lee and my great kids Adrian and Ellena.

Cheers to Peter Bargh for all his hard work making this title the
success it already is and my thanks to him for allowing me to
carry on the tradition he started.

Thanks also to the enthusiastic and very supportive staff at Focal
Press including Marie Hooper, Christina Donaldson, Emma
Baxter, Margaret Denley, Georgia Kennedy and Stephanie Barrett.

My appreciation goes to Bryan O'Neil Hughes at Adobe for his
support, technical advice and kind Foreword. And thanks once
more to Adobe for bringing image enhancement and editing to us
all through their innovative and industry-leading products, and
the other hardware and software manufacturers whose help is an
essential part of writing any book of this nature. In particular I
wish to thank technical and marketing staff at Adobe, Microsoft,
Canon, Nikon, and Epson. Also to Manfred 'Grids Rule!' Huber for
his design guidance.

And finally my thanks to all the readers who continue to inspire
and encourage me with their generous praise and great images.
Keep emailing me to let me know how your imaging is going.

Adobe Photoshop CS2 A–Z

Tools and features illustrated ready reference

Philip Andrews

AMSTERDAM • BOSTON • HEIDELBERG • LONDON • NEW YORK • OXFORD
PARIS • SAN DIEGO • SAN FRANCISCO • SINGAPORE • SYDNEY • TOKYO
Focal Press is an imprint of Elsevier

ELSEVIER

Focal Press

Focal Press
An imprint of Elsevier
Linacre House, Jordan Hill, Oxford OX2 8DP
30 Corporate Drive, Burlington MA 01803

First published 2005

British Library Cataloguing in Publication Data
A catalogue record for this book is available from the British Library

Library of Congress Cataloguing in Publication Data
A catalogue record for this book is available from the Library of Congress

ISBN   0 240 52002 5

For information on all Focal Press publications visit our website at: www.focalpress.com

Printed and bound in Italy

Layout and design by Philip Andrews in Adobe InDesign CS

Contents ....

A B C D E F G H IJK L M N O PQ R S T U V W XYZ

Foreword ....

I've been using Photoshop fanatically since version 3.0 and have worked on the Photoshop team at Adobe since before version 6.0; and yet, a week doesn't pass without finding new functionality in this amazing application of ours. This is a testament to both the power and complexity of the program.

I've also tech-edited several titles over the years, but none are as quick to reference or as intuitive as Philip Andrews' *Adobe Photoshop CS2 A–Z*. A dictionary of terms is a wonderful addition to any imaging library; one specific to Photoshop that wrangles complex concepts and offers intuitive solutions, as this book does, is invaluable.

Fresh off the Photoshop CS2 development cycle, I was well versed in the many new features of the application. Upon my first readings, I was surprised and extremely pleased to find new, relevant and very in-depth sections for all of our new features in this text.

Having read and reread this book, I can tell you that it has and will continue to be an extension of my Photoshop user experience. As with so many things related to Photoshop, this book will be a complement to my life at and beyond work.

I hope that you discover and learn often, as I have, with the help of this essential book.

Bryan O'Neil Hughes
Adobe Quality Engineer
Adobe Systems Inc.

Introduction ·················

Now in its ninth release
Photoshop is undoubtedly the
King of photo-editing software
and considering the host of
new and revamped features included in the CS2 version of the program its position at
the top of the heap is assured.

The software is so popular with photographers, designers and illustrators that it is
truly hard to recall a time when we didn't have Photoshop at the centre of our creative
endeavors. With the massive upsurge of digital camera owners there is now a host of
new photographers who are just discovering the pure editing and enhancement power
afforded by the program.

Given the success of previous editions it would have been easy for Adobe to sit back
and bask in the reflected glory of the program's popularity but instead Adobe has been
hard at work improving what was already a great product. The CS2 version, just like
the releases before it, is a state-of-the-art image-editing program full of the features
and functions that digital photographers and desktop image makers desire the most.

In fact, the program has become so comprehensive that producing an illustrated A–Z
book like this one is not just a nicety, but has became a necessity. The software covers
so many areas that Photoshop users needed a quick ready-reference guide to all the
major tools and features. Peter Bargh, in the first few editions of this text, provided
just such a comprehensive guide to the program and here I add to his excellent work.
As was Peter's approach, I haven't stopped at simply describing the tool or feature, I
accompany the text with illustrations of the software in action together with before
and after pictures of the applied changes.

All entries include shortcut keys, menu locations and are cross-referenced to other
Photoshop features that relate. Many features also include step-by-step guides to their
usage and extended visual examples of the effects of using different settings on your
pictures.

Keep this ready reference handy for all those occasions when you ask yourself 'What
does that do?'

But most of all keep enjoying your digital image making!

Philip Andrews

How to use this book...

In order to make the most out of this book, take a couple of minutes to read the following. This will let me introduce a few of the special features that I have included to help you find the information that you need fast. Apart from the basic A–Z structure that lists the topics, features and tools alphabetically, I have also used the following design devices to make 'search and locate' missions speedier and more productive.

Feature summary

Each feature and tool entry is headed with a summary table that details the menu where the feature can be found, any keyboard shortcuts associated with the tool, the version of Photoshop that contains the feature and any other features that are linked to the feature.

Edge tabs

The colored edge tabs change for each letter section. They can be used in conjunction with the contents page to quickly thumb through the book to locate a particular group of entries.

Before and after examples

The before and after examples illustrate how features, tools and techniques can be used to change the way that your pictures look.

Tips and reminders

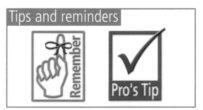

Important ideas and techniques are highlighted with the 'Remember' icon and the tips and tricks used by working professionals are noted with the 'Pro's Tip' ticked box.

CS2 features highlighted

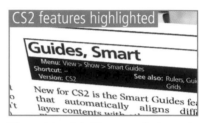

The entries detailing new features in Photoshop CS2 are highlighted in red and lableled 'New for CS2'.

Online extensions

Don't forget about the book's website – **www.photoshop-a-z.com**. Here you will find video tutorials on how to use the top new features in Photoshop CS2, the example pictures used in the step-by-step guides, links to all the featured plug-in vendors and much more.

Step-by-step application

Selected features include step-by-step guides designed to demonstrate how to use the tool or feature. These mini-tutorials can be used to extend your understanding as well as build your editing and enhancement skills.

© www.alamistock.com 2005

Accented Edges filter

Menu: Filters > Brush Strokes > Accented Edges
Shortcut: Ctrl F   **See also:** Ink Outlines filter
Version: 6.0, 7.0, CS, CS2

The Accented Edges filter searches out the edges within a picture and then highlights them with a line. The size of the line is controlled by the Edge Width slider (1) in the filter's dialog. The darkness or lightness of the line is determined by the Edge Brightness slider (2). A high value produces a lightly colored edge that appears like chalk and a low value, like the one used in the illustration here, creates an ink-like outline. The Smoothness slider (3) is used to even out the roughness of jagged edges of the line.

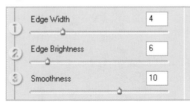

Actions

Menu: Window > Actions
Shortcut: Alt/Opt F9   **See also:** Batch command,
Version: 6.0, 7.0, CS, CS2   Droplet

An action is a way of automatically applying a technique to an image using a pre-recorded series of commands. Actions are triggered either by pressing one or a combination of keys or selecting the action from the Actions palette (1). Many actions are already supplied with Photoshop and can be found at the bottom of the Actions menu (2) by clicking on the side-arrow at the top right of the Actions palette.

An action can be as simple as opening a new canvas or as advanced as creating a drop shadow on an existing picture or as in our example making snow.

Ready-made actions can be downloaded from the internet, saved to your hard drive and then installed in Photoshop. Use the Load Actions command (3) in the Actions menu to search for and install the downloaded ATN or Photoshop Actions file.

You can also create your own Photoshop actions using the Record mode, so if there are techniques you find particularly fiddly or ones you'll want to use again, record the commands as you run through them and assign the action a shortcut key.

1. Actions can also be applied to several images in one go using the Batch command or created into droplets.

2. If a command cannot be recorded you can insert it manually using the Insert Menu command.

3. If you make a mistake, keep going, you can edit the script later.

4. Some settings may need modifying for different images. Clicking on the box to the left of the action will stop the script at that point and bring up the dialog box so that you can manually adjust before continuing the script.

Before

After

Active layer

Menu: –
Shortcut: –   See also: –
Version: 6.0, 7.0, CS, CS2

The Layers feature is great for creating pictures that are made up of a variety of parts. But the way in which the feature works means that it is only possible to edit or enhance one layer at a time. You must activate the layer first before applying changes.

To select the layer, click on its thumbnail in the Layers palette. At this point the layer will change to a different color from the rest in the stack. The layer is now active and can be edited in isolation from the others that make up the picture.

Add Noise filter

Menu: Filter > Noise > Add Noise
Shortcut: Ctrl F   See also: Grain filter,
Version: 6.0, 7.0, CS, CS2   Texturizer filter

Many photographers like to replicate the look of film grain in their digital photographs. Using the Add Noise filter is one way to introduce this texture into your digital pictures. The filter adds random speckled pixels to your picture. A small amount of noise can be applied to gradients to prevent banding when printed.

The filter uses a single Amount slider to control the strength of the texture effect. The higher the setting the more obvious the results will be. Two different types of texture are provided – Uniform and Gaussian. The Uniform option adds the noise evenly across all the tones in the picture. In contrast the Gaussian setting concentrates the noise in the midtones with fewer changes being applied to the highlight and shadow areas. Selecting the Monochrome option restricts the noisy pixels added to white, black and gray only.

Adjustment layers

Menu: Layer > New Adjustment Layer
Shortcut: Layers palette button   See also: Grain filter,
Version: 6.0, 7.0, CS, CS2   Fill Layers

These special layers alter the look of the layers that are arranged below them in the stack. They act as a filter through which the lower layers are viewed. You can use adjustment layers to perform many of the enhancement tasks that you would normally apply directly to an image layer without changing the image itself.

CS2 contains twelve different adjustment layers which are grouped with the Fill layers under the Create Adjustment Layer button (1) in the Layers palette. They are:

Levels – Adjusts the tones in the picture.

Curves – Adjust the tones in the picture.

Color Balance – Used for adding or removing color casts from images.

Brightness/Contrast – Lightens, darkens and controls contrast.

Hue/Saturation – Changes the color and strength of color in photos.

Selective Color – Adjusts the hue of a single group of colors.

Channel Mixer – Changes the color makeup of individual channels and in the monochrome mode creates great black and white conversions from color pictures.

Gradient Map – Changes the photo so that all the tones are mapped to the values of a selected gradient.

Invert – Reverses all the tones in a picture, producing a negative effect.

Threshold – Converts the picture to pure black and white with no grays present at all.

Photo Filter – Reproduces the color changes of traditional photo filters.

Posterize – Reduces the total number of colors in a picture and creates a flat paint (or poster)-like effect.

Adobe Online

Menu: Help > Photoshop Online
Shortcut: –   See also: –
Version: 6.0, 7.0, CS, CS2

Users can be transported directly to Adobe's official Photoshop (and ImageReady) website by clicking on the picture icon (feather for CS and CS2) at the top of the toolbar (1). This action displays your default web browser and automatically loads the Photoshop home page.

The same web page is displayed if you select Help > Photoshop Online (2).

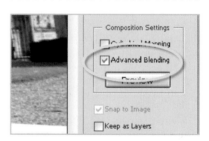

Advanced Blending

Menu: File > Automate > Photomerge
Shortcut: –   See also: Photomerge
Version: CS, CS2

The Advanced Blending option in the Photomerge workspace provides an automatic approach to balancing the color and tone of sequential pictures in a composition. The feature is designed to even out slight exposure or color differences that can occur when creating source images. When used in conjunction with the Preview button the results can be reviewed on screen before proceeding to the creation of the full panorama. On some occasions it is difficult to assess the accuracy of the blending action via the preview. If this occurs then create several different panoramas applying different Blending, Perspective and Mapping settings for each.

Aliased text

Anti-aliased text

Before

After

Airbrush

Menu: –
Shortcut: B then Airbrush button from the options bar   **See also:** Brush tool
Version: 6.0, 7.0, CS, CS2

A painting tool that applies a color in much the same way as a real airbrush. The airbrush moved from the toolbar in Photoshop 7.0 and now appears in the brush options bar. Now you simply choose airbrush as a style and select how you want it to work from the Brush palette.

Hold down the mouse and drag it around to spray color evenly onto the canvas. Hold it in the same place and color builds up while spreading outwards. Covering an area that's already sprayed increases color depth.

As with all brush modes you can specify size, blending mode and opacity from the bar that appears at the top of the page when you click on a brush. There's also an option to adjust flow.

Pro's Tip

1. Select a start point, hold down the Shift key and then click an end point to paint a straight line.

2. Use the airbrush on low pressure with black paint to create shadows.

3. Press the Caps lock key to turn the airbrush standard cursor into a precision cross hair.

Aliasing

Menu: –
Shortcut: –   **See also:** Anti-aliasing fonts,
Version: 6.0, 7.0, CS, CS2   Anti-aliasing selections

Even though the lettering system in Photoshop is based on smooth-edged (vector) technology, when type layers are flattened into the background, or the PSD file is saved in the JPEG format, the type is converted to pixels. One of the drawbacks of using a pixel system is that curves and diagonal lines are recreated with a series of pixel steps. When viewed closely, or printed very large, these steps can become obvious and appear as a saw-tooth pattern. This is called 'aliasing'.

Anti-aliasing is a system where the effects of these 'jaggies' are made less noticeable by partially filling in the edge pixels. This technique produces smoother looking type overall and should be used in all print circumstances and web applications.

Align Linked

Menu: Layer > Align
Shortcut: –   **See also:** Arrange
Version: CS, CS2

The Aligned Linked feature was introduced in Photoshop CS to make it easier to align items within layers.

Select this option and one of the six align options to make objects on linked layers align to the top, center or bottom edge in either horizontal or vertical directions.

In CS2 the Align option also functions with multi-selected layers that are not linked.

The Align options are located in the Layer menu (1) and are also present on the options bar (2) when multi-layers are selected.

Aligning type

Menu: –
Shortcut: –   See also: Channels
Version: 6.0, 7.0, CS, CS2

The terms alignment and justification are often used interchangeably and refer to the way that a line or paragraph of text is positioned on the image.

The left align feature will arrange all text to the left of the text frame. When applied to a group of sentences the left edge of the paragraph is organized into a straight vertical line whilst the right-hand edge remains uneven or ragged.

Right align works in the opposite fashion, straightening the right-hand edge of the paragraph and leaving the left ragged.

Selecting the center text option will align the paragraph around a central line and leave both left and right edges ragged.

Select the type alignment before entering the text into your document. Do this by pressing the appropriate alignment button in the Type tool options bar.

To change the alignment of existing text use the cursor to highlight the letters and then press the chosen alignment button.

Before

After

All command

Menu: Select > Select All
Shortcut: Ctrl/Cmd A   See also: Selections
Version: 6.0, 7.0, CS, CS2

The All command, found under the Select menu, encompasses the whole picture with a selection marquee. This command is

Alpha channel

Menu: –
Shortcut: –   See also: Channels
Version: 6.0, 7.0, CS, CS2

These are ideal for saving selections separate from the RGB or CMYK channels. Carefully draw round a subject and choose Select > Save Selection once you're happy with the selection. The selection is stored at the base of the Channels palette as a separate channel – the Alpha channel. It can be recalled and the selection applied to the image at any time by calling up Load Selection from the Select menu. This saves you having to reselect a subject later.

Over 50 Alpha channels can added to an RGB image allowing you to produce very complex selections that can be recalled to make changes to a variety of detailed parts of the image at any time.

Alpha channels can also used to create depth maps which can be loaded into Lens Blur.

the first step in a simple border creation technique that also uses the Stroke feature. See below.

Open a suitable photo into the Editor workspace. Use the Select > All command to place a marquee around the whole canvas.

With the selection still active choose Edit > Stroke. In the Stroke dialog that appears, pick the width of the stroke (line) and its color. Next select the Inside option as the location. Click OK to draw the colored border.

Angle gradient tool

Menu: –
Shortcut: G (Gradient tool)   See also: Gradients
Version: 6.0, 7.0, CS, CS2

Photoshop has no less than five gradient types for you to play with. All the gradient options gradually change color and tone from one point in the picture to another. The Angle gradient (1) gradually changes the color in a counterclockwise direction around the starting point.

Angle option – Brush

Menu: –
Shortcut: B (Brush tool)   See also: Brush Presets
Version: 6.0, 7.0, CS, CS2

One of the strengths of Photoshop as a drawing package is the flexibility of its brush engine. Rather than just supplying a series of pre-made brushes Adobe includes the ability to create and save custom brushes.

The Brushes palette, which is opened with the Brushes palette button on the Brush options bar, contains controls for changing dozens of different brush characteristics. The brush angle is one of these custom characteristics.

Changing the angle will rotate the brush tip resulting in a diagonal stroke when dragged across canvas. To make the brush tip slant, select the Brush Tip Shape option from the list on the left, alter the angle value (1). The change in brush shape is previewed on the bottom right of the dialog (2).

Angled Strokes filter

Menu: Filter > Brush Strokes > Angled Strokes
Shortcut: Ctrl F   **See also:** –
Version: 6.0, 7.0, CS, CS2

The Angled Strokes filter, as one of the group of Brush Strokes filters, repaints the picture using diagonal strokes. The brush strokes in the light area of the photo are drawn in one direction and those in the darker parts in the opposite direction.

The Direction Balance (1), Stroke Length (2) and Sharpness (3) of the brush effect are controlled by the sliders in the filter dialog.

Animated GIFs

Menu: File > Save for Web
Shortcut: Alt/Opt Shft Ctrl/Cmd S   **See also:** GIF format
Version: 6.0, 7.0, CS, CS2

One of the characteristics of the GIF file format is that it is capable of storing and displaying simple animations. To take advantage of this feature Adobe has merged traditional techniques with the multi-layer abilities of its PSD file structure to give Photoshop users the chance to produce their own animations.

Essentially, the idea is to make an image file with several layers, the content of each being a little different from the one before. The layers are then converted to frames in frames using the Animation palette (new for CS2). Other options in the palette enable you to change the frame delay setting and indicate whether you want the animation to repeat (loop) or play a single time only. The file is then saved in the animation friendly GIF format.

As the GIF is a format used for small animations on the Net, the moving masterpiece can be viewed with any web browser, or placed on the website to add some action to otherwise static pages.

The easiest way to save a GIF file is via the Save for Web feature. The Save for Web dialog contains the original image and a GIF compressed version of the picture.

Create a Photoshop file with several layers of differing content. Display the Animation palette and convert the layers to frames with the Make Frames From Layers option in the side-button menu (top right).

Adjust the frame delay option (1) to control the length of time each individual image is displayed. Select the number of times that the animation will play from the drop-down menu (2).

Select the Save for Web option from the File menu. Choose GIF as the file type. Preview the animation by clicking the browser preview button at the bottom of the screen or by clicking the VCR buttons to the right of the preview. Select OK to save the file.

Animation, Photoshop

Menu: Window > Animation
Shortcut: –   **See also:** Animated GIFs
Version: CS2

In CS2, the boundaries between Photoshop and ImageReady continue to blur with the introduction of the Animation palette into the Photoshop workspace.

Now it is possible to create simple animation sequences using the separate layers of a Photoshop document. The time that each frame is displayed and the sequence that they are shown in is easily altered in the palette. There is even an option of automatically 'tweening' from one key frame to another.

The Animation palette includes the following options:

Looping controls (1), VCR type play, stop, previous/next frame and first frame buttons (2), tweening control (3), duplicate selected frame (4) and delete selected frame (5). Extra animation options are located on the fly-out menu accessed via the sideways arrow on the top right of the palette (6).

Animation controls and options can also be displayed in the Layers palette (7) by selecting this option from side-arrow menu.

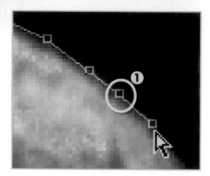

Anchor points

Menu: –
Shortcut: –   **See also:** –
Version: 7.0, CS, CS2

Anchor points (1) are the small square boxes that are placed around an object when you make a selection with the Pen tool.

The points can be moved when they've been placed using the Direct Selection tool (2).

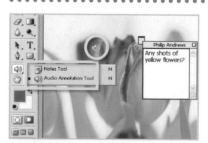

Annotations

Menu: –
Shortcut: N   **See also:** –
Version: 7.0, CS, CS2

Photoshop contains two annotation tools that can be accessed directly from the toolbox.

Anti-aliasing, fonts

Menu: –
Shortcut: –   **See also:** Aliasing
Version: 6.0, 7.0, CS, CS2

To make the edge of text appear less jagged, select one of the anti-aliasing options in the drop-down menu located on the Type tools option bar. This feature smooths out the saw-tooth edges that appear on letter shapes that have diagonal or circular sides.

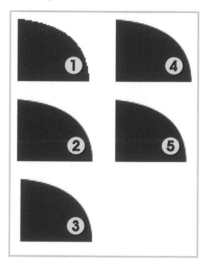

The *Notes Tool* allows users to add typewritten notes to the surface of a photograph. These sticky notes are saved with the file and are present when the picture is reopened. The author, size and color of the note can be altered via the settings in the options bar.

The *Audio Annotation Tool* provides you with the ability to record and attach a small sound file to the picture. Again this file is saved with the original picture and is available after reopening. After selecting the tool, click onto the picture surface and then press the Start button in the pop-up dialog. Speak your message and then press the Stop button.

The Annotations feature is supported by the PDF, PDP, PSD and PSB file formats.

Anti-aliasing, selections

Menu: –	
Shortcut: –	**See also:** Feather command,
Version: 6.0, 7.0, CS, CS2	Aliasing

Selections can be created with sharp or soft edges. You can soften the edge in two ways – by feathering, or by using the anti-aliasing feature in the Selection tool's options bar (which is activated by default when the tool is first selected).

Like the anti-aliasing effect for type-faces this feature softens the edges of the selection by smoothing the transition between selected and non-selected areas. The option must be selected before making the selection. Unlike feathering it cannot be applied later on.

Use this feature to help conceal the edges of pasted picture parts in newly created compositions.

The anti-aliasing option works with the Lasso, Polygonal Lasso, Magnetic Lasso, Elliptical marquee and the Magic Wand tool.

Arrange

Menu: Layer > Arrange	
Shortcut: –	**See also:** Bring to Front, Bring
Version: 6.0, 7.0, CS, CS2	Forward, Send Backward, Send to Back, Reverse, layer order

The order of layers in the layer stack can be altered by selecting a layer to move and then choosing an option from those listed in the Layer > Arrange menu.

In the example the 'Top' text layer was selected and then the Send Backward option was chosen from the Layer > Arrange menu. This results in the 'Top' layer moving below the 'Middle' layer in the stack with the consequence that the 'Middle' layer text now partially obscures the contents of the 'Top' layer.

Arrowhead options

Menu: –	
Shortcut: U (Line tool)	**See also:** Shape tools
Version: 6.0, 7.0, CS, CS2	

The Line tool is one of the vector-based or sharp-edged shape tools in Photoshop. Along with settings for color, weight and style the Line tool's option bar also contains a drop-down menu with controls for creating arrowheads on the lines you draw.

From within the dialog you can select to apply the head to the start or end of the line, adjust the width and length of the arrow as well as control its concavity. The percentages used here are based on the line weight.

These options need to be set before drawing the line on the canvas surface. The example arrows below are drawn with the following settings:

(1) End, Width 500%, Length 1000%

(2) End, Width 500%, Length 1000%, Concavity 50%

(3) Start and End, Width 500%, Length 1000%, Concavity 50%

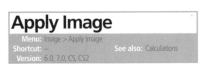

Apply Image

Menu: Image > Apply Image	
Shortcut: –	**See also:** Calculations
Version: 6.0, 7.0, CS, CS2	

Used to blend one image layer and channel with another. The source and destination image have to be the same size.

I found the effect works well using the same image with the blend option. It's

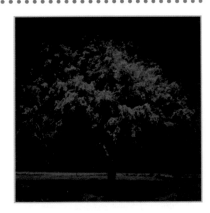

very much a trial and error process but well worth the effort as seen here, as I've appeared to change the time of day in one simple step.

Before

Overall

Before

After

Detail

After

Art History Brush

Menu:	–	
Shortcut:	Y	See also: History Brush
Version:	6.0, 7.0, CS, CS2	

This is a feature that was first introduced in version 5.5 and continues to appeal to artists as, with a little experimentation, it can create some stunning painterly effects.

You can choose from a variety of patterns, Blending modes and opacity settings before painting over an existing image. The more you paint over the same area the more pronounced the effect will be. The larger the brush, the bigger the paint daub texture becomes and the less realistic the final results.

Pro's Tip

Using one of the other custom brush tips from Photoshop's brush presets will produce more unusual effects.

Artifacts

Menu:	–	
Shortcut:	–	See also: JPEG artifact
Version:	–	removal

Digital photography, like any form of image capture, can produce faults and these are referred to as artifacts. They can be caused by a number of problems including flare from the camera's lens, electrical interference or low resolution CCDs. Low resolution CCDs cause curved edges to appear jagged as the curve takes on the square edges of each pixel – known as aliasing.

But the most common of all artifacts present in digital photographs are those produced by saving the image with a high compression setting. Notice the halos around the contrasty sections of the example picture.

Artistic filters

Menu:	Filter > Artistic, Filter > Filter Gallery > Artistic	
Shortcut:	–	See also: Filters
Version:	6.0, 7.0, CS, CS2	

Change your picture into a painterly image using this collection of filters that mimic natural or traditional artists' effects. Each filter has a selection of sliders which control the strength and style of the effect. I'll explain the Colored Pencil filter below.

For a little more control over the effects try using the Edit > Fade option with a Blend mode after having applied the filter.

In the example, the Colored Pencil filter has produced a rough crosshatch effect by drawing in a pencil style over the original using the background color. Edges are retained and the original background image shows through the pencil strokes. Moving the pencil width slider to the left makes the pencil lines thin while sliding to the right makes them thick.

Stroke pressure controls the accuracy of the lines over the original image.

The paper brightness slider affects the color of the pencil. Move it to the right for the maximum color. Moving the slider to the middle produces a progressively gray pencil effect and to the left it goes black.

Before

After

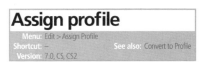

Aspect ratio

Menu: –
Shortcut: –   See also: Constrain Proportions
Version: 6.0, 7.0, CS, CS2

The aspect ratio or Constrain Proportions option is usually found in dialog boxes concerned with changes of image size and refers to the relationship between width and height of a picture.

The maintaining of an image's aspect ratio means that this relationship will remain the same even when the image is enlarged or reduced.

For example, failing to select the Constrain Proportions option in the Image > Image Size dialog will result in pictures that are squashed or stretched out of proportion.

Assign profile

Menu: Edit > Assign Profile
Shortcut: –   See also: Convert to Profile
Version: 7.0, CS, CS2

You can choose to attach a different ICC profile to an image by selecting the Edit > Assign Profile option. This feature lets you assign the chosen color space to the picture without changing the value of the image's colors to the profile.

In contrast, the Convert to Profile option available from the same menu changes the color values of the original image to match the newly selected color space.

Auto Color Correction

Menu: Image > Adjustments > Auto Color
Shortcut: Shft Ctrl\Cmd B   See also: Auto Levels
Version: 6.0, 7.0, CS, CS2

The Auto Color Correction feature works in a similar way to tools like Auto Levels and Auto Contrast, providing a one-click fix for most color problems.

Unlike these other tools it concentrates on correcting the color in the midtones of the picture and adjusting the contrast by reassigning the brightest and darkest pixels to white and black.

Sometimes such automatic fixes do not produce the results that you expect. In these scenarios use the Undo (Edit > Undo) command to reverse the changes and try one of the manual correction tools such as Color Balance or Variations.

Before

After

y: 100% ▶ ☑ Auto Erase

Before

After

Auto Contrast

Menu: Image > Adjustments > Auto Contrast
Shortcut: Ctrl/Cmd Alt/Opt Shft L   **See also:** Auto Levels
Version: 6.0, 7.0, CS, CS2

Auto Contrast is designed to correct images that are either too contrasty (black and white) or too flat (dull and lifeless).

Unlike the Auto Levels feature, Auto Contrast ensures that the brightest and darkest pixels in the picture (irrespective of their colors) are converted to pure white and black. In doing so all the tones in between are expanded or contracted to fit.

Apply Auto Contrast to grayscale photos like the example or pictures whose contrast needs improving but have a strong color tint that you wish to retain.

Pro's Tip

This feature is a good correction option if Auto Levels creates more color cast problems than it corrects.

Auto Erase, pencil

Menu: –
Shortcut: N (Pencil)   **See also:** Pencil tool
Version: 6.0, 7.0, CS, CS2

The Pencil tool draws hard-edged lines using the foreground color. Selecting the Auto Erase feature in the options bar changes the way the tool applies this color.

When drawing over any color other than the foreground color the pencil will draw in the foreground color (1). In Auto Erase mode starting a drawing on a picture part that is the foreground color will cause the pencil to switch to the background color (2). The tool draws over all other picture parts with the foreground color.

Auto Levels

Menu: Image > Adjustments > Auto Levels
Shortcut: Ctrl/Cmd Shft L   **See also:** Auto Contrast
Version: 6.0, 7.0, CS, CS2

The Auto Levels command is similar to Auto Contrast in that it maps the brightest and darkest parts of the image to white and black. It differs from the previous technique because each individual color channel is treated separately.

In the process of mapping the tones (adjusting the contrast) in the Red, Green and Blue channels, dominant color casts can be neutralized.

This is not always the case; it depends entirely on the makeup of the image. In some cases the reverse is true; when Auto Levels is put to work on a neutral image a strong cast results. If this occurs, undo (Edit > Undo) the command and apply the Auto Contrast feature instead.

Auto Select Layer

Menu: –
Shortcut: V (Move tool)   **See also:** Bounding Box,
Version: 6.0, 7.0, CS, CS2   Move tool

The Move tool is often used for repositioning contents of different layers. The layer to be moved is first selected in the layer stack and then the tool is clicked and dragged to move the layer contents.

Picking the Auto Select Layer mode (1) from the Move tool's options bar can make the layer selection process easier and more interactive.

Clicking onto the picture surface whilst in this mode will automatically select the uppermost layer that has a picture part positioned under the pointer.

In CS2, when the Auto Select Layer feature is chosen, you have a further option of Auto Select Groups (2) which allows users to automatically select groups of layers with a single click.

Automate

Menu: File > Automate
Shortcut: –   **See also:** Automate, Bridge
Version: 6.0, 7.0, CS, CS2

The options listed under the Automate menu are designed to make complex editing, enhancement and presentation jobs easier.

The *Contact Sheet II, PDF Presentation, Picture Package* and *Web Photo Gallery* options all take a series of photographs and convert them into a finished presentation document by walking the user through several wizard-like dialogs.

The *Batch* command automatically applies a previously recorded Photoshop Action to a folder of photos. The *Create Droplet* option extends this ability by generating an editing utility based on an action. The droplet sits on the desktop and pictures are processed by dragging the image file onto the droplet icon.

The *Photomerge* feature creates wide landscape images from a series of overlapping source pictures that are stitched together.

Merge to HDR is a new automate feature and is designed to combine differently exposed source images of the same location to produce a 32 bits per channel high dynamic range file.

Conditional Mode Change and *Fit Image* are two utilities that are often incorporated into actions as a way to ensure consistent color results and predictable image sizes.

Automate, Bridge

Menu: Bridge: Tools > Photoshop
Shortcut: –   **See also:** Automate
Version: CS2

Many of the options that are available under the File > Automate menu in Photoshop can also be selected from the Tools > Photoshop heading in Bridge.

Though when these features are selected they open the Photoshop workspace in order to complete their tasks, having them situated in Bridge means that you can multi-select the files to enhance directly from the browser workspace.

The Tools menu is also the place where extra features that are based on scripts and written by third party providers are displayed.

bB

Background color

Menu: –
Shortcut: –   See also: Foreground color,
Version: 6.0, 7.0, CS, CS2   Eyedropper tool

Photoshop bases many of its drawing, painting and filter effects on two colors – the foreground and background colors. The currently selected foreground and background colors are shown at the bottom of the toolbox as two colored swatches. The topmost swatch (1) represents the foreground color, the one beneath (2) the hue for the background.

The default for these colors is black and white but it is possible to customize the selections at any time. Click the swatch and then select a new color from the color picker window (5).

To switch foreground and background colors click the double-headed curved arrow at the top right (3) and to restore the default (black and white) click the mini swatches bottom left (4).

Background Eraser tool

Menu: –
Shortcut: E   See also: Eraser tool
Version: 6.0, 7.0, CS, CS2

The Background Eraser is used to delete pixels around the edge of an object. This tool is very useful for extracting objects from their surrounds. The tool pointer is made of two parts – a circle and a cross hair. The circle size is based on the brush size.

To use the tool, the cross hair is positioned and dragged across the area to be erased, whilst at the same time the circle's edge overlaps the edge of the object to be kept. The success of this tool is largely based on the contrast between the edge of the object and the background. The greater the contrast, the more effective the tool.

The Tolerance slider is used to control how different pixels need to be in order to be erased. The Limits options set the tool to erase only those pixels that are linked, or sitting side by side (contiguous) or all the pixels within the circle that are a similar color.

In addition to these controls the options bar also houses buttons for three different sampling modes:

Continuous (1) – The sampled area changes according to where the cross hair pointer is positioned.

Once (2) – Samples and uses the color where the cross hair is first positioned.

Background Swatch (3) – Uses the current background color as the sample.

Background layer

Menu: –
Shortcut: –   **See also:** Layers,
Version: 6.0, 7.0, CS, CS2   Layers palette

An image can only have one background layer. It is the bottom-most layer in the stack. No other layers can be moved or dragged beneath this layer. You cannot adjust this layer's opacity or its blending mode. The background layer is locked (1) from these changes.

You can convert background layers to standard image layers by double-clicking the layer in the Layers palette, setting your desired layer options in the dialog provided and then clicking OK.

If the document that you are working on doesn't contain a background layer, it is possible to change any layer into a background layer by selecting the layer in the Layers palette and then choosing Layer > New > Layer From Background.

If the selected layer is not the bottom-most layer changing it to a background layer will force it to the bottom of the stack and this could dramatically alter the look of the image.

To create a matted web image, choose the web page color you want to use and then create a picture with a transparent background.

Background matting

Menu: –
Shortcut: –   **See also:** Save for Web
Version: 6.0, 7.0, CS, CS2

Most photos that are optimized for use on the Internet are saved in the JPEG format. As part of the construction process of a web page, the pictures are then placed on top of a colored background. The JPEG format does not contain a transparency option and so when an irregularly shaped graphic is saved as a JPEG and placed onto a web page it is surrounded by a plain colored box, usually white (1).

Background matting is a technique for adding the web page color to the background of the object at the time of web optimization. When the matted object is then used to create the web page, it appears to be sitting on the background as if it was surrounded by transparency (2). The transparent pixels surrounding the object are replaced with the matte color and the semi-transparent pixels are blended.

The Matte option is located in the settings area of the File > Save for Web feature (3).

Choose File > Save for Web. In the dialog select the JPEG option as the file format. Select the web page color from the Matte pop-up menu. Click OK to save.

Bas Relief filter

Menu: Filter > Sketch > Bas Relief
Shortcut: –   **See also:** Emboss filter
Version: 6.0, 7.0, CS, CS2

The Bas Relief filter, as one of the group of Sketch filters, simulates the surface texture of the picture using the current foreground and background colors. Changing the colors will result in dramatically different results.

The edges in the picture are used as the basis for the effect with the three settings in the dialog providing control over how the colors are applied.

The Detail slider (1) alters the amount of the original photo detail used to create the end result. Higher numbers create more detailed results. The Smoothness slider (2) alters the sharpness of the detail and the Light menu (3) contains a series of options for the direction of the light that is used to create the textured look of highlights and shadows.

Now construct the web page and add in the new matted graphic. When the page is displayed the background of the object will seamlessly merge with the page color.

14

B

Batch command

Menu:	File > Automate > Batch	
	Bridge: Tools > Photoshop > Batch	
Shortcut:	–	See also: Actions,
Version:	6.0, 7.0, CS, CS2	Batch Rename

If you've ever had to deal with enhancing a group of pictures using the same settings or converting a pile of images from one format or color mode to another you'll welcome this feature.

The Batch command takes a selection of images from a folder (2) and performs action sequences (1) that you've pre-recorded in the Actions palette.

You can specify whether you want the processed files to replace the existing ones or create new versions in a different destination folder (3). There are also options for renaming (4) the processed files and a series of checkbox settings that help manage the automation process (5).

The Batch command can be accessed from the File > Automate menu in Photoshop and the Tools > Photoshop menu in Bridge. Choosing the feature in Bridge means that you can apply the editing changes to multi-selected files in the browser workspace rather than complete folders which is the case when selecting the option in Photoshop.

The Batch feature automatically applies actions that have been previously recorded. So essentially the first step in using the Batch command is recording an editing action.

Batch Processing

Menu:	–	
Shortcut:	–	See also: Batch Rename, Image
Version:	6.0, 7.0, CS, CS2	Processor

Batch processing is a term use for applying the same editing or enhancement sequence to a folder or a series of selected images.

There are several places where batch processing occurs within Photoshop. The most obvious examples are:

Batch (File > Automate > Batch) – This feature takes a folder (or a group of selected images if used in Bridge) and applies a pre-recorded action to them.

Batch Rename (Bridge: Tools > Batch Rename) – Using this utility several pictures can be renamed via a single dialog.

Image Processor (Bridge: Tools > Photoshop > Image Processor) – This feature converts Raw files with the Camera Raw feature and then saves the processed pictures in a variety of file formats.

Batch processing is a terrific way to speed up the process of applying the same edits or enhancements to a bunch of photos.

Batch Rename

Menu:	Bridge: Tools > Batch Rename	
Shortcut:	Ctrl/Cmd Shft R	See also: Batch Processing,
Version:	CS2	Image Processor

Several files can be renamed in a single action using the Tools > Rename option in Bridge.

After multi-selecting the files in the browser workspace choose Tools > Batch Rename, add in the name (2), destination settings (1), select the output options (3) and check the preview section (4) in the Batch Rename dialog and click Rename.

The New Filenames section contains three drop-down menus that provide a variety of options for creating useful filenames. The menu items cover the name, extension and case of the filename (5).

Behind blend mode

Normal blend mode

Behind blending mode

Menu: –
Shortcut: –   **See also:** Blend modes
Version: 6.0, 7.0, CS, CS2

Along with the standard blend modes that are available for most painting and drawing tools and layers, Photoshop also contains two other options, Behind and Clear.

The Behind blend mode is used for drawing or painting on the transparent areas of selected layers. The result looks like the picture has been painted from behind and in the process the layer content has been preserved.

To use the mode select a layer, ensure that the Lock Transparency option is off and then select a drawing or painting tool. Now choose Behind from the mode list in the tool's options bar. Finally paint onto the selected layer.

Bevels

Menu: Layer > Layer Style > Bevel and Emboss
Shortcut: –   **See also:** Layer Styles
Version: 6.0, 7.0, CS, CS2

A layer style that you can use to produce stylish type that will leap off your page. It can also be used on colored shapes to create 3D panels and buttons.

Using the Bevel and Emboss section of the Layer Style dialog you can adjust the highlight and shadow of the bevel to create shallow or deep 3D effects.

Results vary depending on the resolution of your image so experiment with the settings to find a suitable effect. Turn Preview on so you can see the changes as you play.

Here are several I made using a 7×3 cm canvas with a resolution of 300 ppi and 50 point text.

Bézier curves

Menu: –
Shortcut: –   **See also:** Pen tool
Version: 6.0, 7.0, CS, CS2

Curves created using Photoshop's Pen tool are called Bézier (bay-zee-ay) curves, named after French mathematician Pierre Bézier.

The shape of a curve is created by the position of anchor points and direction lines that can be moved to change its shape and direction. They're used to make perfect selections around smooth or curved objects.

15

B

Low resolution original

© www.ablestock.com 2005

Bicubic

Bicubic - Sharper

Bicubic - Smoother

Bilinear

Nearest Neighbor

Bicubic interpolation

Menu: Image > Image Size
Shortcut: –
Version: CS, CS2
See also: Bilinear interpolation, Nearest Neighbor, interpolation

Digital photos are made up of pixels. These are discrete blocks of color and tone arranged in a grid fashion. The number of pixels in a picture is determined when the photo is taken or the print scanned. Occasionally it is necessary to change the number of pixels in the picture to make it either bigger or smaller. This task is usually handled by the Image Size feature where there are controls to increase or decrease the pixel dimensions (1), resample the pixels (2) and choose the method of resampling (3).

The process is often called resampling or interpolating the picture, and makes use of a mathematical algorithm to generate the newly sized picture.

Bicubic is one of the algorithms you can select to resize your picture. It takes the longest to process the file, but provides smooth graduations in the final photo.

Bicubic – Sharper interpolation

Menu: Image > Image Size
Shortcut: –
Version: CS, CS2
See also: Bicubic – Smoother interpolation

As well as standard Bicubic interpolation Adobe includes two other options: Bicubic – Sharper and Bicubic – Smoother.

Bicubic – Sharper is specifically designed for occasions when you are reducing the size of a picture. It retains the detail of the original image and sharpens the picture as it resizes. If the sharpening results are too harsh then Edit > Undo the process and try the standard Bicubic approach.

Bicubic – Smoother interpolation

Menu: Image > Image Size
Shortcut: –
Version: CS, CS2
See also: Bicubic – Sharper interpolation

As well as standard Bicubic Photoshop has two other approaches for increasing and decreasing the size of your pictures. Both options are based on the Bicubic algorithm but they have been optimized for different picture resizing operations. The Bicubic – Smoother option should be used for increasing the size of photographs, whereas the Bicubic – Sharper option is for making pictures smaller.

Bilinear interpolation

Menu: Image > Image Size
Shortcut: –
Version: CS, CS2
See also: Bicubic interpolation, Nearest Neighbor, interpolation

Apart from the Bicubic options examined here Photoshop can also resize pictures using two other interpolation options – Bilinear and Nearest Neighbor.

Nearest Neighbor is the fastest to apply but produces the coarsest results. Bilinear is a compromise in speed and quality between Bicubic and Nearest Neighbor.

Interpolation Quick Guide:

Action	Original	Method
Enlarge (Quality)	Photo	Bicubic – Smoother
Reduce (Quality)	Photo	Bicubic – Sharper
Enlarge (Speed)	Photo	Bilinear
Reduce (Speed)	Photo	Bilinear
Enlarge	Screen shot	Nearest Neighbor
Reduce	Screen shot	Bicubic – Sharper

Bitmap color mode

Menu: –	
Shortcut: –	**See also:** Mode, Threshold
Version: 6.0, 7.0, CS, CS2	filter

It is possible to change the color mode of your picture by selecting a different mode from the Image > Mode menu. When converting a color photograph to Bitmap mode in Photoshop the file must be flattened and changed to a grayscale first and from there to pure black and white. In the process you can choose the approach used for this conversion via the Method pop-up menu.

50% Threshold – Creates broad areas of flat black and white with a 50% tone used as the separation point.

Pattern Dither – Uses a black and white dot pattern to simulate tones.

Diffusion Dither – Examines each pixel in the picture before converting it to black or white resulting in a grain-filled photo.

Halftone Screen – This option recreates the look of the halftone dots used in traditional lithographic printing process.

Custom Pattern – Use this option to select a specific pattern to simulate the tone in the picture. You can select from the patterns preinstalled in Photoshop or even create and use your own pattern with the Edit > Define Pattern feature.

Bitmap images

Menu: –	
Shortcut: –	**See also:** Pixels
Version: 6.0, 7.0, CS, CS2	

Confusingly the term bitmap images does not refer to the pure black and white pictures that result from converting your photos to Bitmap mode. Instead a bitmap picture is one that is made up of rectangular pixel blocks which could just as easily be in color or grayscale. In this way all digital photographs are bitmap images as their color, brightness and detail are created from a grid of pixels. In most applications the pixel structure of the photograph is not apparent as the individual blocks are so small that they become invisible to the viewer's gaze. To see the underlying bitmap structure of your pictures magnify the image on screen using the View > Zoom In command until the photo is at 1600% magnification.

• •

Blend modes

Menu: –	
Shortcut: –	**See also:** –
Version: 6.0, 7.0, CS, CS2	

The way that layers interact with other layers in the stack is determined by the blending mode of the upper layer. By default the layer's mode is set to normal which causes the picture content on the upper layer to obscure the picture parts beneath, but Photoshop has many other ways to control how these pixels interact.

Called blend modes, the different options provide a variety of ways to control the mixing, blending and general interaction of the layer content.

The modes are grouped into several different categories based on the type of changes that they make (1).

The layer blend modes are located in the drop-down menu at the top left of the Layers palette (2). Blend modes can also be applied to the painting and drawing tools via a drop-down menu in the tool's options bar (3).

After – 50% Threshold

After – Pattern Dither

After – Diffusion Dither

Before

After – Halftone Screen

After – Custom Pattern

18

B

In the following blend mode examples the picture has two layers – 'Top' (1) and 'Bottom' (2). In each example the blend mode of the top layer has been changed to illustrate how the two layers blend together.

Normal

The pixels in the top layer are opaque and therefore block the view of the bottom layer. Adjusting the opacity of the top layer will make it semi-transparent causing it to blend with the top layer.

Dissolve

Combines the top layer with the bottom using a pattern of pixels. There is no effect if the top layer is at 100% opacity. Reduce the opacity to see the effect. Example set to 80% opacity.

Darken

Compares the color of the top and bottom layers and blends the pixels where the top layer is darker than the bottom.

Multiply

Multiplies the color of the bottom layer with the top layer producing an overall darker result. There is no image change when the top layer is white.

Color Burn

Darkens or 'burns' the image using the contents of the top layer. There is no image change if the top layer is white.

Linear Burn

Uses the same approach as the Color Burn mode but produces a stronger darkening effect. There is no image change when the top layer is white.

Lighten

Compares the color in the top and bottom layers and blends the pixels if the top layer is lighter than the bottom.

Screen

The opposite to the Multiply mode as it multiplies the inverse of the top layer with the bottom layer producing a much lighter image.

Color Dodge

Makes the picture lighter using the top layer to dodge the bottom layer. There is no effect if the top layer is black.

Linear Dodge

Similar to the Screen mode but produces a much stronger lightening effect. There is no effect if the top layer is black.

Overlay

Combines the effect of both the Multiply and Screen modes whilst blending the top layer with the bottom. There is no effect if the top layer is 50% gray.

Soft Light

Similar to the Overlay mode but produces a more subtle effect. There is no change if the top layer is 50% gray.

Hard Light

Uses the same approach as the Overlay mode but the change is more dramatic. Here the top layer is either Screened or Multiplied depending on its color. There is no effect if the top layer is 50% gray.

Vivid Light

Combines the effects of both Color Burn and Color Dodge modes and applies the blend based on the color of the top layer. There is no effect if the top layer is 50% gray.

Linear Light

Similar to the Vivid Light mode but produces a more dramatic result. There is no effect if the top layer is 50% gray.

Pin Light

Blends the light colors in the top layer using the Lighten mode and blends the dark colors using the Darken mode. There is no effect if the top layer is 50% gray.

Hard Mix

Creates a flat toned picture with limited colors and lots of posterization. The luminosity of the top layer is blended with the color of the bottom.

Difference

Displays the tonal difference between the contents of the two layers by subtracting the lighter pixels from either of the layers. This results in a dark and sometimes reversed image.

Exclusion

Similar to the Difference mode but produces less dramatic effects.

Hue

Combines the Hue (color) of the top layer with the Saturation (color vibrancy) and Luminance (tones) of the bottom layer.

Saturation

Combines the Saturation (color vibrancy) of the top layer with the Hue (color) and Luminance (tones) of the bottom layer.

Color

Combines the Hue (color) and Saturation (color vibrancy) of the top layer with the Luminance (tones) of the bottom layer.

Luminosity

Combines the Luminance (tones) of the top layer with the Saturation (color vibrancy) and Hue (color) of the bottom layer.

Before

After

Before

After

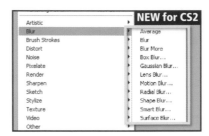

NEW for CS2

Artistic	
Blur	Average
Brush Strokes	Blur
Distort	Blur More
Noise	Box Blur...
Pixelate	Gaussian Blur...
Render	Lens Blur...
Sharpen	Motion Blur...
Sketch	Radial Blur...
Stylize	Shape Blur...
Texture	Smart Blur...
Video	Surface Blur...
Other	

B

Bloat tool, Liquify filter

Menu: Filter > Liquify
Shortcut: B (whilst in Liquify filter)   **See also:** Liquify filter
Version: 7.0, CS, CS2

The Bloat tool is one of several tools in the Liquify filter that allows you to stretch, twist, push and pull your pictures. It spreads the pixels apart in the center of a circle equal to the size of the current brush tip. The result is like the picture part has been blown up or 'bloated'.

To bloat your pictures, select the tool, then adjust the brush size so that it is the same dimensions as the area to be changed and then hold down the mouse button until the picture has changed the required amount. You can drag the mouse across the canvas bloating the pixels as you go.

To reverse the tool's effect either select the Revert button (top right) or paint over the surface with the Reconstruct tool.

Blur filters

Menu: Filter > Blur
Shortcut: –   **See also:** Filters, Box Blur filter, Surface
Version: CS2   Blur filter, Shape Blur filter

Photoshop CS2 contains a extensive array of blur filters including the new Box, Shape and Surface Blur options. It might seem strange for image makers to actually want to destroy the sharpness of their photos but many interesting enhancement effects make use of these filter options.

Box Blur – Fast blur option that is great for large pictures and special effects work.

Surface Blur – The Surface Blur filter is an edge preserving filter that produces results faster than Smart blur.

Shape Blur – A blur filter that creates its effect based on a user selected shape. The amount of blur is determined by the size of the shape which is adjusted via the slider control.

 Box, Shape and Surface Blur options all work in 16 bits and 32 bits per channel (HDR) modes.

Average – Averages all the color in the picture and then fills the canvas with this color.

Blur and Blur More – Smooths transitions and softens details. Blur More is stronger.

Gaussian Blur – Slider controlled blurring based on the Gaussian distribution of pixel changes.

Motion Blur – Blurs the image in a specific direct. Great for speed enhancing effects.

Radial Blur – Creates either spinning or zooming blur effects.

Smart Blur – Provides more control over the type and placement of blur using Radius, Threshold, Quality and Mode adjustments.

Lens Blur – This filter is used to simulate realistic depth of field blur effects that traditionally are created via camera and lens techniques. In CS2 Lens Blur now works in the 16 bits per channel mode.

✓ Pro's Tip   Before applying a blur filter to a layer with transparency, make sure that Lock Transparency option is turned off.

Blur tool

Menu: –
Shortcut: R   **See also:** Blur filters
Version: 6.0, 7.0, CS, CS2

Along with the extensive range of blur filters available in Photoshop, the program also includes a Blur tool.

The tool is used like a paintbrush but instead of laying down color on the canvas the image is blurred.

The Size (brush tip), Mode (blend mode) and Strength settings for the tool are all controlled in the options bar.

Original

Box Blur

Gaussian Blur

More Blur

Motion Blur

Shape Blur – bow tie

Smart Blur

Lens Blur

Radial Blur – zoom

Surface Blur

Average

Borders

Menu: Select > Modify > Border
Shortcut: –   **See also:** Modify
Version: 6.0, 7.0, CS, CS2

It's easy to add a border to your whole image or a selection. With an area selected choose the Select > Modify > Border command and enter a width in pixels. The mode will be grayed out from the menu if you haven't made a selection.

The thickness of border is relative to the original image size – a 3 pixel border on a 300 pixel wide image will look much smaller when applied to a picture with a 600 pixel width.

When applied you'll have a second set of marching ants which you can fill using the Bucket tool or Edit >Fill command. Choose the color border you want and set this as the foreground color before applying the fill.

• •

Borders, printing

Menu: File > Print with Preview
Shortcut: Ctrl/Cmd Alt/Opt P   **See also:** Print options
Version: 6.0, 7.0, CS, CS2

You can add a border 'on the fly' when making prints with Photoshop. The Border option is part of the extended print features found in the Print Preview dialog that is displayed when the Output option is selected.

The size of the border can be set and the color is always black.

Bounding box, Move tool

Menu: –
Shortcut: V (Move tool)
Version: 6.0, 7.0, CS, CS2
See also: Move tool, Free Transform command

For versions prior to CS2 the Show Bounding Box setting is located on the options bar for the Move tool.

Selecting this setting displays a bounding box complete with edge and side handles (small boxes) around the currently selected layer.

The handles can be used to scale, distort, skew, rotate and apply perspective changes interactively. See the Free Transform tool entry for the keystroke combinations for these changes.

In CS2 the Bounding Box option has been replaced by the Show Transformation Controls (1).

Box Blur filter

Menu: Filter > Blur > Box Blur
Shortcut: –   **See also:** Filters, Blur filters
Version: CS2

The Box Blur filter (1) is one of the range of blur filters contained in Photoshop. Like all the blur filters the box blur adds a degree of unsharpness to the picture. The filter contains a slider control (2) that is used to adjust the level of blur it produces. Higher values create less distinct results.

The Box Blur filter tends to work very quickly, especially when used with large pictures and is often recommended for the creation of blur in special effects techniques.

Bridge Center

Menu: Enhance > Adjust Lighting > Levels
Shortcut: Ctrl/Cmd Alt/Opt Shft L   **See also:** Bridge
Version: CS2 (with Creative Suite installed)

For those users who have the Adobe Creative suite installed Bridge contains another mode for the feature called Bridge Center. This is the pivot point for information, file management and integration of the various components in the Creative Suite.

In Bridge Center mode you can view news group posting and other web content (1), catch up on the latest tips (2) and tricks, create a new Version Cue project (3), synchronize color management settings across a range of Adobe applications (4), save files in groups (5) and access recently used files and folders (6).

If Bridge Center is not displayed in the Favorites panel then open the Edit > Preferences > General dialog and select the option from the Favorite Items section.

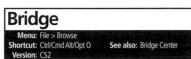

Look In menu (1). Favorites panel (2). Folders panel (3). Preview panel (4). Metadata and Keywords panel (5). Content area – thumbnails (6). Display modes and thumbnail size slider (7). Content area – preview (8). Delete, rotate, new folder, compact mode and show options (9).

Bridge

Menu: File > Browse	
Shortcut: Ctrl/Cmd Alt/Opt O	**See also:** Bridge Center
Version: CS2	

The Bridge feature, Adobe's new super browser, replaces the standard file browser option found in previous versions of Photoshop. Selecting File > Browse displays Bridge and the fastest way to open a file from your picture library is to search for, and select, the file from within Bridge and then press Ctrl/Cmd O. If Photoshop is not the default program used for opening the file, select File > Open With > Photoshop. Multi-selected files in the browser can also be opened in this way.

Bridge is a separate application to Photoshop (stand alone), has its own memory management system and can be opened and used to organize and manage your photo files without needing to have Photoshop running at the same time.

Using Bridge

To locate files – Files can be located by selecting the folder in which they are contained using either the Favorites or Folders panel or the Look In menu. Alternatively, the Edit > Find command can be used to search for pictures based on filename, file size, keywords, date, rating, label, metadata or comment.

To manage files – Bridge is more than just a file browser it is also a utility that can be used for sorting and categorizing your photos. Using the options listed under the Label menu, individual or groups of photos can be rated (with a star rating) or labeled (with a colored label) and these tags can be used as a way to sort and display the best images from those taken at a large photoshoot or grouped together in a folder. Labels and ratings are applied by selecting (or multi-selecting) the thumbnail in the Bridge workspace and then choosing the tag from the Label menu. Shortcut keys can also be used to quickly attached tags to selected files.

Viewing thumbnails – One of the real bonuses of the Bridge is the multitude of ways that the thumbnails can be viewed in the workspace. Two different controls alter the way that Bridge appears – Workspace and View.

Workspace controls the overall look of the Bridge window and the Window > Workspace menu provides a variety of preset spaces that you can choose as well as allowing you to save your own design.

View options are specifically used to alter the way that the thumbnails are displayed in the Bridge workspace (see above). Photoshop provides four basic view modes

(Thumbnails, Filmstrip, Details and Versions and Alternatives), all of which are available via the View menu or in button form at the bottom right of the Bridge window.

Tools used in Bridge – Although no real editing or enhancement options are available in the Bridge feature it is possible to use the browser as a starting point for many of the operations normally carried out in Photoshop. For instance, photos selected in the workspace can be batch renamed, printed online, used to create a Photomerge panorama, compiled into a contact sheet or combined into a PDF-based presentation all via options under the Tools menu. Some of these choices will open Photoshop before completing the requested task whereas others are completed without leaving the browser workspace.

Processing Raw inside Bridge – One of the real bonuses of Bridge is the ability to open, edit and save Raw files from inside the browser workspace. Now there is no need to open the files to process via Photoshop. The conversions to DNG, TIFF, JPEG or PSD files can be handled directly from the Bridge by selecting (or multi-selecting) the files and then choosing File > Open in Camera Raw.

NEW for CS2

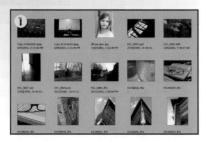

Bridge – View modes

Menu: Bridge: View > As	
Shortcut: –	**See also:** Bridge, Compact
Version: CS2	Mode, Sort files, Workspace

Bridge contains a range of ways that your images can be displayed and browsed. Listed under the View menu are options for viewing your pictures as thumbnails (1), in a filmstrip (2), with details (3) and with saved versions or alternates (4). To switch between view modes you can select the desired option from the View menu or press one of the view buttons at the bottom right of the Bridge screen. Also included in the View menu are options for displaying selected photos in a slide show, sorting images according to a variety of criteria and switching Bridge to its Compact Mode. Another way to organize the look of the Bridge work area is with the options found under Window > Workspace.

Before

After

Brightness/Contrast

Menu: Image > Adjustments > Brightness/Contrast	
Shortcut: –	**See also:** Curves, Shadow/
Version: 6.0, 7.0, CS, CS2	Highlight

The Brightness/Contrast command helps you make basic adjustments to the spread of tones within the image.

When opened you are presented with a dialog containing two slider controls. Click and drag the slider to the left to decrease brightness or contrast, to the right to increase the value.

Keep in mind that you are trying to adjust the image so that the tones are more evenly distributed between the extremes of pure white and black. Too much correction using either control can result in pictures where highlight and/or shadow details are lost.

As you are making your changes, watch these two areas in particular to ensure that details are retained.

Before

After Bring Forward

Bring Forward

Menu: Layer > Arrange > Bring Forward	
Shortcut: Ctrl]	**See also:** Layers palette
Version: 6.0, 7.0, CS, CS2	

To change the order of layers in the layer's stack you can either click on the layer in the palette and drag it to the new position or make use of the commands in the Layer > Arrange menu.

Layers can be moved up and down the stack using these options. Here we selected the Bottom layer and then chose Bring Forward. The layer then moves up one place in the stack, positioning the layer in between the Top and Middle layers.

After Bring to Front

Bring to Front

Menu: Layer > Arrange > Bring to Front	
Shortcut: Shft Ctrl }	**See also:** Layers palette
Version: 6.0, 7.0, CS, CS2	

As well as options for moving layers up or down one position at a time, the Layer > Arrange menu also contains items for placing the selected layer at the very top (or bottom) of the stack.

Here the Bring to Front option was used to move the Bottom layer to the top of the stack, effectively making it above both the Middle and Top layers.

Browse

Menu: File > Browse
Shortcut: Ctrl/Cmd Alt/Opt O   **See also:** Bridge
Version: 6.0, 7.0, CS, CS2

In CS2 this option takes the user directly to the Bridge workspace. In previous versions of the program it was this command that opened the Photoshop File Browser. Bridge now replaces this feature and in doing so provides much more power and control than a simple thumbnail browser utility.

If it is simple, no-frills file browsing that you are after then CS2 provides the option of a customized Adobe file open (and save) dialog (1).

Brush Presets

Menu: –
Shortcut: B (Brush tool)   **See also:** Brush tool
Version: 6.0, 7.0, CS, CS2

Photoshop is shipped with a wide range of pre-made brushes which are stored in several groups in the Brush Presets palette.

To access a specific brush from the library first display the pop-up palette by clicking the down arrow next to the brush stroke preview in the options bar. Select a group of brushes from the menu accessed via the side-arrow (top right). Now scroll through the brush types and click to select the brush you want to use.

Ready-made Photoshop brush libraries can be downloaded from sites on the Internet that specialize in providing free imaging resources. After downloading the file, click on the side-arrow in the top right of the Brush Preset dialog and select the Load Brushes item from the menu. Locate the library file and click OK to incorporate the new brushes into the palette.

Pro's Tip

www.graphicxtras.com

To create a new brush select the Brush tool from the toolbar and then display the Brush Preset dialog by clicking the down-arrow next to the brush stroke preview in the options bar. Choose a brush set from the menu accessed via the side-arrow (top right) and then click on a specific brush to modify.

Modify the characteristics of the selected brush by adjusting the various settings in the options bar. For more creative changes alter the slider controls for the brush dynamics in the Brushes palette (Window > Brushes Palette).

Display the Brush Presets again and select the side-arrow in the top right of the pop-up. Choose New Brush Preset from the menu items. Type a name into the Brush Name dialog and click OK. The newly created brush is added to the bottom of the brush library.

Brush tool

Menu: –
Shortcut: B
Version: 6.0, 7.0, CS, CS2

See also: Airbrush, Pencil tool, Paint Bucket tool

The Photoshop Brush tool lays down color in a similar fashion to a traditional paint brush.

The color of the paint is set to the current foreground color. The size and shape of the brush can be selected from the list in the Brush Presets list (1) in the options bar. Changes to the brush characteristics can be made by altering the settings in the options bar and the More Options palette.

In addition to changes to the size, blend mode (2), opacity of the brush (3) and the flow rate (4), which are made via the options bar, you can also alter how the brush behaves via the Brushes palette (5).

Pro's Tip To draw a straight line click to start the line and hold down the Shift key then click the mouse button a second time to mark the end of the line.

Brushes palette

Menu: Window > Brushes
Shortcut: F5
Version: 6.0, 7.0, CS, CS2

See also: Brush tool

The palette is displayed by selecting Window > Brushes or pressing the Brushes Palette button located at the right end of the Brush tool options bar. The palette is used to creatively control the following brush characteristics or dynamics:

Brush Tip Shape – Design and change the shape of the painting tip of your brush.

Shape Dynamics – Control the size, angle and roundness jitters (automatic variation).

Scattering – Set the scattering options.

Texture – Select specific textures to paint with and control their scale and depth.

Dual Brush – Creates a second brush tip that is combined with the first to produce a single stroke.

Color Dynamics – Set hue, saturation, brightness and foreground/background jitters.

Other Dynamics – Adjust opacity and flow jitters.

Noise – Add noise characteristics to the painted areas.

Wet Edges – Create water color type effects where the paint builds up around the edges of the stroke.

Air Brush – Applies gradual buildup of color.

Smoothing – Produces strokes with smoother curves and edges.

Protect Texture – Maintains the same texture across all brushes.

Burn tool

Menu: –
Shortcut: O
Version: 6.0, 7.0, CS, CS2

See also: Dodge tool

The Burn tool darkens specific areas of a photograph when the tool tip is clicked and dragged across the picture surface.

The tool's attributes are based on the settings in the options bar and the current brush size. The strength of the darkening is governed by the exposure setting. Most professionals choose to keep this value low and build up the tool's effect with repeated strokes over the same area.

You can also adjust the precise grouping of tones, highlights, midtones or shadows that you are working on at any one time by setting the option in the Range menu.

Button mode

Menu: –
Shortcut: –
Version: 6.0, 7.0, CS, CS2

See also: Actions

This is a pretty looking interface that's an alternative to the normal Actions palette and is selected from the black triangle drop-down menu. Each Action is assigned a color, making it easy to group similar Actions.

This mode is useful for less experienced users of the Actions feature, but scripts can't be edited so more advanced users should stay clear.

27

C

Cache, Bridge

Menu: Bridge: Tools > Cache
Shortcut: –   **See also:** Bridge
Version: CS2

The cache in the Bridge application is a portion of hard disk memory that is used to store thumbnail, metadata and file information. Caching these details means that loading times for folders and files that have already been displayed are much shorter.

Caches are built for specific folders when the contents are first displayed in Bridge. Alternatively the cache building process can occur before display by selecting the folder and then choosing Tools > Cache > Build Cache for Subfolders. This action speeds up the display of the contents in the subfolders when they are first viewed.

When copying images to a CD or DVD the cache for the files can be added to the disk to help speed up display when the photos are first viewed. If you have selected the Use A Centralized Cache File in the Preferences dialog then to include the cache data in the picture folder you will need to select the Tools > Cache > Export Cache option before copying the folder to CD or DVD.

Two purge options are also available in the Tools > Cache Menu.

Purge Cache for this Folder clears the memory of the data saved for the folder selected. This is a good option for removing a corrupted cache and then rebuilding a new one.

Purge Central Cache deletes the whole centralized cache freeing up space on the hard drive.

Calculations

Menu: Image > Calculations
Shortcut: –   **See also:** –
Version: 6.0, 7.0, CS, CS2

This mode lets you merge two channels from one or two images and save the result as a new channel in one of the existing images or create a new image.

The Calculations palette gives you various options including Blend method and is useful if you want to combine masks or selections.

Calibrate monitor

Menu: –
Shortcut: –   See also: Color Settings
Version: 6.0, 7.0, CS, CS2

Photoshop has a color management system
that will help ensure that what you see on
screen will be as close as possible to what
you print and what others see on their
screens.

For this reason, it is important that you
set up your computer to use this system
before starting to make changes to your
images. The critical part of the process is
the calibration of your monitor. To achieve
this, use the following steps:

To start the calibration process make sure
that your monitor has been turned on for
at least 30 minutes.

Check that your computer is displaying
thousands (16-bit color) or millions (24- or
32-bit color) of colors.

Remove colorful or highly patterned
backgrounds from your screen, as this can
affect your color perception.

Start the Adobe Gamma utility.
In Windows, this is located in the Control
Panel. For Macintosh users, use Apple's own
Display Calibrator Assistant, as Adobe
Gamma is not used with the new system
software.

Use the step-by-step Wizard to guide you
through the setup process. If a default
profile was not supplied with your
computer, contact your monitor
manufacturer or check their website for
details.

Save the profile, including the date in the
filename. As your monitor will change with
age, you should perform the Gamma setup
every couple of months. Saving the setup
date as part of the profile name will help
remind you when last you used the
utility.

(1) Filmstrip area.
(2) Preview area.
(3) Histogram.
(4) Conversion settings.
(5) Saving (workflow) options.
(6) Shadow/Highlights clipping warnings.
(7) Cropping, color sampling and straightening tools.
(8) Synchronize setting button.
(9) File formats for saving.
(10) Rating stars.

Camera Raw

Menu: –	
Shortcut: –	**See also:** Camera Raw
Version: CS, CS2	– Bridge

When you open a Raw file into Photoshop you are presented with an editing dialog containing a full color, interpolated preview of the sensor data. This editor is called Adobe Camera Raw.

Using a variety of menu options, dialogs and image tools in this dialog you will be able to interactively adjust image data factors such as tonal distribution and color saturation. Many of these changes can be made with familiar editing tools like levels and curves controls. The results of your editing can be reviewed immediately via the live preview image and associated histogram graphs.

After these general image editing steps have taken place you can apply some enhancement changes such as filtering for sharpness using an Unsharp Mask tool, removing moiré effects and applying some smoothing.

The final phase of the process involves selecting the color space, color depth, pixel dimensions and image resolution with which the processed file will be saved.

Clicking the OK button sets the utility into action applying your changes to the Raw

file, whilst at the same time interpolating the Bayer data to create a full color image and then opening the processed file into the full Photoshop workspace.

New for CS2

• Camera Raw can also be used outside of Photoshop from within the Bridge workspace.

• Multiple files can be selected (either via the File > Open dialog or with Bridge) and edited in Camera Raw.

• Pressing Ctrl/Cmd R after selecting several Raw files opens Camera Raw in Filmstrip mode (1). Settings can be applied to individual files or 'Synchronized' across all photos in the filmstrip (8).

• Processed files can be saved directly from Camera Raw in a variety of formats – DNG, TIFF, PSD or JPEG (9).

• Camera Raw now contains both crop and straighten tools (7).

• Pictures can be rated inside the Camera Raw dialog (when in Filmstrip mode) by selecting the thumbnail and then pressing Ctrl/Cmd 1 through 5 (10).

• A new Curves control has also been added to Camera Raw. The function works in a similar way to the Curves feature located in the Image > Adjustment menu and is located under the Curves tab.

Camera Raw – batch

Menu: Bridge: Tools > Photoshop > Image Processor
Shortcut: –   **See also:** Camera Raw
Version: CS2

The Image Processor located in both Bridge and Photoshop can be used to batch process and save multiple Raw files.

The utility can also save and size in several different formats (1) at the same time providing a fast and efficient workflow for processing images that have been captured in a single session.

Camera Raw, Bridge

Menu: Bridge: File > Open in Camera Raw
Shortcut: Ctrl/Cmd R   **See also:** Camera Raw
Version: CS2

In CS2, Raw files can be opened directly into Camera Raw from inside Bridge (1) without needing to open the full Photoshop application first. This makes for a workflow where downloaded Raw photographs start as thumbnails in Bridge, suitable images are then multi-selected, opened and processed with the Camera Raw editor. This whole procedure takes place inside Bridge.

The revised Camera Raw workspace can now process several photos without having to open and close each in turn. The multi-selected photos are loaded into the feature and wait to be processed in the new Filmstrip section (2) of the dialog.

 When processing several images that were photographed under the same lighting conditions, the Camera Raw settings from the first image can be copied and pasted to all other files using the options found under the Edit > Apply Camera Raw menu (3). In the same way the default or previously used settings can also be applied to several photos at once.

Camera Raw – clear settings

Menu: Bridge: Right-Click > Clear Camera Raw Settings
Shortcut: –   **See also:** Camera Raw
Version: CS2

You can clear the Camera Raw settings that have been applied or pasted to a picture by selecting the thumbnail in Bridge and then choosing the Clear Camera Raw Settings from the right-click menu (Ctrl-click for Mac users).

Camera Raw, copy/ paste settings

Menu: Bridge: Right-Click > Copy Camera Raw Settings
          Bridge: Right-Click > Paste Camera Raw Settings
Shortcut: –   **See also:** Camera Raw
Version: CS2

Whilst working within Bridge it is possible to copy and paste the Camera Raw settings from one picture to another.

Simply select the thumbnail with the settings to copy and then choose the Copy Camera Raw Settings option (1) from the right-click menu (Ctrl-click for single button Mac users). Next click on the thumbnail that you wish to transfer the settings to and choose the Paste Camera Raw Settings (2) to the file. You can choose which settings to apply in the dialog that pops up.

Camera Raw – Done

Menu: –
Shortcut: –   See also: Camera Raw
Version: CS2

After applying all the conversion settings to your Raw file the Camera Raw dialog provides you with six different options of what to do next.

Done – Applies the Raw conversion settings and then closes Camera Raw without opening the picture fully in Photoshop.

Save... – Processes the file and then displays a Save dialog that contains naming, file format and destination folder options.

Open – Processes the files and then opens the completed picture in Photoshop.

Cancel – Quits the dialog and applies no changes to the selected file.

Reset (Alt/Opt-click the Cancel button) – Resets all the settings in the dialog from their current position.

Save (Alt/Opt-click the Save button) – Bypasses the Save dialog and the options it contains.

Canvas

Menu: –
Shortcut: –   See also: Canvas Size
Version: 6.0, 7.0, CS, CS2

In creating documents in Photoshop the program makes a distinction between the canvas (1), upon which pictures and other content are placed, and the image content (2) itself. This is true even for photos with one layer only. For most newly imported photos the canvas and image size are exactly the same and so the canvas remains hidden from view.

Given this distinction, it is possible to resize, alter the format or change the color of the canvas without affecting the image at all.

Canvas Size

Menu: Image > Canvas Size
Shortcut: Ctrl/Cmd Alt/Opt C   See also: Image Size
Version: 6.0, 7.0, CS, CS2   command

Altering the settings in the Canvas Size dialog changes the dimensions of the background the image is sitting upon. Larger dimensions than the picture result in more space around the image. Smaller dimensions crop the image.

To change the canvas size, select Canvas Size from the Image menu and alter the settings in the New Size section of the dialog.

You can control the location of the new space in relation to the original image by clicking one of the sections in the Anchor diagram. Leaving the default setting here will mean that the canvas change will be spread evenly around the image.

With the picture already open in the Photoshop workspace select Image > Canvas Size.

In the Canvas Size dialog add in the new values for the width and height of the canvas. When making the canvas larger click and drag the white square in the 3 × 3 grid to determine where the new canvas area will be added. Leaving the square in the middle will mean the new canvas area will be added evenly surrounding the current image area.

You can select the color that will be used to fill the new canvas area either by choosing a new background color before starting the Canvas Size feature, or by selecting a Canvas Extension Color option from the drop-down menu at the bottom of the dialog.

Chalk & Charcoal filter

Menu: Filter > Sketch > Chalk & Charcoal filter
Filter > Filter Gallery > Sketch > Chalk & Charcoal
Shortcut: –   **See also:** Filters,
Version: 6.0, 7.0, CS, CS2   Charcoal filter

The Chalk & Charcoal filter is one of several drawing-like filters that can be found in the Sketch section of the Filter menu in Photoshop. The feature simulates the effect of making a drawing of the photograph with white chalk and black charcoal. The tones in the photograph that range from shadow to mid-gray are replaced by the charcoal strokes and those lighter values (from mid-gray to white) are 'drawn' in using the chalk color.

The filter dialog gives you control over the balance of the amount and placement of the charcoal and chalk areas as well as the pressure of the stroke used to draw the picture. Higher values for the Charcoal (1) and Chalk (2) area sliders will increase the number and variations of tones that are drawn with these colors. High settings for the Stroke Pressure slider (3) produce crisper transitions between tones and a more contrasty result.

 Pro's Tip To add a little more color to your Chalk and Charcoal 'drawings' select colors other than black and white for the foreground and background values. Double-click each swatch to open the color picker where you can select the new hue.

Channel Mixer

Menu: Image > Adjustments > Channel Mixer
Shortcut: –   **See also:** Adjustment layers
Version: 6.0, 7.0, CS, CS2

The Channel Mixer is one of those tools in Photoshop that you come to once you have a little more experience.

The mixer gives you control over the color components of a single channel. By adjusting the color of the individual Red, Green and Blue channels you can change the color of an element within the picture (1).

As well as color adjustment, one of the most common uses for the Channel Mixer feature is to control the conversion of colors to black and white. By clicking on the Monochrome option and adjusting the color sliders it is possible to alter the type of gray that specific colors are converted to (2).

When converting color images to black and white using the Monochrome option (3) it is advisable to ensure that the settings used for each of the Source Channels (4) add up to a total of 100%.

The Channel Mixer option is also available as an Adjustment Layer.

Channels

Menu: Window > Channels
Shortcut: –   **See also:** CMYK, RGB
Version: 6.0, 7.0, CS, CS2

Photoshop is made up of channels that store information about the image. A freshly created RGB file has a channel for each of the three colors Red, Green and Blue, and a CMYK file has four channels (Cyan, Magenta, Yellow and Black), while Duotones and Index color images have just one.

You can add channels to store info about the picture. For example, Alpha channels can be added to save selections as masks. Then when you want to perform a similar cutout in the future you load the Alpha channel to bring the marching ants into play on the selected layer.

Channels can also be edited individually so you could blend certain ones, or fiddle with the color of just one channel – useful when you want to make a selection based on a certain color that would be easier to do in its own environment.

Pro's Tip Individual color channels appear as black and white by default. If you prefer to see them in color go to File > Preferences > Displays and Cursors and select the Color Channels in Color option.

Charcoal filter

Menu: Filter > Sketch > Charcoal
Filter > Filter Gallery > Sketch > Charcoal
Shortcut: – **See also:** Chalk & Charcoal
Version: 6.0, 7.0, CS, CS2 filter

Giving similarly textured results to the Chalk & Charcoal filter, the straight Charcoal filter makes use of only one drawing tone to create the sketching effect.

Three sliders control the appearance of the final result. Charcoal Thickness (1) adjusts the density of the drawn areas whereas the Detail slider (2) adjusts the level of detail that is retained from the original picture.

Care should be taken with the settings used for the Light/Dark Balance slider (3) to ensure that some shadow and highlight detail is retained.

Check spelling

Menu: Edit > Check Spelling
Shortcut: – **See also:** –
Version: 6.0, 7.0, CS, CS2

This feature, which was introduced in version 7.0, proves useful if you are using the Type tool to work with text in Photoshop.

Once selected the utility automatically runs through your work and finds anything that isn't spelled correctly or doesn't appear in its dictionary and suggests an alternative.

If, for example, it found the incorrectly spelt 'grassshopper' the feature would suggest the correct 'grasshopper' and you could then click on 'change' to have the word automatically substituted.

This sort of feature is available with all word and DTP (desktop publishing) packages and is a welcome addition to Photoshop.

Chrome filter

Menu: Filter > Sketch > Chrome
Filter > Filter Gallery > Sketch > Chrome
Shortcut: – **See also:** Filters
Version: 6.0, 7.0, CS, CS2

The Chrome filter is another Sketch filter designed to change the appearance of your picture so that it looks like it is created from another surface. In this case the filter converts the detail of the picture to simulate the look of polished chrome.

During the transformation you have control over both the detail (1) that is retained in the filter photo as well as the smoothness (2) of the chromed surface.

In some instances a further levels enhancement to increase the contrast of the final filtered picture will help produce brighter highlights on the silvered surface.

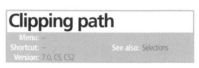

Clear blending mode

Menu: –		
Shortcut: –		See also: Behind blending
Version: 7.0, CS, CS2		mode

The Clear blend mode that is available for the painting and drawing tools in Photoshop removes the image pixels from the layer converting the area to transparent. For instance, when the Brush is set to Clear mode it acts in a similar way to the Eraser tool.

For the Clear mode to be available in the blend mode menu of the options bar, the layer's Transparency Lock must not be selected and the layer itself cannot be a background layer.

Clipboard

Menu: –		
Shortcut: –		See also: Purge
Version: 6.0, 7.0, CS, CS2		

The Clipboard is a part of the computer's memory that is allocated to storing information that is copied and pasted.

In Photoshop the Clipboard memory space is used every time you select a picture part, copy it and paste it back down as a new layer. During this process the copied image is stored on the Clipboard and remains there until it is replaced by a new copied part or is deleted using the Purge command.

Unlike other applications Photoshop uses its own specialized clipboard, not that of the operating system.

Pro's Tip — Clear (purge) the Clipboard often if you regularly copy large pictures, or find that you are always low on memory.

Clipping path

Menu: –		
Shortcut: –		See also: Selections
Version: 7.0, CS, CS2		

Puts an invisible path (2) around an image to ensure the background is transparent when the image is dropped into an illustration or desktop publishing page.

To create a clipping path, first outline the subject with a selection tool such as the Lasso or Magic Wand tools to make a selection then click on the arrow at the right of the Paths palette and select Make Work Path (1), then Save Path. Finally select Clipping Path.

Save the file as an EPS or TIFF which keeps the clipping path data which can then be read by the DTP software to allow a transparent background or text to wrap around the subject (3).

Just like layers and channels, actions for manipulating paths are centered around a single palette – the Paths palette which can be displayed by selecting the Paths option from the Windows menu.

Before

After

© www.adanstock.com 2005

Clone Stamp tool

Menu: –
Shortcut: S   **See also:** Pattern Stamp,
Version: 6.0, 7.0, CS, CS2   Spot Healing Brush,
Healing Brush,
Patch tool

Scanning your prints or negatives is a great way to convert existing pictures into digital, but sometimes during the process you pick up a few unwanted dust marks as well as the picture details.

Or maybe when you photographed your mother you did not realize that the electricity pole in the background would look like it is protruding from her head in your picture. Removing or changing these parts of an image is a basic skill needed by all digital photographers and Photoshop contains just the tool to help eliminate these unwanted areas.

Called the Clone Stamp tool (or sometimes the Rubber Stamp tool), the feature selects and samples an area of your picture and then uses these pixels to paint over the offending marks. It takes a little getting used to but as your confidence grows so too will the quality of your repairs and changes.

There are several ways to use the tool. For starters it acts like a brush so you can change the size, allowing cloning from just one pixel wide to hundreds. You can change the opacity to produce a subtle clone effect. You can select any one of the options from the Blend menu.

The Clone Stamp tool works by sampling a selected area and pasting the characteristics of this area over the blemish, so the first step in the process is to identify the areas in your picture that need repair. Make sure that the image layer you want to copy is selected.

Next locate areas in the photograph that are a similar tone, texture and color as the areas needing to be fixed. It is these areas that the Clone Stamp tool will copy and then use to paint over fence wires.

• •

And, most importantly, there's a choice between Clone align or Clone non-align the sample area.

Select Aligned from the Clone Stamp options palette and the sample cursor will follow the destination cursor around keeping the same distance away. When unaligned is chosen the sample cursor starts where you left off with all ensuing paint strokes. Both choices have their advantages.

Pro's Tip

1. Make sure that you select the layer that you want to clone from, before using Alt/Option + Click to select the sample point.

2. Alternatively if you want to sample from all the image layers in the picture select the Use All Layers option in the tool's options bar.

3. Watch the cursor move over the sampled area as you clone. To avoid unexpected results be sure that the sample cursor doesn't move into unwanted parts of the picture.

4. When cloning fine detail look around for similar areas and try to follow a path that will make the sample look natural.

Select the area to be sampled, or the 'Sample Point'. Do this by holding down the Alt key (Win) or the Option key (Mac) and clicking the left mouse button when the cursor (now changed to cross hairs) is over a part of the image that suits the area to be repaired.

With the sample point selected you can now move the cursor to the area to be fixed. Click on the blemish and a copy of the sample point area is pasted over the mark. Depending on how well you chose the sample area, the blemish will now be blended into the background seamlessly. Continue to click and drag to repair more areas.

You may need to reselect your sample point if you find that the color, texture or tone doesn't match the surrounds of the blemish. You can also change the brush size and hardness to alter the characteristics of both the sample and stamp areas. A softer edge helps blend the edge areas of the newly painted parts of the picture with the original image.

Switching between aligned and non-aligned (when the Aligned option is not selected) can really help when you are rebuilding missing parts of your restoration project. 'Aligned' sets the sample point so that it remains the same distance from the stamped area no matter where on the picture you start to click, and 'Non-aligned' repositions the sample point back to the original sample spot each time the mouse is moved and then clicked.

NEW for CS2

Close

Menu: File > Close
Shortcut: Ctrl/Cmd W   **See also:** Close All
Version: 6.0, 7.0, CS, CS2

To close a single open file from the Photoshop workspace select File > Close.

If the file is not saved or changes have been made to the document since the last time it was saved you will then be presented with a Save pop-up window.

●●●●●●●●●●●●●●●●●●●●●●●●●●●●

Close All

Menu: File > Close All
Shortcut: Alt/Opt Ctrl/Cmd W   **See also:** Close
Version: 6.0, 7.0, CS, CS2

To close multiple open picture windows, select File > Close All.

If any of the files are not saved or changes have been made to them since the last time they were saved then a different save confirmation window will be displayed for each file.

Close and Go To Bridge

Menu: File > Close and Go To Bridge
Shortcut: Ctrl/Cmd Shft W   **See also:** Close, Close All
Version: CS2

Close and Go To Bridge is a new option available in CS2. Like the standard close option, this menu selection closes the currently selected open document and then switches windows to display Bridge. If Bridge is not already open then this action opens the feature as well.

If the file is not saved or changes have been made to the document since the last time it was saved you will then be presented with a Save pop-up window (1).

Clouds filter

Menu: Filter > Render > Clouds
Shortcut: –   **See also:** Filters
Version: 6.0, 7.0, CS, CS2

The Clouds filter is one of the options in the Render group of filters.

The feature creates a random cloud-like pattern based on the currently selected foreground and background colors (1).

Apart from altering these colors there are no other options for adjusting the effect created by this filter.

Pro's Tip — This filter is particularly good for creating effects that can be used as effective backgrounds to your pictures. Blue creates natural skies (2) while orange will deliver a sunset effect and black will produce a stormy sky.

If the cloud effect is too harsh use Ctrl/Cmd keys to reduce the image on screen. Then use the transform tool to stretch the clouds.

CMYK

Menu: –	
Shortcut: –	**See also:** RGB, Channels
Version: 6.0, 7.0, CS, CS2	

Most digital photographs are captured using the three channel RGB (Red, Green, Blue) mode. When such files are printed the color is converted from RGB into a CMYK color mode. This usually occurs as a process in the background without you knowing.

CMYK is the standard method of printing for both inkjet and magazine and uses Cyan, Magenta and Yellow inks to make up the various colors.

A 100% combination of C, M and Y should produce black, but in reality it's a murky brown color so the Black ink (K to avoid confusion with the Blue of RGB) ensures black is printed where necessary.

• •

Collage

Menu: –	
Shortcut: –	**See also:** Blend modes,
Version: 6.0, 7.0, CS, CS2	Layers, Masks

Strictly speaking a collage is a collection of photographs mounted together, but Photoshop creates a perfect digital alternative by bringing several photos together to form one larger image that hasn't seen a drop of glue or sticky tape.

It's a great technique to use to create a family tree (1), group photo, promo, surreal image or, as below, a panel to go on a Web site (2) or stationery header.

Using Layers makes the job much easier and more controllable. Here masks and blend modes allow lower layers to react with ones above.

The binary text was created using the text tool and then distorted, skewed and stretched, to give it a forward look.

Color Balance

Menu: Image > Adjustments > Color Balance	
Shortcut: Ctrl/Cmd B	**See also:** Auto Color
Version: 6.0, 7.0, CS, CS2	Correction, Variations

Used to remove or create a color cast. The Color Balance dialog has three sliders to control the color.

Moving the top slider (1) left adds cyan and reduces red. Move it to the right to add red and reduce cyan.

The middle slider controls magenta and green (2) and the bottom, yellow and blue (3).

Precise values can be keyed in the top boxes. You can also select where you want the color to change, placing emphasis in the highlights, shadows or midtones (4).

The final option is to Preserve Luminosity which maintains the original brightness when it's turned on (5).

In practice, the Color Balance option is helpful in correcting the hues in shots taken with mismatched white balance. For example, the Daylight white balance setting is designed to produce a natural looking range of colors for outdoor photography or indoor shots taken with flash. Take a photo indoors without flash and you'll end up with a color cast.

This will be green if the light source is fluorescent or orange if it's tungsten light. Some flashguns are so harsh that they create a blue color cast. The walls in a room can also reflect light to add a color to your subject.

Correct or lessen these cast problems with the Color Balance feature.

Before

After

Before

After

38

C

Color blending mode

Menu: –	
Shortcut: –	See also: Blend modes
Version: 6.0, 7.0, CS, CS2	

The Color option is one of the many blend modes that can be set for both layers and painting/drawing tools in Photoshop.

This mode is particularly useful when creating traditional hand coloring effects (adding color to a black and white picture). Unlike when working with the normal mode, where the color applied by the brush paints over (and replaces) the original color and detail of the photo beneath, the Color mode maintains the detail and replaces the color only.

Pro's Tip

1. Zoom in close and then change your brush's size and edge softness to get into those small and tricky areas of your picture.

2. If you accidentally paint into an area with the wrong color, don't panic. Either use the Edit > Undo command or reselect the surrounding color using the Eyedropper tool and then paint over the mistake.

Most black and white photographs will need to be changed to RGB mode for this technique (Image > Mode > RGB Color). Now click on the foreground swatch in the toolbox and select a color appropriate for your picture. Here I chose a dark green for the leaves.

Select the Brush tool from the toolbox and adjust its size and edge softness using the settings in the options bar. Change the blend mode to Color by clicking on the Mode drop-down menu in the options bar and selecting the Color option from towards the bottom of the list.

Now apply the color and notice that the brush is substituting the color for the gray tones in the picture and it is doing so proportionately: dark grey = dark green, light gray = light green. Once the leaves and stems have been colored, select new colors for the flowers and finally the bucket.

Color Burn blending mode

Menu: –	
Shortcut: –	See also: Blend modes
Version: 6.0, 7.0, CS, CS2	

The Color Burn blending mode is one of the group of modes that darkens the picture.

Here when the upper layer is changed to the Color Burn mode its content is used to darken the bottom layer and in the process mirror the color of the upper layer.

Blending with a white upper layer produces no change.

Before

After

Before

After

Color cast removal

Menu: –	
Shortcut: –	**See also:** Color Balance,
Version: 6.0, 7.0, CS, CS2	Variations, Auto Color Correction, Auto Levels

Photographing under a range of mixed lighting conditions can cause your pictures to have a strange color cast. There are several Photoshop tools that can be used to remove this tint from your photos.

The **Auto Color** and **Auto Levels** options both attempt to redistribute the colors and, in the case of Levels the tones as well, to achieve a neutral result. As with most automatic options there will be occasions when this approach works well and times when the results are not all you expect. If this occurs select Edit > Undo to reverse the changes applied and then try another cast removal approach.

For a more manual approach, both the **Color Balance** and **Variations** features allow incremental color changes to specific tonal areas (shadow, midtones, highlights) of the picture.

Color depth

Menu: Image > Mode	
Shortcut: –	**See also:** 16-bit, 8-bit, High
Version: 6.0, 7.0, CS, CS2	Dynamic Range

Each digital file you create (photograph or scan) is capable of representing a specific number of colors. This capability, usually referred to as the 'mode' or 'color depth' of the picture, is expressed in terms of the number of 'bits'.

Most images these days are created in 24-bit mode. This means that each of the three color channels (red, green and blue) is capable of displaying 256 levels of color (or 8 bits) each. When the channels are combined, a 24-bit image can contain a staggering 16.7 million discrete tones/ hues.

This is a vast amount of colors and would be seemingly more than we could ever need, see, or print, but many modern cameras and scanners are now capable of capturing up to 16 bits per channel or 'high-bit' capture. This means that each of the three colors can have up to 65,536 different levels and the image itself a whopping 281,474,976 million colors (last time I counted!).

Earlier versions of Photoshop were only capable of supporting 8-bit files, but CS2 supports both 8- and 16-bit files and can now open and edit (in a limited way) 32-bit or HDR files as well. Editing pictures in 16-bit or higher bit modes provides far better results (smoother and with more detail) than manipulation in 8-bit. Where possible perform all editing in 16-bit mode.

Color Dodge blending mode

Menu: –	
Shortcut: –	**See also:** Blend modes
Version: 6.0, 7.0, CS, CS2	

The Color Dodge blending mode is one of the group of modes that lighten the picture.

When the top layer is changed to the Color Dodge mode, its content is used to lighten the bottom layer in a dodging fashion. In the process, the bottom layer's color mirrors that of the upper layer.

Blending with a black upper layer produces no change.

40

C

Color Halftone filter

Menu: Filter > Pixelate > Color Halftone
Shortcut: –   **See also:** Filters
Version: 6.0, 7.0, CS, CS2

The Color Halftone filter replicates the look of the CMYK (Cyan, Magenta, Yellow and Black) printing process. The photograph is broken into the four colors and the tone for each of the colors represented by a series of dots. Where the color is strongest the dots are bigger and can even join up. In the lighter tones the dots are small and are surrounded by large areas of white paper.

The controls in the filter dialog are separated into two sections – the size of the dot that makes up the screen (1) and the angle (2) that will be applied to each of the color screens. In practice the best results are obtained when the dot size is altered and the screen angle left alone.

Color Halftone is one of the Pixelate group of filters.

Color jitter

Menu: Window > Brushes
Shortcut: F5   **See also:** Brush tool
Version: 7.0, CS, CS2

The Color Dynamics settings in the brush palette provide a range of options for altering the color jitter of the brush tool. The jitter characteristic controls the amount that the setting fluctuates.

The **Foreground/Background Jitter** (1) adjusts the oscillation between these two colors. The **Hue Jitter** (2) setting changes the hue color as you paint. The **Saturation Jitter** (3) controls variations in color strength and the **Brightness Jitter** (4) fluctuates the lightness of the tone.

In combination these settings control the overall color jitter of the brush tool.

Color management

Menu: –
Shortcut: –   **See also:** Color Settings
Version: 6.0, 7.0, CS, CS2

Good color management is the foundation of consistent color from the time of capture (photographing or scanning) through editing and enhancement tasks and finally to printing. Establishing a workflow that understands the capabilities and limitations of each of the devices in this production process is key to setting up a color managed system. For this reason professionals use an ICC (International Color Consortium) profile-based system to manage the color in their pictures.

The options that govern color management in Photoshop are grouped in a single dialog titled Color Settings. Here you select the working profiles that will be used for each picture type (RGB, CMYK and Grayscale) and determine when and how any color space conversions will occur.

 To ensure that you get the benefits of color management, be sure to turn on color management features for your camera, scanner, monitor, software and printer. Always tag your files as you capture them and then use this profile to help keep color consistency as you edit, output and share your work.

Color management, synchronized

Menu: –
Shortcut: –   **See also:** Bridge
Version: CS2

Over the last few years one of the most pressing issues for the digital photographer has been the question of how to maintain color control of his or her pictures throughout the whole production process. Thankfully companies like Adobe have been working hard on the problem and CS2 provides the best all round color management options for the digital worker that we have seen to date.

One feature that makes this new release stand out in this regard is the synchronized color management offered via Bridge. The Bridge application not only provides a single place to access and manage your media assets it also contains the ability to synchronize the color settings used in all Adobe CS2 applications.

To synchronize your color settings start with Bridge open and the Bridge Center option selected from the Favorites list (1). Next press the Synchronize color management button (2) at the bottom of the window and choose the color setting from those listed in the dialog that is displayed.

The Bridge Center workspace and therefore the Synchronized Color options are only available to Creative Suite 2 owners. The version of Bridge shipped with Photoshop alone does not contain these options.

Color modes

Menu: Image > Mode
Shortcut: Ctrl/Cmd Alt/Opt Shift L   **See also:** Color depth,
Version: 6.0, 7.0, CS, CS2   Bitmap images

Photoshop can create, edit and convert images to and from several different color modes. The mode of a picture document determines the maximum number of colors that can be stored in the file and this in turn affects the size of the file. Generally speaking more colors means a larger file size.

The mode options available in Photoshop are listed under the Image > Mode menu. They are:

Bitmap – Can only contain black and white colors.

Grayscale – Supports up to 256 levels of gray including black and white.

Duotone – A monochrome color mode that is used for printing tinted black and white images. Duotone uses two inks, Tritone three inks and quadtone four inksets.

Indexed Color – Can contain up to 256 different colors and is the default color mode for the GIF file format.

RGB Color – This is the default mode for all photos in Photoshop. It is an 8-bit color mode which means that it can support 256 levels of color in Red, Green and Blue channels: giving a combined maximum total number of hues possible of over 16 million. Colors in this mode are described by three numbers representing the red, green and blue value of the individual pixel.

CMYK – In this essentially 'printing only' color mode the value of each color is represented as a percentage of ink color.

Lab color – This mode is comprised of three channels – Lightness, 'a' color (green-red) and 'b' color (blue-yellow).

Multi-channel – This modes is generally for specialized printing applications and supports 256 levels of gray in each channel.

Color Range

Menu: Select > Color Range
Shortcut: –   **See also:** Selections
Version: 6.0, 7.0, CS, CS2

Photoshop's Color Range is a versatile tool that can be used to help you select and change the color of a part of your picture. This could easily be a model's lipstick, car paint work or, as in this case, red pupils.

With the picture open call up the Color Range dialog (Select > Color Range). To make it easier to see what you're doing click on Selection at the bottom of the palette to turn the preview window into a grayscale image. For this exercise also select Sampled Colors from the menu at the top of the palette.

Now click on the left-hand Eyedropper tool and position your cursor over a part of the red pupil and click once. You'll see areas of white appear on the grayscale preview. These are red pixels that are similar in color to the red you've just clicked. Adjust the Fuzziness slider to control the range of reds that are selected. Click OK when you are happy with your results.

Now with the pupil successfully selected use the Hue slider from the Hue/Saturation control to alter the color to a shade that is more suitable.

The Color Range palette also lets you choose which type of mask to put over the image as you work. We've been using None, but the menu box, labelled Selection Preview at the bottom of the palette, has four other options. Grayscale makes the image look like the palette's preview. Black Matte (right) shows the unselected area black. White Matte makes the unselected area white. Quick Mask puts red over unselected areas.

Before

After

42

C

Color Replacement tool

Menu: –
Shortcut: J
See also: Color Range
Version: 7.0, CS, CS2

The Color Replacement tool appears as the third option under the Brush and Pencil tools (1) in the Photoshop CS2 toolbar. This feature is used to replace the color in the photograph with the current foreground color and acts like a paintbrush that changes the color.

If you set the foreground color to black and the mode to hue it acts like a desaturation brush. You could previously do this by changing a photo from color to grayscale and then back to color, setting the History to the grayscale state and painting in with the History brush. Using the Color Replacement tool is a much quicker way.

It goes one stage further by working like the Magic eraser where it only replaces the color of pixels within the same tolerance range as the first sampled point.

Color Sampler tool

Menu: –
Shortcut: I
See also: Eyedropper tool
Version: 6.0, 7.0, CS, CS2

An Eyedropper tool that is used to place one or several sample points on the photo so you can compare color and density of each spot using measurements displayed in the Info palette.

A second set of measurements appears at the side of the current values, showing the adjustments you make when using controls such as levels, curves, contrast and brightness. In this example I placed four samples in the highlight areas of the waterfall so I could adjust curves and ensure there was still detail in most parts.

Color temperature

Menu: –
Shortcut: –
See also: Color cast removal, Variations, Auto Color Correction, Color Balance, Camera Raw
Version: 6.0, 7.0, CS, CS2

Color temperature refers to the color of the lighting used to illuminate your photos. Most digital cameras have a range of color temperature or white balance (1) settings designed to accommodate changing lighting conditions.

Matching your camera's setting to the light source in the picture will help ensure that the photograph is recorded without a color cast. Alternatively some cameras have an auto white balance option that attempts to match the light source and the way that the sensor records to obtain neutral cast-free pictures.

Photoshop also has Color Temperature sliders in the White Balance part (2) of Camera Raw. This feature is designed to correct imbalances between light source and sensor settings at the time of capture.

Color Settings

Menu: Edit > Color Settings
Shortcut: Ctrl/Cmd Shift K
See also: Color Management
Version: 6.0, 7.0, CS, CS2

Allows you to set up color profiles so that images you open up either use a pre-selected color space or are converted to a specific profile. Spend some time setting this up correctly and you'll maintain consistent color when the image is displayed and printed. Mac OSX users will find the item under the Photoshop menu not the Edit menu.

Colored Pencil filter

Menu: Filter > Artistic > Colored Pencil
Shortcut: –   See also: Filters
Version: 6.0, 7.0, CS, CS2

The Colored Pencil filter is one of the options in the Artistic group of filters. The feature creates a drawn version of the photograph simulating the effect of colored pencils. The detail in the image is retained and different tones are created using crosshatching.

Three slider controls can be found in the filter dialog. The Pencil Width (1) controls the bands of drawn color that replicate the picture's detail, the Stroke Pressure (2) adjusts the amount of color laid down on the paper surface and the Paper Brightness (3) determines the tone of the paper the pencil is drawn on (from black to white).

Colorize

Menu: Image > Adjustments > Hue/Saturation
Shortcut: Ctrl/Cmd U   See also: Hue/Saturation
Version: 6.0, 7.0, CS, CS2

The Colorize option (checkbox) at the bottom right of the Hue/Saturation dialog (1) provides a creative option for toning your photographs.

The option converts a colored image to a monochrome made up of a single dominant color and black and white.

Change the tint color by selecting different Hue values and alter the strength of the toning effect via the Saturation slider.

Hue/Saturation adjustments can also be made non-destructively to your picture by using a Hue/Saturation adjustment layer.

Compact mode

NEW for CS2

Compact mode, Bridge

Menu: Bridge: View > Compact Mode
Shortcut: Ctrl/Cmd Enter   **See also:** Bridge view modes
Version: CS2

As well as the standard operating system options such as maximize and minimize the Bridge window can be viewed in Compact, Ultra Compact and Full modes. These options are available by pressing the Compact (1) or Full mode (2) buttons on the features options bar. Pressing the Compact button while Bridge is already in Compact mode will cause the window to reduce to display just a title bar and folder menu. This view is called Ultra Compact mode.

Ultra Compact mode

Full mode

The options dialog box for the lossy JPEG file format provides a slider control that moves between the two extremes of small file with least image quality and large file with best image quality.

Compression

Menu: –
Shortcut: –   **See also:** JPEG format,
Version: 6.0, 7.0, CS, CS2   JPEG2000, TIFF

The files that hold our digital pictures store information about the color, brightness and position of the pixels that make up the image. As the resolution and color depth of pictures increase so too does the file itself. Some of the more recently released cameras are capable of capturing pictures with file sizes beyond 20 Mb each.

Large files like these take up a lot of storage room and are impossible to email. For this reason a lot of photographers shrink their files by applying a form of compression to their pictures.

Compression is a system that reorders and rationalizes the way in which the information is stored. The result is a file that is optimized and therefore reduced in size.

There are two different types of compression possible:

Lossy – This compression type is capable of shrinking files to very small sizes (file size can be reduced to as little as 1% of the original) but loses picture detail in the process. The JPEG file format uses this type of compression.

Lossless – The lossless approach maintains all the detail of the original but optimizes the file and can reduce file sizes by up to 40%. The TIFF file format is an example of a file format that uses this compression.

 Good compression comes from lossy storage of the image, but images that retain all their original quality are only possible via lossless systems.

Conditional Mode Change

Menu: File > Automate > Conditional Mode Change
Shortcut: –   **See also:** Actions
Version: 6.0, 7.0, CS, CS2

The Conditional Mode Change option is one of the commands located under the Automate menu. It is used to change the color mode of a picture from a 'source' (1) mode to a 'destination' (2) mode.

Add this command to an action sequence to keep the color mode of all files the same when the action is being performed.

This option as well as the Fit Image command are designed to be embedded into Photoshop actions to help facilitate the automation of a wide range of tasks.

Constrain Proportions

Menu: Image > Image Size
Shortcut: –   **See also:** Actions
Version: 6.0, 7.0, CS, CS2

When the Constrain Proportions option in the Image Size dialog is selected any changes will maintain the proportions of the photo's sides. Keeping the sides of a picture in proportion when changing size is also called maintaining the aspect ratio of the picture.

This option should always be selected unless you intentionally wish to squash or stretch the photo.

Contact Sheet

Menu: File > Automate > Contact Sheet II
Bridge: Tools > Photoshop > Contact Sheet II
Shortcut: –   **See also:** Automate
Version: 6.0, 7.0, CS, CS2

The Contact Sheet option creates a series of small thumbnail versions of all the images in a catalog or those that were multi-selected before opening the tool.

These small pictures are arranged on pages and can be labeled with filename caption. Once created it is an easy task to print a series of these contact sheets that can be kept as a permanent record of a folder's images. The job of selecting the best pictures to manipulate and print can then be made with hard copies of your photos without having to spend the time and money to output every image to be considered.

The feature can be accessed via the Tools > Photoshop options in Bridge or the Automate menu in Photoshop. Individual pictures can be multi-selected for inclusion in the feature when working via Bridge. In contrast, complete folders of photos are used when the feature is accessed from within Photoshop.

The options contained within the Contact Sheet dialog allow the user to select the number of columns of image thumbnails and the content of the text labels that are added. The page size and orientation can be chosen via the Page Setup button.

Multi-select the pictures from inside the Bridge. Then select Tools > Photoshop > Contact Sheet II. If Photoshop is not already opened the program will start and the Contact Sheet II dialog will appear.

Set up the document size, color mode and resolution. Choose the number of columns to use (and therefore the total number of thumbnails to place on a single sheet) and pick the Auto-Spacing and Rotate for Best Fit options. Adjust the size and style of the caption text and press the OK button to create the contact sheet document.

Conté Crayon filter

Menu: Filter > Sketch > Conté Crayon
Filter > Filter Gallery > Sketch > Conté Crayon
Shortcut: –   **See also:** –
Version: 6.0, 7.0, CS, CS2

The Conté Crayon filter is one of the options in the Sketch group of filters. The feature replicates the effect of a traditional conté crayon drawing created with dark and light crayons on a textured paper background. The detail in the image is retained and different tones and colors are created using shaded areas of background and foreground color.

The controls for the filter are divided into two sections – one that controls the interaction of the dark and light tones or picture details (1) and a second that houses sliders and drop-down menus for adjusting the surface texture (2).

NEW for CS2

Context menus

Menu: –	
Shortcut: –	**See also:** –
Version: 6.0, 7.0, CS, CS2	

Photoshop contains a context menu system which provides a pop-up menu of options when you right-click (Ctrl-click – Mac) over an image, tool, selection or palette. Context menus are not available for all items in the workspace.

Continuous tone

Posterized tone

Content area, Bridge

Menu: Window > Workspace > Filmstrip Focus	
Shortcut: Ctrl/Cmd F5	**See also:** Bridge View modes
Version: CS2	

When in Filmstrip Focus mode (1) the Bridge browser displays a preview of the currently selected thumbnail in the content area of the screen. This workspace setup allows the user to review a group of images quickly and easily while taking time to overview a larger preview for editing purposes.

Jump to a horizontal version (2) of the Filmstrip Focus mode by clicking the Switch Orientation button at the bottom right of the content area (3).

You can switch to other view modes by making a different selection from the Window > Workspace menu.

Contiguous option

Menu: –	
Shortcut: –	**See also:** Magic Wand tool,
Version: 6.0, 7.0, CS, CS2	Paint Bucket tool

The Contiguous option is available in tools that base their changes or selection on locating pixels of a specific color in a photo. The option can be found in the option bars of both the Magic Wand and Paint Bucket tools and controls how the pixels are selected throughout the image.

Choosing Contiguous will restrict the selection to those pixels adjacent to where the tool was first clicked on the image surface (1).

Turn the setting off and the tools will locate similar colored pixels throughout the whole photo irrespective of whether they are connected to the pixel first selected (2).

Continuous tone image

Menu: –	
Shortcut: –	**See also:** Bitmap images,
Version: 6.0, 7.0, CS, CS2	Halftone Pattern filter

The term continuous tone refers to pictures that have a range of tones and colors that move seamlessly from one to another.

Traditionally this term was used to describe photographs (black and white or color) and to distinguish them from those images printed in magazines, whose tones are created with a series of dots.

Digital photographs whether displayed on screen or output in printed form give the appearance of a continuous tone picture even though the photograph is entirely created of very small blocks called pixels.

It is important to maintain the appearance of continuous tone in our photographs throughout the editing and enhancement process. Sometimes the extreme correction needed for poorly exposed pictures causes the colors and tones of the photograph to lose the continuous appearance and become posterized.

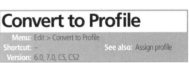

Contract, selection

Menu: Select > Modify > Contract
Shortcut: –   **See also:** Expand selection
Version: 6.0, 7.0, CS, CS2

An active selection can be altered and adjusted using the options listed under the Select > Modify menu.

One option is the Contract command which reduces the size of the selection by the number of pixels entered into the feature's dialog.

If the selection incorporates part of the document edge this part of the marquee will not be changed by the command.

Contrast, image

Menu: –
Shortcut: –   **See also:** Brightness/Contrast,
Version: 6.0, 7.0, CS, CS2   Shadow/Highlight,
Auto Levels, Auto
Contrast, Levels
command, Curves

The contrast of a picture refers to how the tones are distributed between black and white points.

A low contrast photograph can appear dull and generally contains no pure black or white points anywhere in the image. A high contrast picture does contain the black and white tones but in extreme examples, where too much contrast exists, subtle shadow and highlight details disappear as they are represented as either black or white.

Picture contrast can be adjusted in Photoshop by using features such as Auto Levels, Curves, Auto Contrast, Brightness/Contrast, Levels and Shadows/Highlights.

Convert to Profile

Menu: Edit > Convert to Profile
Shortcut: –   **See also:** Assign profile
Version: 6.0, 7.0, CS, CS2

The Edit > Convert to Profile (1) option changes the color values of the original image to match the newly selected color space. The dialog displays the current space of the image – Source Space (2), provides a drop-down menu of choices for the Destination Space (3), Engine (4) and Intent (5) conversion options as well as checkboxes for Black Point Compensation, Dither and Flatten Image (6).

You can also choose to attach a different ICC profile to an image by selecting the Edit > Assign Profile option. This feature lets you assign the chosen color space to the picture without changing the value of the image's colors to the profile.

Convert to 8 Bits/Channel

Menu: Image > Mode > 8 Bits/Channel
Shortcut: –   **See also:** 8-bit, 16-bit, HDR
Version: 6.0, 7.0, CS, CS2

Photoshop contains many features that work with 16-bit files (and a few that work with 32-bit documents as well), but there are other tools and options that can only be applied to an 8-bit file.

To use these features you will need to convert your file to 8 bits per channel before accessing the tool. Do this by selecting Image > Mode > 8 Bits/Channel.

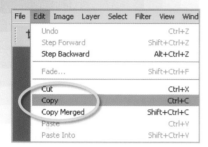

Copy command

Menu: Edit > Copy
Shortcut: Ctrl/Cmd C   **See also:** Copy Merged
Version: 6.0, 7.0, CS, CS2   command,
                                            Paste command

Just like other computer software (word processing and spreadsheet software) Photoshop contains the standard Copy and Paste commands.

Located under the Edit menu, the Copy option duplicates the contents of the picture parts in the current selection and stores it in the Clipboard memory of the computer.

Copying is usually the first step in the process; the next action is usually to paste the picture part into the same or a new document. This step is handled by the Edit > Paste command.

Copy Merged command

Menu: Edit > Copy Merged
Shortcut: Ctrl/Cmd Shft C   **See also:** Copy command,
Version: 6.0, 7.0, CS, CS2   Paste command

Just like the Copy command, the Copy Merged option copies the contents of a selection, but the difference is that this command also copies and merges the content of all the layers in the document.

This feature is particularly helpful for creating a single layer copy of a multi-layered composition but without merging or flattening the original.

To make a single layer copy of the content of a multi-layered Photoshop document without flattening or merging start by selecting the whole canvas area using Select > All.

Now copy the merged layers using Edit > Copy Merged and then create a new document the size of the copied layers with File > New > Blank File and paste down the merged copy using Edit > Paste.

Craquelure filter

Menu: Filter > Texture > Craquelure
          Filter > Filter Gallery > Texture > Craquelure
Shortcut: –   **See also:** Filters
Version: 6.0, 7.0, CS, CS2

The Craquelure filter is one of the options in the Texture group of filters. The feature creates an effect that looks as if the picture has been created on a surface of cracked mud.

Three slider controls can be found in the filter dialog. The Crack Spacing (1) controls the distance between crack edges, the Crack Depth (2) adjusts the width of the crack line and its shadow, and the Crack Brightness (3) determines how dominant or strong the crack lines will appear in the final result.

Before

After

Image Size...	Alt+Ctrl+I
Canvas Size...	Alt+Ctrl+C
Pixel Aspect Ratio	▶
Rotate Canvas	▶
Crop	
Trim...	
Reveal All	

Crop and Straighten Photos

Menu: File > Automate > Crop and Straighten Photos
Shortcut: –   **See also:** Crop tool
Version: CS, CS2

This feature, new to the Photoshop CS edition of the program, appeared a few years ago in the software that was used with flatbed scanners.

It automatically detects the edges of a photo, which may have been scanned a little crooked and with too much background surroundings, and crops off the waste pixels. It also rotates the image if the picture was scanned at an angle like this example.

Crop command

Menu: Image > Crop
Shortcut: –   **See also:** Crop tool
Version: 6.0, 7.0, CS, CS2

An on-the-fly cropping technique that is an alternative to using the Crop tool starts with drawing a regular rectangular selection or marquee to define the size and shape of the crop (1).

Once the area has been selected the Crop option is chosen from the Image menu (2).

The picture parts outside the selection marquee are removed or cropped.

Crop marks printing E

Menu: File > Print with Preview
Shortcut: Ctrl/Cmd Alt/Opt P   **See also:** Print options
Version: 6.0, 7.0, CS, CS2

One of the many print options available in the Photoshop Print with Preview dialog is the ability to add crop marks to a print. These vertical and horizontal lines provide a visual indication where the edge of the picture is on the paper.

The crop marks are generally used to aid with trimming the excess paper from the surrounds of the print.

To add crop marks to your print check the Corner Crop Marks option from the Output settings in the Print Preview dialog.

Before

After

50

Crop tool

Menu: –
Shortcut: C **See also:** Crop command
Version: 6.0, 7.0, CS, CS2

The act of cropping or removing parts of a picture that are unwanted is a skill that most digital photographers use regularly.

Photoshop has a specially designed cropping feature called the Crop tool. Cropping is a simple matter of drawing a rectangle around the parts of the picture that you wish to keep leaving the sections that will be removed outside of the marquee. The areas outside the cropping marquee are shaded a specific color (usually semi-transparent black) to allow the viewer to imagine the results of the crop.

To help with fine adjustments the edges and corners of the cropping marquee contain small squares called handles. The marquee can be resized or reshaped at any time by click-dragging one of the handles. When you are satisfied with your crop you can execute the command by double-clicking your cursor inside the cropping marquee, pushing the Enter key or clicking on the 'tick' in the options bar.

Pro's Tip

1. The settings entered into the width, height and resolution sections of the Crop tool option bar remain until you click the Clear button.

2. If you want the dimensions and resolution of an image to become the settings used to crop a second picture then select the original and click the Front Image button. The picture's characteristics are input into the settings area of the tool ready for the next crop.

1

To start a new crop select the Crop tool and click-drag a marquee over the parts of the picture you want to keep. You don't have to be exact with this first rectangle as you can adjust the size and shape of the marquee by click-dragging the corner and side handles.

By dragging the cursor whilst it is outside the marquee it can be rotated to crop and straighten at the same time.

2

To help you imagine how your cropped picture will appear Photoshop shades the area of the picture that is to be removed. You can alter the color and opacity of this shading (called the 'Shield') using the settings in the option bar.

The crop is executed by clicking the 'tick' in the options bar.

• •

Extension technique

You can make a crop of a specific size and resolution by adding these values to the options bar before drawing the cropping marquee. Using this feature you can crop and resize in one step.

With the dimensions and resolution values set when you click-drag the Crop tool it will only draw rectangles the size and shape of the values you have entered.

When you execute the crop, Photoshop will automatically crop and resize the picture. Here we have prepared the image to be printed on a sheet of 10 × 8 inch paper at a resolution of 200 pixels per inch.

Crosshatch filter

Menu: Filter > Brush Strokes > Crosshatch
Filter > Filter Gallery > Brush Strokes > Crosshatch
Shortcut: – **See also:** Filters
Version: 6.0, 7.0, CS, CS2

The Crosshatch filter is one of the options in the Brush Strokes group of filters. The feature recreates the color and different tones in the picture using crosshatching or a series of overlapping strokes.

Three slider controls can be found in the filter dialog. The Stroke Length (1) controls the length of the crosshatching stroke, the Sharpness (2) adjusts how crisp the edge of the stroke appears and the Strength (3) determines how obvious the effect is to the viewer.

Cursors, tool pointer

Menu: Edit > Preferences > Display & Cursors
Shortcut: –   **See also:** Preferences
Version: 6.0, 7.0, CS, CS2   Photoshop

The tool pointer or cursor that is displayed when working with Photoshop tools can be changed to a range of options. Setting up the default pointer style is controlled via the options in the Edit > Preferences > Displays & Cursors dialog. Here you can select from the following cursor options:

Standard – The pointer is displayed as the tool icon.

Precise – The pointer is displayed as a set of cross hairs.

Normal Brush Size – The pointer is displayed at 50% of the size of the brush tip.

Full Size Bush Tip – The pointer is displayed in the size and shape of the current brush tip.

Show Cross hair in Brush Tip – Places the cross hair at the center of the currently selected brush tip.

The **Caps Lock** key switches the cursor between Brush Size and its original setting.

Other tools - Standard

Other tools - Precise

Painting cursor - Full size

Painting cursor - Precise

Painting cursor - Standard

Painting cursor - Normal

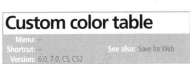

Custom color table

Menu: –
Shortcut: –   **See also:** Save for Web
Version: 6.0, 7.0, CS, CS2

Images produced to be used on the Web need small file sizes. Photoshop reduces the number of colors from millions down to just 256 when it saves files as GIFs and the colors that are used can be saved as a custom table. This photo of canal boats would contain these 256 colors when reduced.

Curves

Menu: Image > Adjustments > Curves
Shortcut: Ctrl/Cmd M   **See also:** Levels command,
Version: 6.0, 7.0, CS, CS2   Shadow/Highlight

Curves is an advanced tonal control that is a favorite with experienced users and offers the most accurate contrast, color and brightness adjustments of any Photoshop feature.

Its dialog (1) has a graph with vertical and horizontal scales representing input and output brightness. When you first open this you'll see a straight line running through the graph at 45° from the bottom left to the top right.

The bottom left represents the shadow area (2), top right is highlights (4) and the midpoint is midtones (3). You can drag the line by clicking on it and holding down as you move the mouse. Moving the midpoint up has a lightening effect (5) and down darkens the image. Use the Eyedropper tool and Ctrl/ Cmd click anywhere on the image and its brightness value will appear as a point on the line. You can then move this point up or down to darken or lighten that part of the image. The picture will look natural, providing you create either a straight line or an arc. The best results are usually achieved with a very shallow S-shaped curve (6), and is the reason why it's called Curves. The

usual Curve to make is a slight downward direction of the 3/4 shadow areas and a slight upward movement of the first quarter highlight areas, creating a very gentle S shape. This gives a boost to contrast without clipping shadow or highlight detail that could occur when Levels or Brightness/ Contrast is used.

You can reverse the graph if you prefer the shadow detail to be at the top right and the highlights at the bottom left by clicking on the arrow on the horizontal bar.

In Photoshop CS2 curves also appears as an adjustment option in the Camera Raw feature.

Before

After

Custom Shape tool

Menu: –
Shortcut: U   See also: Shape tools
Version: 6.0, 7.0, CS, CS2

The Custom Shape tool is one of the group of shape tools that includes rectangle, ellipse, rounded rectangle, polygon and line. All these drawing options create hard-edged, or vector-based, graphics.

The Custom Shape tool allows you to draw a variety of pre-made shapes. After selecting the tool and picking the fill color, you draw the shape by clicking and dragging the mouse. Different shapes can be selected from the drop-down thumbnail list under the Shape preview in the options bar. A new layer is created automatically for each new shape. This layer is made up of two parts – the 'Fill' and the 'Path'. Double-clicking the Fill icon will give you the opportunity to change the color. After clicking the Path icon you can edit the shape using the Direct Selection Tool.

The tool's options include:

Unconstrained – Set width and height by dragging the mouse.

Defined Proportions – Only allows shape drawings of a specific proportion.

Defined Size – Draws the shape at the size that the shape was initially created.

Fixed Size – The shape is drawn according to the size settings you input.

From Center – Draws the shape from the center outwards rather than from a corner.

Cut command

Menu: Edit > Cut
Shortcut: Ctrl/Cmd X   See also: Copy command,
Version: 6.0, 7.0, CS, CS2   Paste command

As part of the standard editing control group, which also includes the Paste and Copy commands, the Cut option removes image parts to the clipboard. A selection must be made first before using the command. After cutting the selection, the contents of the selection area are filled with the background color (1) or in the case of cutting a background layer the selection area is filled with transparency.

The picture parts cut to the clipboard can then be pasted down as a new layer in the same file or used as a basis for the creation of a new document. With a selection still active, pressing the Delete key will perform the same function as the Edit > Cut command except that using the Cut command will put the image on the clipboard, whereas pressing the Delete key will not.

Custom filter

Menu: Filter > Other > Custom
Shortcut: –   See also: Filters
Version: 6.0, 7.0, CS, CS2

The Custom filter is one of the options in the Other group of filters. The feature allows the user to create, save, load and share their own customized filter effects.

The filter dialog contains a grid of text boxes into which you can enter numbers that will alter the brightness of the pixels that the filter is applied to. Values from −999 to +999 can be entered into any of the boxes. Values don't have to be entered into all boxes.

The central box (1) represents the pixels being evaluated with the values placed in those around the center being adjustments made to the surrounding pixels.

Cutout filter

Menu: Filter > Artistic > Cutout filter
Shortcut: –   See also: Filters
Version: 6.0, 7.0, CS, CS2

The Cutout filter is one of the options in the Artistic group of filters. The feature recreates the tone and shape of the original photo using a series of flat areas of color similar to pieces of 'cutout' paper. Three slider controls can be found in the dialog. The Number of Levels (1) controls the number of colors, Edge Simplicity (2) adjusts how much detail will be in the edge of the flat areas and the Edge Fidelity (3) determines how flat the edge detail will be.

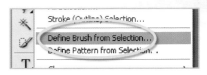

53

D

Darken blend mode

Menu: –		
Shortcut: –	**See also:** Blend modes	
Version: 6.0, 7.0, CS, CS2		

The Darken blending mode is one of the group of modes that darken the picture.

When the top layer is changed to the Darken mode both layers are examined at each part of the picture. When the darkest color is located – it can be from either layer – it is selected as the final color.

Next the pixels in the top layer are compared to the final color; if they are lighter then they are replaced, if darker they are left unchanged.

Define Brush

Menu: Edit > Define Brush Preset		
Shortcut: –	**See also:** Brush tool	
Version: 6.0, 7.0, CS, CS2		

Photoshop includes a sophisticated Brush engine that when combined with the program's ability to make a brush tip from almost any image allows the user unlimited drawing options to play with.

At the center of brush customization is the Define Brush Preset feature. After using any of the selection tools to outline a part of a picture that will be the new brush tip, select Define Brush Preset under the Edit menu. Name the new brush and click OK. The new tip will now be available at the bottom of the list of brushes in the tool's options bar.

In the example below a customized Holly Brush tip is created to be used to help decorate a Christmas card. See over.

Open the source picture containing the image part that you want to use as a base for the new brush tip. Using one of the selection tools outline the image part. Here I selected a single holly leaf.

With the selection still active pick Edit > Define Brush Preset and enter a new name for the Holly brush. Click OK to add the brush to the current set of brush tips.

Select the new brush tip from the bottom of the brush list thumbnails. Set the foreground color to black and click and drag to draw with the brush.

To further refine the look and characteristics of the new brush click on the Brushes Palette button in the options bar. Apply new settings for the Shape and Color dynamics and add some Scattering options before changing the fore- and background colors. Click and drag to test the new brush tip.
When completed select the Save Brush option from the pop-out menu in the Brushes palette.

Define Custom Shape

Menu: Edit > Define Custom Shape
Shortcut: –   **See also:** Custom Shape
Version: 6.0, 7.0, CS, CS2   tool

The Custom Shape tool in Photoshop draws a variety of vector-based shapes. The package ships with a variety of pre-made graphic shapes to choose from but you can also add to this group with shapes that you create yourself.

As the Shape tool uses vector-based artwork as its base, to create your own shape you must use the Pen tool to draw the outline of the design (1).

With the path that outlines your shape complete select the Define Custom Shape option from the Edit menu and add a name for the shape in the Shape Name dialog that pops up (2).

The newly created shape can now be accessed like an other shape from the Custom Shape Tool library (3).

Custom shapes can also be used in the Shape Blur filter which is new for Photoshop CS2.

Define Pattern

Menu: Edit > Define Pattern
Shortcut: –   **See also:** Define Brush
Version: 6.0, 7.0, CS, CS2

Working in a similar way to the Define Brush Preset feature, this option creates and saves a pattern tile for use with tools such as the Pattern Stamp and the Fill command.

To create a new pattern pick Rectangular Marquee tool from the selection tools in the toolbar. Make sure that the Feather and Anti-aliased options are both turned off. Select the picture part that will become the new pattern. Choose the Edit > Define Pattern option and add a new pattern name in the pop-up dialog.

The pattern you create is saved to the bottom of the Pattern Picker (1) menu and becomes available for use immediately after its creation.

Before

After

After De-interlacing

Defringe

Menu: Layer > Matting > Defringe	
Shortcut: –	**See also:** –
Version: 6.0, 7.0, CS, CS2	

No matter how hard you try, when cutting round a subject you usually leave a few pixels from the old background. When you paste the cutout to the new background the unwanted pixels may stick out like a sore thumb. This orange flower, for example, cut out from a typical green foliage background has a few dark green pixels around the edge that show up when it's pasted to its new blue background.

The Defringe command changes these green pixels to orange to produce a cleaner effect. Like most commands, you can enter a pixel value, in this case, a width of between 1 and 200 pixels, depending on the nature of your original selection.

The picture above left is the straight cutout and above right is after a defringe value of 50 was applied to the pasted image.

De-interlace filter

Menu: Filter > Video > De-interlace	
Shortcut: –	**See also:** –
Version: 6.0, 7.0, CS, CS2	

Photoshop has the ability to manipulate and edit single video frames captured from movies, but the photos derived from video sources often need extra processing other than the steps usually involved with still pictures.

The process used to record digital video means that photos captured in this way may contain some missing pixels (every second video line). The De-interlace filter is designed to replace this missing picture detail by either interpolating the pixels or duplicating the ones surrounding the area (1). Interpolation provides the smoothest results and duplication the sharpest.

Also included in the filter dialog is the option to select which video field to keep and which to eliminate (2). If you are unsure which option to select apply the filter to the image with different options set creating two example photographs and then compare the results.

Delete, layers

Menu: Layer > Delete Layer	
Shortcut: –	**See also:** Layers, Layers palette
Version: 6.0, 7.0, CS, CS2	

There are four ways to delete a single layer from the layer stack in Photoshop.

1. Select the layer in the Layers palette and then drag it to the dustbin icon (Delete Layer button) at the bottom of the palette.

2. Select the layer in the palette, click on the dustbin icon and then select Yes in the confirmation dialog box. To avoid this dialog box hold down the Alt/Option key when clicking the dustbin.

3. After selecting the layer to be discarded, choose Layer > Delete Layer.

4. Make sure that the layer to remove is selected in the palette then choose Delete Layer from the pop-up menu displayed via the sideways button (top right of the palette).

Before

Full color

oshop

| Layer | Select | Filter | View | Window | Help |

All   Ctrl+A
Deselect   Ctrl+D
Reselect   Shift+Ctrl+D
Inverse   Shift+Ctrl+I

All Layers   Alt+Ctrl+A
Deselect Layers
Similar Layers

Color Range...

Feather...   Alt+Ctrl+D
Modify   ▶

Grow
Similar

Transform Selection

Load Selection...
Save Selection...

After

Fully desaturated (-100)

Delete selection

Menu: –	
Shortcut: Delete	**See also:** Cut command,
Version: 6.0, 7.0, CS, CS2	Copy command

The contents of active selections can be deleted by pressing the Delete key. This action results in the pixels contained within the selection being converted to the current background color.

The results are the same as selecting Edit > Cut with an active selection with the exception that deleting does not store a copy of the selected area on the clipboard.

In the example, a rectangular selection was made on the surface of the picture before hitting the Delete key. To soften the edges the selection was feathered (1) first before deleting.

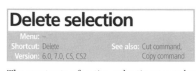

| er | Select | Filter | View | Window |

Feather: 50 px   ☐ Anti-alias

①

Partially desaturated (-50)

Desaturate

Menu: Image > Adjustments > Desaturate	
Shortcut: Shft Ctrl/Cmd U	**See also:** Grayscale images,
Version: 6.0, 7.0, CS, CS2	Grayscale Mode

The term saturation refers to the vividness of the color in the picture. Desaturating the color reduces the color's strength in the photograph. Desaturating the image totally removes all color from the picture leaving a grayscale image.

The Hue/Saturation feature (1) in Photoshop is the key control for adjusting the saturation of colors. Moving the middle slider (Saturation) in the dialog to the left allows gradual desaturation of the colors in the picture. Moving the control completely to the left produces an image with no color.

Color can also be removed or its vibrancy enhanced during Raw file editing via the Saturation slider in the Camera Raw feature.

The Desaturate option in the Image > Adjustment menu creates the same effect.

Most professionals don't convert images to grayscale via the desaturation route, instead they preferred to use techniques that have more control such as those that use the Channel Mixer otpion.

Deselect

Menu: Select > Deselect	
Shortcut: Ctrl/Cmd D	**See also:** Selections
Version: 6.0, 7.0, CS, CS2	

To remove an active selection from the canvas choose Select > Deselect from the menu bar or use the key combination Ctrl/Cmd D.

Alternatively, you can click anywhere on the canvas outside of the current selection area. This may cause a new selection to be created if you are in the middle of using a selection tool such as the Magic Wand.

Hue/Saturation

Edit: Master

Hue: 0
Saturation: -50
Lightness: 0

OK
Cancel
Help

☐ Colorize
☑ Preview

Deselect Layers

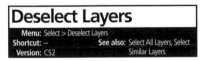

Menu: Select > Deselect Layers
Shortcut: –   **See also:** Select All Layers, Select
Version: CS2   Similar Layers

Photoshop CS2 introduces some changes to the way that layers are linked/grouped. You can now Shift-click layers in the Layers palette to multi-select groups of layers.

The Select > Deselect Layers menu item is one of the new commands that can be used in conjunction with the multi-selection of layers. Selecting the option deselects all currently selected layers and leaves no layer active or selected in the Layers palette.

Pro's Tip Another way to select multiple layers is to choose the Auto Select Layer and Auto Select Groups options in the move tool's options bar and then drag a selection marquee around the layers in the workspace.

Despeckle filter

Menu: Filter > Noise > Despeckle
Shortcut: –   **See also:** Reduce Noise
Version: 6.0, 7.0, CS, CS2

The Despeckle filter is one of the options in the Noise group of filters. The feature smooths the speckled appearance of photos taken with high ISO settings whilst trying to retain as much detail in the original as possible.

The filter isolates the edges and areas of high contrast in the picture before applying its smoothing changes.

As no controls, or preview, are provided with the filter, using the feature is a matter of 'try it and see'. If the results are unsatisfactory then you can undo the filter changes by selecting Edit > Undo Despeckle.

Generally, better results are obtained using the more sophisticated and controllable Reduce Noise filter. So as a general rule use the Reduce Noise filter for color noise problems and Despeckle for larger areas of more uniform noise.

Diamond gradient

Menu: –
Shortcut: G (Gradient tool)   **See also:** Curves, Shadow/
Version: 6.0, 7.0, CS, CS2   Highlight

Photoshop has five different gradient options. All the gradient types gradually change color and tone from one point in the picture to another.

The Diamond gradient (1) changes color from a center point outwards in a diamond shape.

D

D

Difference blend mode

Menu: –
Shortcut: –   **See also:** Blend modes
Version: 6.0, 7.0, CS, CS2

The Difference blending mode is one of the group of modes that compare and highlight the differences between the top and bottom layers.

By changing to the Difference mode both layers are compared and the color values in the layer (top or bottom) where pixels are brightest are subtracted from the other layer's colors. In this way, colors in the top layer can be subtracted from the bottom, or values in the bottom layer can be taken away from the top based on layer brightness.

Blending with a black upper layer produces no change. Blending with a white upper layer inverts the bottom layer's colors.

Difference Clouds filter

Menu: Filter > Render > Difference Clouds
Shortcut: –   **See also:** Filters
Version: 6.0, 7.0, CS, CS2

The Difference Clouds filter is one of the options in the Render group of filters. The feature fills the document with randomly drawn clouds based on variations in hues ranging from the foreground to background colors.

Applying the filter once creates a basic cloud pattern (1) with colors fluctuating between the foreground and background hues. Applying the filter several times creates a more random effect with new colors and textures entering the picture (2).

Diffuse Glow filter

Menu: Filter > Distort > Diffuse Glow
       Filter > Filter Gallery > Distort > Diffuse Glow
Shortcut: –   **See also:** Filters
Version: 6.0, 7.0, CS, CS2

The Diffuse Glow filter is one of the options in the Distort group of filters. The feature adds a strong softening and diffusion effect to the photograph. As a result large areas of tone appear to glow and the whole photograph takes a lighter, more high-key look.

Three slider controls can be found in the filter dialog. The Graininess slider (1) controls the amount of grain-like texture in the resultant photo, the Glow Amount (2) adjusts the degree that bright colors bleed into the surrounding areas and the Clear Amount (3) determines the strength of the diffusion effect.

Diffuse filter

Menu: Filter > Stylize > Diffuse
Shortcut: –   **See also:** Filters
Version: 6.0, 7.0, CS, CS2

The Diffuse filter is one of the options in the Stylize group of filters. The feature softens and diffuses the look of the picture by moving the image pixels around. The effect can be quite subtle and generally more control over the application of diffusion can be obtained using the Diffuse Glow filter.

Four different settings (1) and a preview window are available in the filter dialog.

Normal – Applies the effect randomly throughout all the pixels in the picture.

Darken Only – Replaces light pixels in the photograph with darker ones.

Lighten Only – Replaces darker pixels with lighter ones.

Anisotropic – Applies the soften to all pixels in the picture.

Original

Before

Directional lighting

Direct Selection tool

Menu:	–
Shortcut: A	See also: Paths
Version: 6.0, 7.0, CS, CS2	

The Direct Selection tool is one of a pair of selection tools (1) used for manipulating paths.

Direct Selection tool – This tool is used to select path segments as well as picking up the anchor points on a path made by the Pen tool. Once selected the anchor points can be used to move the entire path, change a point or create a Bézier curve around the subject (2).

To select a path segment with the tool either click onto one of the anchor points or drag a marquee over the segment area.

Path Selection tool – Use this tool to select the whole path by clicking anywhere inside the path boundaries.

Pro's Tip

1. To select the whole path with the Direct Selection tool Alt/Opt-click inside the path.

2. Ctrl/Cmd-click on an anchor point to activate the Direct Selection tool.

3. To select additional path segments hold down the Shift key whilst clicking on the segment.

Directional option, Lighting Effects filter

Menu:	Editor: Filter > Render > Lighting Effects
Shortcut: –	See also: Filters
Version: 6.0, 7.0, CS, CS2	

The Lighting Effects filter provides a vast array of options to adjust the way that light is distributed in, or projected on, your photos. One of the options is the lighting type. The choices are:

Omni – Shines light in all directions like a naked light bulb.

Spotlight – Shines light in a beam shaped like an ellipse.

Directional – Shines light as if the light source is far away from the picture.

You can adjust a directional light type in the following ways:

1. Drag the center circle to move the light.

2. To change the direction of the light drag the square end and move it to a separate angle or position in the photograph.

3. To adjust the strength of the light, click and drag the end circle to make the line longer. The shorter the line the brighter the light source.

Displace filter

Menu:	Editor: Filter > Distort > Displace
Shortcut: –	See also: Filters
Version: 6.0, 7.0, CS, CS2	

The Displace filter changes the look of a photo by shifting the position of pixels in the original image. The position and amount of the shift are determined by a displacement map picture which is combined with the original photo as part of the filtering process.

To displace a picture, start by selecting the filter from the Distort menu. Next set the values in the filter dialog (1). In this example I used 100% for both scales, Stretch To Fit and Repeat Edge Pixels settings. Click OK and then choose a displacement map from those saved in the Photoshop/Plug-ins/Displacment Map folder (2).

After displacement

Displacement map

After DIY displacement

Displacement maps

Menu: –
Shortcut: –   See also: Displace filter
Version: 6.0, 7.0, CS, CS2

Displacement maps are Photoshop files (PSD) that have been designed for use with the Displace filter. The program ships with several examples but you can also make your own.

The amount of displacement in the final picture is based on the tonal value of the map. Dark areas or those pixels with values approaching 0 give the maximum negative shift. Light areas or those with values near 255 produce the maximum positive shift. Middle values (around a value of 128) produce no displacement.

Use the filters and painting tools in Photoshop to create your own maps.

After displacement – B

Displacement map – B

Start creating a displacement map by resetting the fore- and background colors to default (black and white). Then create some artwork. Here I filled a new document with a linear gradient.

Next, to add a bit more of a graphic edge to the map I used the Distort > Wave filter to convert the gradient to tall black and white spikes.

The finished map was then saved as a Photoshop (PSD) file to the Photoshop/ plug-ins/displacement maps folder.

The example image was opened and the Distort > Displace filter selected. Both scales were set to 100% and the Stretch To Fit and Repeat Edge Pixel options were selected. After clicking OK I browsed for and located my newly created 'spike' map which was then used as a basis for the picture's distortion.

Before

After

Dissolve blend mode

Menu: –
Shortcut: –   See also: Blend modes
Version: 6.0, 7.0, CS, CS2

The Dissolve blending mode is one of the group of modes that lighten the picture.

Using the mode blends top and bottom layers using a pattern of pixels. As the opacity of the top layer drops, more of the bottom layer can be seen. The effect is similar to the dissolve transition or editing cut found on many video editing or slide show creation software packages.

Blending when the top layer's opacity is set to 100% produces no effect. Reduce the top layer's opacity setting to see the change. The example uses an 80% opacity for the top layer.

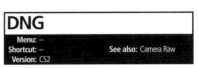

Distorting a layer

Menu: Edit > Transform > Distort	
Shortcut: –	**See also:** Free Transform
Version: 6.0, 7.0, CS, CS2	command, Skew, Scale, Rotate Canvas, Perspective options, Perspective changing, Warp

The Edit > Transform menu contains six options that allow you to change the shape of your pictures from their standard rectangle format. The Distort feature is one of these options and is used to stretch and squeeze your photos.

After selecting Image > Transform > Distort (1) you may be prompted to change the background to a standard layer ready for transformation. Click Yes in this dialog. Next change the shape of your picture by click-dragging the corner handles to new positions in the document. When completed either double-click on the transformed layer or press the Enter key to 'commit' the changes.

To cancel the changes at any time during the distortion process press the Esc key.

Holding down the Alt/Opt key whilst distorting mirrors the changes around the center point of the photo.

Distortion filters

Menu: Filter > Distort	
Shortcut: –	**See also:** Filters
Version: 6.0, 7.0, CS, CS2	

A collection of filters that distort the image in a variety of ways. If you have an older computer be patient, some of these filters are memory intensive and apply to your image at a snail's pace.

Use these filter options with care. If applied to a full image the results can often look a bit naff. When used creatively on selections within an image the filters can be much more valuable. In the example above the Zigzag filter was used was in a selection of just the water.

To control the filtering effect even more try using the Edit > Fade command directly after applying the filter to the picture.

DNG

Menu: –	
Shortcut: –	**See also:** Camera Raw
Version: CS2	

Many medium to high level digital cameras support saving images in a Raw file format. The format has many advantages for photographers offering them greater control over the tone and color in their files but there is only one standard available for the Raw files. Each camera manufacturer has their own flavor of the file format.

Adobe developed the DNG or Digital Negative format to help promote a common Raw format that can be used for archival as well as editing and enhancement purposes. As well as including output DNG options in both Photoshop CS2 and Photoshop Elements 3.0 Adobe provides a free DNG converter that can change proprietary camera Raw formats to DNG. The converter can be downloaded from www.adobe.com.

To save your Raw files in the DNG format select this option as the file type when saving from the Camera Raw editor (1).

In addition to providing a common Raw file format the DNG specification also includes a lossless compression option which, when considering the size of some Raw files, will help reduce the space taken up with the thousands of images that photographers accumulate.

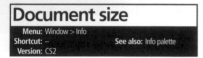

Document size

Menu: Window > Info
Shortcut: –   **See also:** Info palette
Version: CS2

The Info palette contains a variety of details regarding the document that is currently open in the workspace as well as the position of any selected tool. Added to the bottom of the palette for CS2 is another information panel that displays a range of document and program data (1).

By clicking the side-arrow and then selecting Document Sizes it is possible to set up the panel to display. The figure on the left represents an estimate of the file's size when flattened and saved in the Photoshop format (PSD). The number on the right is the approximate size of the current open file including all layers. As was the case in previous editions of Photoshop you can also find this detail on the left-hand side of the Status Bar at the bottom of the screen (2). To change the display select a different option from the pop-up menu.

A picture with the same pixel dimensions can be printed to two different sizes by altering the number of pixels per inch that are used in the output process.

In this way the same file can be used to output a 5 × 4 inch print (2), or a 10 × 8 inch photo (1), by altering the picture's resolution (pixels per inch) within the Image Size dialog (3).

Dodge tool

Menu: –
Shortcut: O   **See also:** Burn tool, Sponge tool,
Version: 6.0, 7.0, CS, CS2   Shadow/Highlight

The Dodge tool lightens specific areas of a photograph when the tool tip is clicked and dragged across the picture surface. The tool's attributes are based on the settings in the options bar and the current brush size.

The strength of the lightening is governed by the exposure setting. Most professionals choose to keep this value low and build up the tool's effect with repeated strokes over the same area.

You can also adjust the precise grouping of tones, highlights, midtones or shadows that you are working on at any one time by setting the option in the Range menu.

DPI (dots per inch)

Menu: –
Shortcut: –   **See also:** Resolution,
Version: 6.0, 7.0, CS, CS2   Color Halftone filter

The term 'dots per inch' started as a measurement of the screen size used by offset printers when converting continuous tone pictures to a series of colored ink dots. It literally refers to the number of dots that would be used in a single inch of a printed picture. The higher the DPI value, the finer the screen and, therefore, the smaller the dot size. Typically newspapers use a DPI value of around 85 and good quality magazines 150.

More recently the term has been used to represent the digital resolution of a photo as well as a measure for scanning resolution. Even though most readers will understand what others mean when they say 'What is the DPI of that photo?' or 'What DPI do you have your scanner set to?', this is an incorrect use of the term.

PPI – For digital photos the correct unit of measure is PPI or pixels per inch as this describes the resolution of the picture in terms of its primary component – pixels. The picture will only be converted to dots per inch when printed.

SPI – The unit that should be used when discussing scanner settings is SPI or samples per inch. This describes how often the scanning head will sample the information in the photo original per inch.

DPI – As dots per inch started life as a printing term it still has a place in this part of the digital photography process. In fact, in inkjet technology the number of dots laid down by the printer head is often called DPI.

Before

Before

After

After

Drop shadow

Menu: Layer > Layer Style > Drop Shadow
Shortcut: –   **See also:** Layer Styles
Version: 6.0, 7.0, CS, CS2

This feature was first introduced in Photoshop 6.0 and was designed to automatically apply a drop shadow to the content of a layer.

All you do is select the layer and then choose the option from the Layer > Layer Styles menu. From the dialog menu (1) you can choose the Blend mode, opacity, angle, distance, blur, contour and intensity – play around until you're happy with the results. Apply the effect by clicking OK.

If the drop shadow style will be used again later use the New Style button to create a new drop shadow style that can be selected from the Layers Style palette.

The Drop Shadow layer style can also be select by clicking the layer style button at the bottom of the Layer palette (2).

Droplet

Menu: File > Automate > Create Droplet
Shortcut: –   **See also:** Actions
Version: 6.0, 7.0, CS, CS2

This feature first appeared in version 6.0 and creates an automated way of applying a prerecorded action.

The droplet is an icon that appears on the desktop that you drag a picture onto to automatically process the prerecorded action.

You may want to set it up to adjust a digital camera picture. Here you could prerecord an action that changes the resolution from 72 ppi to 240 ppi, and adds a faint orange hue to give a feeling of warmth and a touch of Unsharp Mask to improve the clarity of the digital image.

After recording the action select File > Automate > Droplet (1) and alter the settings in the Create Droplet dialog (2) to suit. This action creates the droplet (3).

Duotone

Menu: Image > Mode > Duotone
Shortcut: –   **See also:** Colorize
Version: 6.0, 7.0, CS, CS2

Eight-bit grayscale images display up to 256 shades of gray, but a printing press only reproduces around 50 levels per ink. This means that grayscale images printed with black ink look coarser than ones printed with two or more inks.

Duotones are images with two colors (inks) that increase the tonal range of a grayscale image and look stunning when subtly applied. When black is used for shadows and gray for midtones and highlights you produce a black and white image. Versions printed using a colored ink for the highlights produce an image with a slight tint that significantly increases its dynamic range.

You need to be in grayscale mode before you can enter the world of Duotones (Image > Mode > Grayscale). Choose a Duotone preset by clicking on Load and locate it in the Presets folder, or create your own color by clicking on the colored ink squares to call up the color wheel.

Select a color you like and watch the bar at the base of the palette appear as a range of hues from black to white. If you stumble across a Duotone color effect you'd like to keep click on save and put the *.ado file in a folder. It can then be called up from the Load option when required.

Pro's Tip

If you're new to color tone adjustments and only intend printing out on an inkjet printer it would be safer and easier to use the Variations or Hue/Saturation features to tint your RGB files.

Duplicate image

Menu: Image > Duplicate
Shortcut: – **See also:** –
Version: 6.0, 7.0, CS, CS2

Duplicate Layer

Menu: Layer > Duplicate Layer
Shortcut: – **See also:** Layers
Version: 6.0, 7.0, CS, CS2

Dust & Scratches filter

Menu: Filter > Noise > Dust & Scratches
Shortcut: – **See also:** Filters
Version: 6.0, 7.0, CS, CS2

The File > Duplicate command makes an exact copy of the current open document in the workspace (1). As well as the picture itself being copied and opened in a new window the feature also duplicates any metadata associated with the photo.

The picture can also be duplicated by right-clicking on the title bar of the document and then selecting the duplicate option (2) from the pop-up menu.

All duplicated files are added to the current folder and are automatically given a file name ending with 'copy'.

Any layer can be copied and inserted into the current document with the Layer > Duplicate Layer command. Simply select the layer to be copied, choose Duplicate Layer from the Layer menu, insert a new name (2) and choose the destination of the new layer (3) in the Duplicate Layer dialog.

An alternative method to copy a layer is to click-drag the layer from its position in the stack onto the New Layer button in the Layers palette (4). This approach bypasses the Duplicate Layer dialog and simply adds 'copy' to the name of the original layer.

A final method for copying a selected layer is to choose the Duplicate Layer (5) option from the right-click menu (Cmd-click – Mac).

The Dust & Scratches filter in Photoshop helps to eliminate annoying spots and marks by blending or blurring the surrounding pixels to cover the defect. The settings you choose for this filter are critical if you are to maintain image sharpness whilst removing small marks. Too much filtering and your image will appear blurred, too little and the marks will remain.

To find settings that provide a good balance, first try adjusting the Threshold setting to zero. Next, use the preview box in the filter dialog to highlight a mark that you want to remove. Use the zoom controls to enlarge the view of the defect (1).

Now drag the Radius slider to the right. Find, and set, the lowest Radius value where the mark is removed (2).

Next, increase the Threshold value gradually until the texture of the image is restored and the defect is still removed (3).

64

Exit command

Menu: File > Exit
Shortcut: Ctrl/Cmd Q   **See also:** Blend modes
Version: 6.0, 7.0, CS, CS2

To exit or close the Photoshop program select File > Exit or File > Quit for Macintosh users. If any files are open at the time of selecting the Exit command, a confirmation dialog will be shown asking the user if they want to save the file before quitting or cancel the action (1).

Expand selection

Menu: Select > Modify > Expand
Shortcut: —   **See also:** Contract selection
Version: 6.0, 7.0, CS, CS2

An active selection can be altered and adjusted using the options listed under the Select > Modify menu. One option is the Expand command which increases the size of the selection by the number of pixels entered into the feature's dialog. If the selection incorporates part of the document edge this part of the marquee will not be changed by the command.

Exclusion blend mode

Menu: —
Shortcut: —   **See also:** Blend modes
Version: 6.0, 7.0, CS, CS2

The Exclusion blending mode is one of the group of modes that base their effects on the differences between two pictures.

This option is similar to the Difference mode but produces less dramatic and less contrasty results. When the upper layer is changed to the Exclusion mode the result displays the tonal difference between the two layers.

The difference is calculated by locating the lighter and darker pixels and then subtracting these from either of the two layers producing the resultant color.

Blending with a black top layer produces no change. Blending with a white top layer inverses the value of the bottom layer.

EXIF data

Menu: File > File Info
   Bridge: View > Metadata Panel
Shortcut: Ctrl/Cmd Alt/Opt Shft I   **See also:** Metadata Panel
Version: 6.0, 7.0, CS, CS2

EXIF, or the Exchangeable Information Format, is a data format that is used for recording camera capture details and then displaying them inside software applications such as Photoshop. The information recorded by the camera and saved in this format can include shutter speed, aperture, camera model, date and time the photo was taken, exposure mode that the camera was set to and much more.

There are two places where you can view the available EXIF data for a picture:

In Bridge EXIF details are displayed as part of the greater metadata available for the picture. To display the metadata panel select the option from the View menu (1).

When working in the Photoshop workspace selecting the File > File Info option will display all the metadata associated with the picture including the camera related EXIF data (2).

EXIF data is one part of a set of metadata information that can be viewed and, to some extent, edited and even created in Photoshop. Other metadata options include File Properties, IPTC or copyright information, edit history and any GPS details.

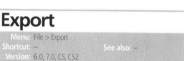

Export

Menu: File > Export
Shortcut: –   **See also:** –
Version: 6.0, 7.0, CS, CS2

The File > Export menu contains several different options for transporting information created or edited in Photoshop into formats that can be used by other programs or displayed on different hardware. The options are:

Data sets as files – Exports the data sets used in Photoshop files that contain data driven graphics options as files suitable for importing into a database or spreadsheet program.

Paths to Illustrator – Saves Photoshop paths as Illustrator documents.

Send Video preview to Device – Outputs the current image to a Firewire connected video device using the settings that were previously set in the Video Preview dialog.

Video Preview – Allows you to set the preview options that will be used to display the current image on a connected (via Firewire) video device.

ZoomView – This option converts the current image into the components necessary display a ZoomView image in a web browser. The format is designed to deliver high resolution pictures via the web and this export option creates the ZoomView components.

Export from Clipboard

Menu: Enhance > Adjust Lighting > Levels
Shortcut: Ctrl/Cmd Alt/Opt Shft L   **See also:** Curves, Shadow/
Version: 6.0, 7.0, CS, CS2   Highlight

As with most programs that handle pictures and text, when you copy an item it is saved in the program's clipboard. Photoshop is just the same, so pictures can be copied, stored temporarily on the computer's clipboard and then pasted into other programs.

To use this option in Photoshop make sure that the Export Clipboard item is selected in the Edit > Preferences > General dialog (1).

As the storing of data on the clipboard takes up RAM there is also an option to remove copied pictures using the Edit > Purge > Clipboard command (2).

Unlike other applications Photoshop manages its own clipboard and doesn't use the one that is maintained by the operating system.

Exposure

Menu: Image > Adjustments > Exposure
Shortcut: –   **See also:** HDR, 32-bit files
Version: CS2

Designed to be used exclusively with the new 32 bits per channel files the Exposure feature provides a mechanism for adjusting the contrast and brightness of the new HDR files.

The dialog contains three slider controls plus three eyedropper buttons. The Exposure (1) slider essentially controls the highlight and midtone areas of the picture and the Gamma (3) option adjusts the overall contrast. The Offset control (2) alters the shadow and midtone areas without affecting the highlights.

The Eyedropper tools are used to set or 'peg' black, white and middle tone values and can be used in the same way that they are in the Curves and Levels features (4).

After

Extract filter

Menu: Filter > Extract
Shortcut: Ctrl/Cmd Alt/Opt X   See also: Filters
Version: 6.0, 7.0, CS, CS2

The Extract filter was first included in Photoshop back in version 5.5 of the program. Here it was hidden away under the Image menu. Now the feature has pride of place in the first section of the Filter menu and provides users with a specialist selection tool that removes the background from the surrounds of an object.

The concept is simple, draw around the outside of the object you want to extract, making sure that the highlighter overlaps the edge between background and foreground and then fill in the middle. The program then analyses the edge section of the object using some clever fuzzy logic to determine what should be kept and what should be discarded, and 'Hey Presto' the background disappears.

The tool provides extracted objects faster than using the lasso or pen tools as you don't need to be as accurate with your edge drawing, and it definitely handles wispy hair with greater finesse than most manual methods.

Extraction tips

1. When previewing the results you can refine the edges left by the extraction process using the Cleanup and Edge Touch up Tools.

2. Make sure that the highlight slightly overlaps the object edges and its background.

Select the layer you wish to extract. Choose Filter > Extract from the Photoshop Menus. Use the edge highlighter tool to draw around the edges of the object you wish to extract.

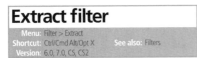

Select the fill tool and click inside the object to fill its interior. Click preview to check the extraction. Click OK to apply the final extraction.

3. For items such as hair, use a larger brush to encompass all strands.

4. Make sure that the highlight forms a complete and closed line around the object before filling.

5. Use the Smart Highlighting option to automatically locate the edge between foreground and background objects and to adjust the size of the highlighter to suit the clarity of the edge.

Extrude filter

Menu: Filter > Stylize > Extrude
Shortcut: –   See also: Filters
Version: 6.0, 7.0, CS, CS2

The Extrude filter, as one of the group of Stylize filters, projects the photo onto a series of extruded shapes that seem to explode from the middle of the document.

By altering the settings in the filter's dialog you can choose the shape of the extrusions – blocks or pyramids (1). The size (2) and depth (3) of the extruded shapes can be set in pixels. Partly completed blocks can be masked or shown as part of the final image (4).

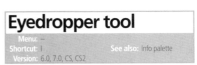

Eyedropper tool

Menu: –
Shortcut: I   See also: Info palette
Version: 6.0, 7.0, CS, CS2

The Eyedropper tool is used to sample colors in a picture. After selecting the tool click on the color in the picture to set a new foreground color and Alt-click (Option-click for Macintosh) for a background color. The size of the area sampled can be adjusted using the options in the Sample Size menu in the options bar. Large pixel samples average the color and tone of the areas they select.

fF

ABCDE PQRSTU
VWXYZABCDEFGHIJKLM
...ABCDEFGHIJKLMNOPQRSTU...
YZABCDEFGHIJKLMNOPQRSTUV
WXYZABCDEFGHIJKLMNOPQRSTUVWXYZA...
BCDEFGHIJKLMNOPQRSTUVWX
YZABCDEFGHIJKLMNOPQRSTU
VWXYZABCDEFGHIJKLMNOPQR
STUVWXYZABCDEFGHIJKLM
NOPQRSTUVWXYZABCDEFGHI
KLMNOPQRSTUVWXYZABCDEF
GHIJKLMNOPQRSTUVWXYZABCDEFGHIKLMN
OPQRSTUVWXYZABCDEFGHI
KLMNOPQRSTUVWXYZABCDEF
GHIJKLMNOPQRSTUVWXYZABC
DEFGHIKLMNOPQRSTUVWXYZABCDEFGHI
LMNOPQRSTUVWXYZABCDEFGHIKLMNOPQRST
VWXYZABCDEFGHIJKLM

F

Facet filter

Menu: Filter > Pixelate > Facet	
Shortcut: –	**See also:** Filters
Version: 6.0, 7.0, CS, CS2	

The Facet filter, as one of the group of Pixelate filters, simulates the look of a hand-worked painting by recreating the photo with blocks of color.

The filter contains no controls to alter the strength or appearance of the effect. Some changes in end results are possible by altering the image size before applying the filter. The filtering process produces more dramatic results when applied to low resolution files than when used with pictures with large pixel dimensions.

As the filter doesn't have an image preview option it may be necessary to filter the picture several times with different resolution settings before deciding on the best values to use. Use Edit > Undo to reverse the last filter change.

Fade command

Menu: Edit > Fade	
Shortcut: Ctrl/Cmd Shft F	**See also:** Undo
Version: 6.0, 7.0, CS, CS2	

The Fade command allows any filter or color change to be reduced in strength using this fade control.

In its standard mode the slider in the feature gradually applies (or takes away) the filter's effect. Another approach is to use the Fade option in conjunction with a Blend mode selection (also included in the dialog) making the filter appear as though it's on a separate layer to give a completely different feel. Definitely one to experiment with.

The Fade command moved to the Edit menu on version 6.0. Version 5.5 users will find it in the Filter menu.

In the example shown here the Fresco filter from the Artistic menu has created a moody oil painting (1). The Fade command, set to Luminosity Blend mode, gives added sparkle in the greens which is further enhanced by increasing brightness and contrast (2).

NEW for CS2

Without feather

Before

With feather

© www.allstock.com 2005

Faux fonts

Menu: –
Shortcut: –   **See also:** Font selecting
Version: 6.0, 7.0, CS, CS2

Some font families include several different versions of the typeface that you can use in conjunction with the Type tool. Typically the typeface options or styles include Bold, Italic and Bold Italic as well as the standard Regular faces (1). Each of the font faces share the same basic letter design but a different alphabet is installed for each face option (i.e. a different set of letters for bold, italic and bold italic options).

For fonts that don't have these face or style options Photoshop has several 'faux' font choices (2) (available from the Character palette) that can be used as a substitute.

Faux fonts simulate the look of different font faces and include Bold (3), Italic (4), Underline (5) and Strikethrough (6).

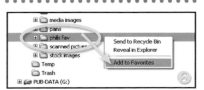

Favorites Panel, Bridge

Menu: Bridge: View > Favorites Panel
Shortcut: –   **See also:** Bridge
Version: CS2

The Favorites Panel, like all Bridge panels, is located on the left-hand side of the window.

Along with the standard My Computer, Adobe Stock Photos, Version Cue, Collections and Bridge Center (Creative Suite only) options you can optimize the list of entries included in the panel to store your own selections. This is a handy place to position entries for regularly used folders of images or project directories. Rather than repeatedly searching for often used locations through the folder panel add these folders to your favorites list for quicker file access.

Two quick ways to add locations to the Favorites panel are:

1. Locate the directory in the Folders Panel and then click-drag the folder to the Favorites Panel. Once the folder is dropped on the panel Bridge will automatically create a new entry (1).

2. Again locate the directory in the Folders Panel and then right-click the folder name and select Add to Favorites from the options in the pop-up menu (2).

Feather command

Menu: Select > Feather
Shortcut: Alt/Opt Ctrl/Cmd D   **See also:** Selections
Version: 6.0, 7.0, CS, CS2

By default most selections are created with a sharp edge that marks the parts of the picture that are included within the selection and those areas that are outside. When changes are made to a photograph via these sharp-edged selections the distinction between edited and non-edited sections of the image is very obvious.

The Feather command softens the transition between selected and non-selected areas.

The example shows a vignetting or edge darkening effect created with a sharp selection (1) and then the same effect repeated with a feathered selection (2).

You can feather a selection in two ways:

Before making a selection – Add a feather amount in the options bar of the selection tool before drawing the selection.

After a selection is created – To feather an existing selection, draw the selection and then choose the Select > Feather (3) command and add a feather amount in the dialog that appears.

The greater the value used for the Feather Radius the smoother the transition will be.

After

File Browser – Windows

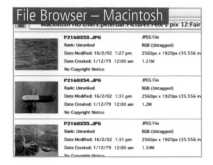

File Browser – Macintosh

Fibers filter

Menu: Filter > Render > Fibers
Shortcut: –   **See also:** Filters
Version: CS, CS2

A useful background creating filter, introduced with Photoshop CS, that produces a fiber style effect from the foreground and background colors. Once created you can adjust the pattern using blur and transform tools, as seen here. The filter has been upgraded to work in 16 bits/channel mode in CS2.

It may come in useful for producing scratched metal effects, worn wood and various cloth styles, making it suitable as another background creator.

The filter contains two slider controls – Variance (1) that controls the contrast of the final results and Strength (2) that alters the extent of fibers in the picture. The Randomize produces a variety of variations of fiber designs (3).

The filter does not use any of the picture information in open documents to create its effect, instead the results are based solely on the current foreground and background hues and the settings in the filter dialog.

 Once you have created your Fibers picture go to Filter > Blur > Motion Blur and add a horizontal blur. Then soften the whole composition with a slight Gaussian Blur and add some texture with the Add Noise filter to create a weather look (4).

Pro's Tip

File Browser

Menu: File > Browse Folders
Shortcut: Shft Ctrl/Cmd O   **See also:** Bridge, Info palette
Version: 6.0, 7.0, CS,

The File Browser was first introduced in Photoshop 7.0 and with the release of CS2 has been replaced with the Bridge application. The File Browser in its original form looked much like a Windows Explorer interface, with folders on the left that open up on the right when you double-click on them to view the contents. Selecting a folder displayed the contents as easy to view thumbnails that could be changed in size and layout.

The layout options included viewing small, medium or large thumbnails, and text alongside the pictures. Clicking a thumbnail created a larger preview and information about the photograph was shown on the left.

It was possible to rename thumbnails in the browser, this altered the name of the original in its folder. In addition the orientation could be changed from horizontal to vertical or vice versa and when you next open the image in Photoshop it will automatically rotate to the correct format.

• •

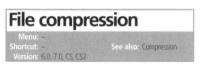

File compression

Menu: –
Shortcut: –   **See also:** Compression
Version: 6.0, 7.0, CS, CS2

Compression is a file format option that reduces the size of images so that they can be more easily transmitted on the web or take up less space when stored.

Two types of general compression are available when saving picture files – Lossy and Lossless.

The Lossy option reduces file sizes dramatically but removes image detail in the process. The JPEG format uses this type of compression to optimize the size of files for internet use. The TIFF format in contrast makes use of lossless compression which makes the file smaller but without the loss of any of the original picture detail.

File conversion

Menu: File > Save As
Shortcut: Ctrl/Cmd Shft S   **See also:** Save As
Version: 6.0, 7.0, CS, CS2

Photoshop files, or any other files that can be opened in the program, can be converted into other formats suitable for different uses.

When you save an image, select File > Save As and pull down the Format menu (1) in the dialog to see a list of file formats to choose from. Then select the one you want to save in that format and choose any other format options from the section at the bottom of the dialog.

File format

Menu:	–
Shortcut:	–
Version:	6.0, 7.0, CS, CS2

See also: File extension,
File Type Associations,
Save As

Photoshop can open and save files in a multitude of different file formats.

The format you use will be determined by the end use of the photo. If the picture is destined for the internet then the JPEG format is the best option. In contrast, photos used in publishing are often saved in the TIFF format.

For most editing and enhancement work the Photoshop, or PSD, format should be used. It provides the best combination of features and image quality. Pictures in the PSD format can be duplicated in other formats for specific uses by resaving the file via the File > Save As option.

File Type	Compression	Layers	Metadata	Uses
Photoshop (.PSD)	✗	✓	✓	Desktop publishing (DTP), internet, publishing, photos
GIF (.GIF)	✓	✗	✗	Internet
JPEG (.JPG)	✓	✗	✓	DTP, internet, publishing, photographic work
TIFF (.TIF)	✓	✓	✓	DTP, internet, publishing, photographic work
PNG (.PNG)	✓	✗	✗	Internet
Digital negative (.DNG)	✓	✗	✓	Archival storage of Raw files
Acrobat (.PDF)	✓	✓	✓	DTP, internet, publishing, photographic work
Raw (various)	✗	✗		Primary camera capture format
Photoshop large document (.PSB)	✗	✓	✓	Photoshop format for documents larger than 2 Gb in size
High Dynamic Range	✗	✗	✓	A file type that can contain up to 32bits/channel of tone and color data. Can be saved in PSB, PSD, HDR and TIFF formats.

JPEG

(Joint Photographic Experts Group) – This format is the industry standard for compressing photos destined for the World Wide Web (www) or for storage when space is limited. JPEG compression uses a 'lossy compression' (image data and quality are sacrificed for smaller file sizes when the image files are closed).

The user is able to control the amount of compression. A high level of compression leads to a lower quality image and a smaller file size. A low level of compression results in a higher quality image but a larger file size.

It is recommended that you only save to the JPEG file format for web work and only after you have completed all your image editing.

TIFF

(Tagged Image File Format) – This file type is the industry standard for images destined for publishing (magazines and books).

TIFF uses a 'lossless' compression (no loss of image data or quality) called 'LZW compression'.

Although preserving the quality of the image, LZW compression is only capable of compressing images a small amount.

PSD/PSB

(Photoshop Document) – PSD is the default format used by both Photoshop and Photoshop Elements. An image that is composed of 'layers' may be saved as a Photoshop document. It is good practice to keep a PSD document as the master file from which all other files are produced depending on the requirements of the output device. PSB is the same as PSD but is used for storing files larger than 2 Gb.

GIF

(Graphics Interchange Format) – This format is used for logos and images with a small number of colors and is very popular with web professionals. It is capable of storing up to 256 colors, animation and areas of transparency. Not generally used for photographic images.

PNG

(Portable Network Graphics) – A comparatively new web graphics format that has a lot of great features.

Like TIFF and GIF the format uses a lossless compression algorithm that ensures what you put in is what you get out. It also supports partial transparency (unlike GIF's transparency off/on system) and color depths up to 64-bit.

PDF

(Portable Document Format) – The Adobe Acrobat format created so that pictures and desktop published documents could be viewed and displayed accurately on a wide variety of computer systems with the associated Acrobat reader.

Now the format is the industry default for publishing, web document delivery and is also used by photographers to secure their photo files.

EPS

(Encapsulated PostScript) – Originally designed for complex desktop publishing work, it is still the format of choice for page layout professionals. Not generally used for storing of photographic images but worth knowing about.

JPEG2000

Dubbed JPEG2000, this format is designed as an upgrade to the aging JPEG format. It provides 20% better compression, less image degradation than JPEG, full color management profile and 16-bit support, can store saved selections and has the ability to save the file with no compression at all.

SVG

(Scalable Vector Graphics) – Unlike the two most popular web formats today, JPEG and GIF, SVG is a vector-based file format. In addition to faster download speeds, SVG also contains many other benefits such as high-resolution printing, high-performance zooming and panning inside of graphics and animation.

DNG

(Digital Negative) – Adobe's new archival format used to store the Raw data captured by a wide range of mid to high end digital cameras. Raw files can be converted to the DNG format via the free converter published by Adobe or saved in this format from the Camera Raw editor in Photoshop.

Raw

The Raw format is used to store the primary data that is captured by mid to high range digital cameras. Raw files need to be converted to other formats before they can be edited and enhanced in programs like Photoshop. The Camera Raw editor in both Photoshop and Bridge handles this conversion and can save the processed files as TIFF, PSD, JPEG and DNG files.

File Formats:

File extension

Menu: –	
Shortcut: –	See also: File format
Version: 6.0, 7.0, CS, CS2	

A file extension is the three letter abbreviation (2) of the file format that is added after the file's name (1). Windows programs use the extension as a way of recognizing the content of the file as well as the way that it is structured. For example, if you save a file named 'Image1' in the TIFF format then the full filename would be 'Image1.tif' and a JPEG version of the same file would be 'Image1.jpg'. Most programs automatically add an extension to the file as it is being saved. This occurs even if the extensions are hidden from view when viewing filenames in browser. In Windows XP the extension is hidden by default. To view the extension in any folder, choose Tools > Folder Options > View, and deselect 'Hide extensions for known file types'.

File Groups, Bridge

Menu: –	
Shortcut: –	See also: Bridge,
Version: CS2	Bridge Center

A new feature that is available in Bridge is the ability to collate open files in Photoshop into a single easily accessible file group (1). The files can then be located and opened quickly by selecting the group heading in Bridge.

To group pictures that are currently open in Photoshop, switch to Bridge and then select the Bridge Center option from the Favorites panel. Now choose the 'Save open files into a file group' text heading and enter a name for the group in the dialog that pops up. To reopen the pictures saved in the group into the Photoshop program simply select the group title from the Saved File Groups area of the Bridge Center workspace and then press the folder icon. All the photos will then be opened and displayed in Photoshop (2).

The Bridge Center feature and therefore the File Group option are only available for users of the Creative Suite 2 group of programs. The version of Bridge that is shipped with Photoshop CS2 doesn't contain this feature.

Create a File Group from those pictures currently opened in Photoshop by swithcing to Bridge, displaying the Favorites panel and then selecting the Bridge Center option (only available for Creative Suite 2 users).

Click on the Save open files into a file group text in the Saved File Groups section of the window. Input a file group heading or title in the dialog that appears and click OK.

The new file group is displayed as an option in the Saved File Groups section of the Bridge Center workspace. The pictures can now be quickly opened into Photoshop by selecting the group title and then clicking on the folder icon.

File Info command

Menu: File > File Info
Shortcut: Ctrl/Cmd Alt/Opt Shft I   See also: Metadata panel
Version: 6.0, 7.0, CS, CS2

The File Info command displays the meta-data associated with the currently open picture.

This includes data recorded from the camera (EXIF) at the time the picture was created as well as any copyright information, description and authorship details (1).

The dialog also lets you add customized information to the picture such as adding a document title, description and copyright notice but no changes can be made to the Camera Data 1 or Camera Data 2 sections. Repetitive file information can be added saved after the first time of entry and then loaded and applied to new files via the options in the side-arrow menu located in the top right of the dialog (2).

The File Info dialog is displayed by selecting File > File Info or by right-clicking a thumbnail in Bridge and then choosing File Info from the context menu. The details displayed in the File Info dialog can also be seen in the Metadata panel of the Bridge (3).

File optimizing

Menu: File > Save for Web
Shortcut: Ctrl/Cmd Alt/Opt Shft S   See also: Save for Web
Version: 6.0, 7.0, CS, CS2

You should always optimize pictures when saving them for web use.

The idea is to remove any color that can't be seen by a web browser as well as resizing to suit the viewing conditions (usually Mac or PC monitor) and saving it all in the most suitable, web-friendly, format (usually JPEG or GIF).

Ensuring that you balance all these concerns and still maintain image quality is made easier when you use the Save for Web option in Photoshop.

● ●

NEW for CS2

File Type Associations

Menu: Bridge: Edit > Preferences > File Type Associations
Shortcut: –   See also: File extension
Version: CS2

When first installing Photoshop you get a choice of the file types that are associated with both Photoshop and ImageReady programs. After installation is complete double-clicking the associated file types will automatically open the document in Photoshop (or ImageReady).

To change the files type associations for the Adobe suite of products, alter the programs that are attached to different file types in the Edit > Preferences > File Type Associations dialog. Click on the down-arrow on the right of the Program entry to select from a list of suitable applications or to browse for software not listed.

Fill command

Menu: Edit > Fill
Shortcut: F5   See also: Paint Bucket tool
Version: 6.0, 7.0, CS, CS2

When there is no active selection in the open picture the Fill command overpaints the contents of the whole layer with a selected color or pattern. When a selection is active the Fill command paints the color in the area of the selection only.

The content of the fill is selected from the drop-down Use menu (1) where the choices include Foreground, Background Colors, Black, White, 50% Gray or a Pattern. You can also select a specific color by choosing the Color option and then selecting the hue from the Color Picker dialog that is displayed.

Other options in the dialog include the ability to apply the color via a range of blend modes (2) and an adjustment for the opacity (3) of the fill paint that is applied to the layer.

The Solid Color adjustment layer works in a similar way to the Fill command but applies the color in a separate editable layer (4). This option has the advantage of not destroying the contents of the original layer when the fill is applied.

Solid Color

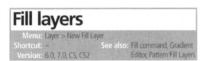

Solid Color...
Gradient...
Pattern...

Layer Style
New Fill Layer   Solid Color..
New Adjustment Layer Gradient...
Change Layer Content Pattern...
Layer Content Options...

Film Grain

Grain   11
Highlight Area 2
Intensity   8

Fill layers

Menu: Layer > New Fill Layer
Shortcut: –   See also: Fill command, Gradient
Version: 6.0, 7.0, CS, CS2   Editor, Pattern Fill Layers

Photoshop contains the options to create three different types of fill layers (1, 2):

Solid Color – Creates a new layer filled with a color selected from the pop-up color picker (3).

Gradient – Creates a new layer filled with a gradient that gradually changes from one color to another or to transparency. Pick from preset gradient types or create your own (4).

Pattern – Creates a layer filled with a pattern that you choose from the palette (5).

A fill layer is created by selecting the specific fill type from the list available under the Layer > New Fill Layer menu, or by clicking the New Fill or Adjustment Layer button in the Layers palette. The new fill layer is always created above the current active layer in the layer stack.

Gradient

Gradient Fill
Gradient: OK
Style: Linear   Cancel
Angle: 90 °
Scale: 100 %
☐ Reverse ☐ Dither
☑ Align with layer

Pattern

Pattern Fill
Scale: 100 %   OK
                 Cancel
☑ Link with Layer
Snap to Origin

Filling a selection

Menu: Edit > Fill
Shortcut: Shft F5   See also: –
Version: 6.0, 7.0, CS, CS2

When the Edit > Fill option is applied whilst a selection is active the feature works like the Paint Bucket tool and drops color into the selection area only (1).

Choose to fill using the foreground or background color in the palette.

You can also adjust opacity and select a blend mode to vary the result.

The same approach can be used with the Solid Color Adjustment layer. Make a selection of the area to be filled first and then add a Solid Color adjustment layer to the picture. The selection will be used as the basis for a layer mask that is linked to the adjustment layer.

The mask can be edited (painted on or erased from) to adjust the area that the color is applied to.

Pro's Tip

When filling a selection, use the feather control first to get a softer fill effect (2).

Press the Ctrl/Cmd Delete keys to fill the canvas or selection with the foreground color.

Press the Alt/Opt Delete keys to fill the selection or canvas with the background color.

Film Grain filter

Menu: Filter > Artistic > Film Grain
        Filter > Filter Gallery > Artistic Film Grain
Shortcut: –   See also: Filters
Version: 6.0, 7.0, CS, CS2

The Film Grain filter, as one of the group of Artistic filters, simulates the texture that was typical of 'grainy', high-speed films of old.

The three settings in the dialog provide control over the grain strength and how it is applied.

The Grain slider (1) alters the strength and size of the grain that is added to the picture. A higher value produces a more pronounced result with less of the detail in the photo being retained. The Highlight Area control (2) alters the amount of highlight tones, with higher values producing a lighter and more posterized result. The Intensity slider (3) works like a contrast slide, creating more defined results as the control is moved to the right.

Filter Gallery

Menu: Filter > Filter Gallery
Shortcut: –   See also: Filters
Version: 6.0, 7.0, CS, CS2

The Filter Gallery is an extended filter dialog that is designed to allow the user to apply several different filters to a single image or the same filter multiple times to the same photo.

The dialog consists of a preview area (1), a collection of filters that can be used with the feature (2), a settings area with sliders to control the filter effect (3) and a list of filters that are currently being applied to the picture (4).

Multiple filters are applied to a picture by selecting the filter, adjusting the settings to suit the image and then clicking the New Effect Layer button at the bottom of the dialog. Filters are arranged in the sequence they are applied.

Applied filters can be moved to a different spot in the sequence by click-dragging them up or down the stack. Click the 'eye' icon to hide the effect of the selected filter from preview. Filters can be deleted from the list by selecting them first and then clicking the 'dustbin' icon at the bottom of the dialog.

Most of the filters that can't be used with the Filter Gallery feature are either applied to the picture with no user settings, or make use of dedicated filter dialog that contains a preview area and several slider controls.

Filters can also be accessed via the Filter menu.

Filters

Menu: Filter
Shortcut: –   See also: Filter Gallery
Version: 6.0, 7.0, CS, CS2

Digital filters are based on the traditional photographic versions, which are placed in front of the lens of the camera to change the way the image is captured. Now, with the click of a button it is possible to make extremely complex changes to our images almost instantaneously – changes that a few years ago we couldn't even imagine.

Most filters in Photoshop can be found grouped under a series of subheadings based on their main effect or feature in the Filter menu. There are four specialized filters that sit about from these groups, which because of their complexity, warrant a single entry for themselves. They are Extract, Liquify, Pattern Maker and Vanishing point.

Selecting a filter will apply the effect to the current layer or selection. Some filters display a dialog that allows the user to change specific settings and preview the filtered image before applying the effect to the whole of the picture. This can be a great time saver, as filtering a large file can take several minutes.

Other filters are incorporated into a Filter Gallery (Filter > Filter Gallery) feature that provides both preview and controls in a single dialog.

Filters, applying multiple

Menu: Filter > Filter Gallery
Shortcut: –   See also: Filters
Version: 6.0, 7.0, CS, CS2

The Filter Gallery is designed to allow multiple filters to be applied to a single picture. Each filter is layered in a stack similar to that found in the Layers palette (1).

Multiple filters are applied to a picture by selecting the filter in the Filter Gallery dialog, adjusting the settings to suit the image and then clicking the New Effect Layer button (2) at the bottom of the dialog. Filters are arranged in the sequence they are applied.

Applied filters can be moved to a different spot in the sequence by click-dragging them up or down the stack. Click the 'eye' icon (4) to hide the effect of the selected filter from preview. Filters can be deleted from the list by selecting them first and then clicking the 'dustbin' icon (3) at the bottom of the dialog.

• • • • • • • • • • • • • • • •

Filters, shortcut keys

Menu: –
Shortcut: –   See also: Filters, Filter Gallery
Version: 6.0, 7.0, CS, CS2

Ctrl/Cmd F – To apply the last filter with the settings used.

Ctrl/Cmd Alt/Opt F – To open the dialog for the last filter used.

The first step to using the Find Edges filter to confine sharpening to just the edges of a picture is to make a copy of the background layer (Layer > Duplicate Layer) and desaturate the color (Image > Adjustments > Desaturate).

Next apply the Find Edges filter (Filter > Stylize > Find Edges) to the grayscale layer and then invert the results (Image > Adjustments > Invert).

Find

Menu: Bridge: Edit > Find
Shortcut: Ctrl/Cmd F   **See also:** Sort files Bridge
Version: CS2

One of the great benefits of organizing your pictures in the Bridge workspace is the huge range of search options that then become available to you.

Selecting Find from the Edit menu displays the Find dialog (1). Here you will be able to nominate what you want to search for (2), the criteria for the search (3), which folder (4) you want to search in, what type of metadata (5) to search and finally what to do with the pictures that match the search criteria (6).

Find Edges filter

Menu: Filter > Stylize > Find Edges
Shortcut: –   **See also:** Filters
Version: 6.0, 7.0, CS, CS2

The Find Edges filter, as one of the group of Stylize filters, searches for and highlights the edges in a picture. The feature classifies edges as being picture parts where there is a major change in tone, color and/or contrast.

The feature outlines the edges it locates with dark lines against a lighter colored background. There are no extra controls of slider adjustments available for this filter.

The edge-finding ability of this filter is used in the following step-by-step technique to isolate the sharpening effects of the Unsharp Mask filter to the edges of a picture.

Now select all of the filtered layer (Select > All) and copy the selection to memory (Edit > Copy). Create a new Levels Adjustment layer (Layer > New Adjustment Layer > Levels) but make no adjustments and click OK. Select the thumbnail of the adjustment layer (Alt/Opt-Click) and then paste (Ctrl/Cmd V) the copied selection into the layer to create a layer mask.

Before edge sharpening

After edge sharpening

Create a new selection using the layer mask by Ctrl/Cmd-clicking the thumbnail. With the selection still active, hide the marching ants (Ctrl/Cmd H) as well as the levels and filtered layers (click on the eye icon). Now choose the picture layer from the layer stack and apply the Unsharp Mask Filter. The filter will be applied through the selection and as the selection is of the edges of the picture only then the sharpening effect will be restricted to these areas.

Find and Replace Text

Menu: Edit > Find and Replace Text
Shortcut: –   **See also:** Check spelling
Version: 7.0, CS, CS2

A word-based feature that was introduced with version 7.0. This is used to search through text and replace one word, punctuation or sentence with another.

Just key in what you want to replace in the 'Find What' box and what you want to change it to in the 'Change To' box. Then click 'Find Next'. The program searches for the words and highlights the first example it comes to. You then can change just the found words or change all occurrences or change the found one and then let it find the next.

Fit Image

Menu: File > Automate > Fit Image
Shortcut: –   **See also:** Automate
Version: 6.0, 7.0, CS, CS2

An automated feature that resizes the image so that it will fit within a certain predetermined canvas space.

If, for example, you have the dialog measurements set to 680 × 480 pixels and apply the Fit image command to a 600 × 600 pixel picture it would reduced it to 480 × 480 pixels.

This feature helps when you need to resize pictures to suit a newsletter or catalogue format with predetermined picture boxes and works well when incorporated into actions.

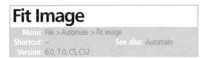

Fixed Size option

Menu: –
Shortcut: –   **See also:** Marquee tools,
Version: 6.0, 7.0, CS, CS2   Crop tool

The Fixed Size option is available in the options bar of both the Marquee (1) and Crop tools (2). This feature allows you to set the size of the selection or cropping area before drawing the shape on the picture's surface.

The size can be nominated in pixels (px), inches (in) or millimeters (mm).

Fixed Aspect Ratio

Menu: –
Shortcut: –   **See also:** –
Version: 6.0, 7.0, CS, CS2

The aspect ratio or Constrain Proportions option is usually found in dialog boxes concerned with changes of image size and refers to the relationship between width and height of a picture.

Fixing an image's aspect ratio means that this relationship will remain the same even when the image is enlarged or reduced.

For example, selecting the Constrain Proportions option in the Image > Image Size dialog will result in pictures where the aspect ratio is maintained when resized.

Flag

Menu: –
Shortcut: –   **See also:** Label Files Bridge
Version: 7.0, CS

The Flag option in the File Browser that was available in Photoshop versions 7.0 and CS was used to distinguish selected images from within the browser workspace. Flags are attached by either clicking on the Flag icon (1) in the File Browser options bar or by selecting the flag option from the right-click menu (2). Typically photographers would attach flags as part of the editing process. Successful images would be flagged and rejected photos would be left without a flag. Flag pictures could then be displayed in isolation from other pictures in the folder by selecting the Show > Flagged option from the drop-down menu in the top right of the File Browser window.

Flags are replaced by Labels in the Bridge workspace for CS2.

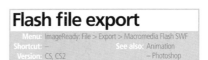

Flash file export

Menu: ImageReady: File > Export > Macromedia Flash SWF
Shortcut: –   **See also:** Animation
Version: CS, CS2   – Photoshop

As well as providing the ability to output animations as GIF files, ImageReady contains an export option to save the file in the Macromedia Flash format.

After creating the animation select the Macromedia Flash SWF option from the File > Export menu (1). Adjust the options in the Export dialog that displays (2) and then press the OK button.

Although Photoshop CS2 contains a new animation palette the export to Flash format option is only available from inside the ImageReady application.

To transport images from Photoshop to ImageReady in order to export as a Flash file click on the Edit in ImageReady button at the bottom of the Photoshop toolbar (3).

Flatten Image

Menu: Layer > Flatten Image
Shortcut: –   **See also:** Merge Layers
Version: 6.0, 7.0, CS, CS2

The Flatten Image command combines the detail of all visible layers into a single layer. In the process transparent areas are filled with white and hidden layers are discarded.

After flattening, text, shape and adjustment layers are no longer present nor are their contents editable.

The file size of the flattened picture will be much smaller than the layered version.

To flatten your image select the option from the Layer menu (1) or from the menu that pops out from the side-button at the top right of the Layers palette (2).

As a general rule you should not flatten the layers in Photoshop documents unless you are absolutely sure that you do not want to edit the picture further. If you are unsure, make a copy of the layered file and flatten the copy, keeping the original safe for editing later.

Flip Canvas Horizontal

Menu: Image > Rotate Canvas > Flip Canvas Horizontal
Shortcut: –   **See also:** Flip Horizontal,
Version: 6.0, 7.0, CS, CS2   Flip Vertical

The Flip Horizontal command rotates the picture (and all its layers) from left to right and creates a result similar to a reflection of the photo in a mirror.

Flip Canvas Vertical

Menu: Image > Rotate Canvas > Flip Canvas Horizontal
Shortcut: –   **See also:** Flip Horizontal,
Version: 6.0, 7.0, CS, CS2   Flip Vertical

The Flip Vertical command rotates the picture (and all its layers) from top to bottom and produces a result similar to the view of the picture if it was flipped upside down.

Flip Horizontal

Menu: Edit > Transform > Flip Horizontal
Shortcut: –   **See also:** Flip Canvas Horizontal,
Version: 6.0, 7.0, CS, CS2   Flip Canvas Vertical

The Flip Horizontal command rotates the selected layer from left to right and creates a result similar to a view of the reflection of the layer contents in a mirror.

Flip Vertical

Menu: Edit > Transform > Flip Vertical
Shortcut: –   **See also:** Flip Canvas Horizontal,
Version: 6.0, 7.0, CS, CS2   Flip Canvas Vertical

The Flip Layer Vertical command rotates the layer from top to bottom and produces a result similar to the view of the layer and its contents when it was flipped upside down.

Focus tools

Menu: –	
Shortcut: R	See also: Blur tool,
Version: 6.0, 7.0, CS, CS2	Sharpen tool

The Focus tool group contains the Blur and Sharpen tools. The tools are used like a paintbrush but instead of laying down color on the canvas the image is blurred (1) or sharpened (2).

The Size (brush tip), Mode (blend mode) and Strength settings for the tool are all controlled in the options bar.

When using these tools most professionals apply repeated low strength strokes to build up the effect rather than a single application using a high strength setting.

Folders Panel, Bridge

Menu: Bridge: View > Folders Panel	
Shortcut: –	See also: Favorites Panel Bridge
Version: CS2	

The Folders Panel (1), on the left-hand side of the Bridge workspace, allows you to navigate through the directories and drives that are resident on your computer.

A small 'plus' icon (3) appears on the left of drives and folders that contain extra folders, called subfolders. Clicking the button reveals the hidden content and replaces the 'plus' with a 'minus' icon. To hide the subfolders again simply click the minus button.

Right-clicking any folder in the panel displays a pop-up menu with the following options (2):

Send to Recycle Bin – Moves the folder and its contents to the system's recycling bin.

Reveal in Explorer – Displays the selected folder in the system's default file browser.

Add to Favorites – Makes the selected folder an entry in Bridge's Favorites panel.

Font menu

Menu: –	
Shortcut: –	See also: Text
Version: CS2	

In CS2, the font menu located in the options bar of the Type tool now displays the word 'Sample' in the actual font design. This addition to the menu list acts as a preview of the letter shapes and style of the typeface.

In addition to this feature the new menu list displays a small icon indicating the base structure of the font. Most fonts are structured as either Postscript (3), TrueType (2) or OpenType (1).

Font size

Menu: –	
Shortcut: –	**See also:** Fonts, selecting
Version: 6.0, 7.0, CS, CS2	

The size of the text you place in your image files is measured as pixels, millimeters or points.

I find the pixel setting most useful when working with digital files, as it indicates to me the precise size of my text in relation to the whole image. Millimeter and points values, on the other hand, vary depending on the resolution of the picture and the resolution of the output device.

Some of you might be aware that 72 points approximately equals 1 inch, but this is only true if the picture's resolution is 72 dpi. At higher resolutions the pixels are packed more closely together and therefore the same 72 point type is smaller in size.

To change the units of measurement used for type, go to the Units & Rulers option in the Preferences menu and then select the Type measure unit you want from the drop-down type menu (1).

To set the size of your font before adding the text to the picture input the value in the Font Size section of the options bar.

To change font size of existing type select the type and then alter the font size value.

Font styles and families

Menu: –	
Shortcut: –	**See also:** Faux fonts
Version: 6.0, 7.0, CS, CS2	

The font family is a term used to describe the way that the letter shapes look. Most readers would be familiar with the difference in appearance between Arial and Times Roman. These are two different families each containing different characteristics that determine the way that the letter shapes appear (1).

The font style refers to the different versions of the same font family. Most fonts are available in regular, italic, bold and bold italic styles (2).

Both font characteristics, family and style, can be altered via the items on the type options bar.

You can download new fonts from specialist websites to add to your system. After downloading, the fonts should be installed into the fonts section of your system directory. Windows and Macintosh users will need to consult their operating system manuals to find the preferred method for installing new fonts on their computer.

Arial - regular
Arial - italic ②

Fonts, selecting

Menu: –	
Shortcut: –	**See also:** Font size, Font styles
Version: 6.0, 7.0, CS, CS2	and families

You can select the typeface or font family to apply to your text in one of two ways:

1. Before adding the text to the picture, by choosing the family along with other type characteristics in the options bar.

2. Alternatively you can select the existing text and then choose a different type-face (1).

Detail

Foreground color

Menu: –
Shortcut: –   See also: Background color
Version: 6.0, 7.0, CS, CS2

Photoshop bases many of its drawing, painting and filter effects on two colors – the foreground and background colors.

The currently selected foreground and background colors are shown towards the bottom of the toolbox as two colored swatches. The topmost swatch (1) represents the foreground color, the one beneath (2) the hue for the background.

The default for these colors is black and white but it is possible to customize the selections at any time. Double-click the swatch and then select a new color from the color picker window (5).

To switch foreground and background colors click the double-headed curved arrow at the top right (3) and to restore the default (black and white) click the mini swatches bottom left (4).

Fragment filter

Menu: Filter > Pixelate > Fragment
Shortcut: –   See also: Filters
Version: 6.0, 7.0, CS, CS2

The Fragment filter, as one of the group of Pixelate filters, breaks the picture into smaller sections and slightly offsets these parts.

The change is often very subtle and only obvious at high magnification or when applied to a low resolution file.

There are no extra controls for altering the look or strength of the effect.

Free rotate layer

Menu: Edit >Transform > Rotate
Shortcut: –   See also: Rotate Canvas
Version: 6.0, 7.0, CS, CS2

The Rotate option allows you to freely spin the contents of a layer around a pivot point.

After selecting the command a bounding box surrounds the layer and the mouse pointer changes to a curved arrow to indicate that it is in rotate mode. When you click-drag the mouse the layer rotates (1).

By default the pivot point is in the center of the layer, but you can select a new position for this point by clicking onto one of the corner or side boxes in the reference point diagram (2) in the options bar.

①

Free Transform command

Menu: Edit > Free Transform
Shortcut: Ctrl/Cmd T   **See also:** Distorting a layer,
Version: 6.0, 7.0, CS, CS2   Skew, Warp

The Edit > Transform menu contains four options that allow you to change the shape of your pictures from their standard rectangle format. The Free Transform feature listed close by in the Edit menu is similar but unlike the other transform options, which tend to only allow one style of change. In contrast, Free Transform can be used to scale, rotate, distort, skew or even apply a perspective change to your picture.

Background layers can't be transformed and so need to be changed to a standard layer before the option becomes available on the menu. Do this by double-clicking the background layer and then naming the layer in the New Layer dialog that pops up before clicking OK (1).

Use the following key stroke combinations to change the shape of your layer:

Scale – Click-drag any of the bounding box handles. To scale proportionally hold the Shift key down whilst dragging.

Rotate – Move the mouse pointer outside the bounding box and click-drag to rotate.

Distort – Ctrl/Cmd-click-drag a bounding box handle to distort.

Skew – Shft-Ctrl/Cmd-click-drag a bounding box handle to skew.

Perspective – Ctrl/Cmd-Alt/Opt-Shft-click-drag to apply perspective changes.

Macintosh users should substitute Command for Control keys and Option for Alt.

Freehand selection

Menu: Enhance > Adjust Lighting > Levels
Shortcut: L   **See also:** Lasso tools
Version: 6.0, 7.0, CS, CS2

Freehand selection is another term for the style of selection created with the Lasso tool, as the effectiveness and accuracy of the selection is largely dependent on the drawing (mouse moving) abilities of the user.

It was for this reason that Adobe developed the Magnetic Lasso, which is designed to stick to the edges of picture parts as you draw.

Professionals whose work regularly requires them to make freehand selections often use a Stylus and Graphics tablet as they find the approach more natural and more akin to drawing with a pencil.

• •

When completed either double-click on the transformed layer or press the Enter key to 'commit' the changes.

To cancel press the Esc key.

Full screen mode

Menu: –
Shortcut: F   **See also:** Standard Screen
Version: 6.0, 7.0, CS, CS2   mode

Full Screen mode is one of the three screen modes that are available for use with Photoshop. With this option the menu bar disappears and the workspace is colored black (1). The options bar, toolbar and any open palettes can be hidden as well by pressing the Tab key. This is a good mode to use to preview your images without the distractions of menus, palettes and toolbars. Switch to this mode by pressing the Full Screen mode button on the toolbar.

• •

Fuzziness setting

Menu: –
Shortcut: –   **See also:** Color Range
Version: 6.0, 7.0, CS, CS2

A similar feature to Tolerance that determines how many colors are selected by the Eyedropper tool in the Color Range mode.

Sliding the control to the right increases the fuzziness and allows a larger range of colors to be picked.

Avoid using high fuzziness settings as they create blurred edges and settings too low can create jagged edges and missing selected pixels.

To continually adjust the selection keep your finger held down on the mouse button as you move the eyedropper around the preview image.

Without Gamut Warning

With Gamut Warning

Radius: 9.7 pixels

gG

87

Gamut Warning

Menu: View > Gamut Warning
Shortcut: Ctrl/Cmd Shft Y   **See also:** Print Space
Version: 6.0, 7.0, CS, CS2

The range of colors a computer monitor can display is known as the gamut and the monitor's gamut has a different range of colors than an inkjet printer can often output. The Photoshop Gamut Warning feature (View > Gamut Warning) shows when the colors on screen are outside of the printer's capabilities by coloring the problem areas.

The Gamut Warning's job is to prevent disappointment when you work in RGB mode. It does so by highlighting all the pixels that are out of gamut or beyond the capabilities of the printer. With the feature turned on you can adjust the colors in the photo until no warning appears and therefore be assured that the colors you see on screen will print.

To adjust the color used for the warning go to Edit > Preferences > Transparency & Gamut.

Gaussian Blur filter

Menu: Editor: Filter > Blur > Gaussian Blur
Shortcut: **See also:** Blur filters
Version: 6.0, 7.0, CS, CS2

The Gaussian Blur filter, as one of the group of Blur filters, softens the look of photos, producing a blur effect that is similar to out of focus pictures.

This filter is often used to blur the background of photographs, producing an artificial shallow depth of field effect. To reproduce these results select the area to be blurred first and then apply the filter.

Unlike the Blur and Blur More options, the Gaussian Blur filter provides a slider control that governs the strength of the effect (1).

Pro's Tip

In recent editions of Photoshop the more sophisticated Lens Blur is more frequently used for depth of field focus effects.

G

GIF – Adaptive

GIF – Perceptual

GIF – Selective

GIF – Restrictive (Web)

88

GIF format

Menu: –
Shortcut: –   **See also:** JPEG format,
Version: 6.0, 7.0, CS, CS2   Save for Web

The GIF format is used to optimize logos and graphics for use on web pages. The format supports up to 256 colors (8-bit), transparency (2), LZW compression and simple animation.

When converting a full color picture to GIF the number of colors is reduced and mixed using one of four options – Selective, Perceptual, Adaptive and Restrictive or Web (1). The Dither option (4) helps simulate continuous tone by mixing patterns of dots. The total number of colors

(3) used in the final file can also be set in the dialog. Save images in the GIF format by selecting the GIF option in the Save for Web feature (1) or via the Compuserve GIF format option in the Save As option.

Global Light

Menu: Layer > Layer Style > Global Light
Shortcut: –   **See also:** Layer Styles
Version: 6.0, 7.0, CS, CS2

The Drop Shadow, Inner Shadow and Bevel and Emboss layer styles use a light source to help define the look of the effect. The direction of the source can be altered via the dialog for each style (1).

The Use Global Light setting forces all layer styles to use the same light source and direction. Using this option gives your styles a more consistent appearance as all shadows and embossing effects are lit in the same way.

To apply the same light settings to all layer styles in a single document select Layer > Layer Style > Global Light and adjust the values in the dialog that pops up (2).

Glass filter

Menu: Filter > Distort > Glass
Shortcut: –   **See also:** Filters
Version: 6.0, 7.0, CS, CS2

The Glass filter, as one of the group of Distort filters, simulates the texture of a picture when it is viewed through rippled glass.

The look and style of the ripple is determined by the various controls in the filter's dialog. The Distortion slider (1) alters the amount of the image that is affected by the glass ripple. The Smoothness control (2) adjusts the sharpness of the ripple detail and the Texture menu (3) contains a series of options for the style of glass used in the filter. The Scaling slider (4) controls the size of the glass elements used to distort the picture and the Invert setting (5) switches the way that the effect is applied.

89

Glow effect

Menu: –	
Shortcut: –	**See also:** Layer Styles
Version: 6.0, 7.0, CS, CS2	

There are two Glow styles available in the Layer Styles menu of Photoshop – Inner Glow and Outer Glow (1). These options add a glow to a selection or the contents of a layer.

Glow styles look particularly effective when produced around type and can be made to appear from inside or outside the selection in any color. The effect is great for creating fancy headlines for websites or newsletters.

The Structure, Elements and Quality settings in the Glow dialogs (2) control the look, size and strength of the glow effect.

Glowing Edges filter

Menu: Filter > Stylize > Glowing Edges	
Shortcut: –	**See also:** –
Version: 6.0, 7.0, CS, CS2	

The Glowing Edges filter, as one of the group of Stylize filters, searches for and draws neon-like colored lines around the edges of picture elements.

The edges in the picture are used as the basis for the effect, with the three settings in the dialog providing control over how these are located and the style of the drawn neon line.

The Edge Width slider (1) alters the size and dominance of the lines drawn around the edges. The Edge Brightness control (2) alters the brightness of the lines and the balance of light and dark in the picture, and the Smoothness slider (3) adjusts the amount of fine detail in the end result.

Gradient adjustment layer

Menu: Layer > New Fill Layer > Gradient	
Shortcut: –	**See also:** Gradients
Version: 6.0, 7.0, CS, CS2	

A Gradient adjustment layer can be added to your picture by selecting the Gradient option from the Layer > New Fill Layer menu (1) or by choosing Gradient from the pop-up menu that appears after pressing the New Fill Layer button at the bottom of the Layers palette. After selecting the option a Gradient Fill dialog appears. Here you can select the gradient colors (2), style (3), angle (4) and scale (5). Clicking OK creates a new layer and fills it with the Gradient type, color and style that you set in the previous dialog.

The example shows the results of adding a gradient adjustment layer whilst a selection (of the white background) is active.

G

Before

After

© www.ablestock.com 2005

Gradient Map

Gradient Editor

Menu: –
Shortcut: G
Version: 6.0, 7.0, CS, CS2   See also: Gradients

The Gradient Editor dialog is used to adjust the existing gradient options found in the Gradient Picker palette or create and save completely new choices to the feature.

To create a new gradient start by displaying the dialog by clicking on the gradient preview (6) in the options bar. Select a preset option (1) to base the new gradient upon. Change colors by double-clicking the color stop (5) and choosing a new color from the Color Picker dialog. Alter the new color's position in the gradient by click-dragging the stop.

Adjust the position of the opacity by click-dragging the opacity stops (2, 3) along the gradient. Change the midpoint of color or opacity changes by click-dragging the midpoint control (4).

To add new color or opacity stops click on the upper or lower side of the gradient. To delete existing stops drag them into the middle of the gradient.

Save the finished gradient by entering a name and pressing the New button. The gradient will be displayed as a new option in the Gradient Picker palette.

Click to edit the gradient

Gradient Map adjustment layer

Menu: Layer > New Adjustment Layer > Gradient Map
Shortcut: –   See also: Gradient Map
Version: 6.0, 7.0, CS, CS2   filter, Gradients

The Gradient Map adjustment layer works in a similar way to the Gradient Map filter in that it swaps the tone of the picture with the colors of the selected gradient.

Applying the changes via an adjustment layer means that the results are always editable later and the original photograph remains untouched. By double-clicking the layer thumbnail (left side) the Gradient Map dialog opens and displays the original settings that were used in the adjustment layer. These settings can be altered and the adjustment layer reapplied.

The Gradient Map feature in either the filter or adjustment layer form is often used to create a custom conversion of a color image to grayscale. By selecting a simple black to white gradient (1) in the feature the tones in the original image are mapped evenly to the grayscale gradient.

Gradient Map filter

Menu: Image > Adjustments > Gradient Map
Shortcut: –   See also: Gradients, Gradient Map
Version: 6.0, 7.0, CS, CS2   adjustment layer

The Gradient Map filter, as one of the group of Adjustment filters, converts the underlying tones (grayscale information) of the photo to the colors and tones of the selected gradient. The dialog contains options for selecting the gradient to use as the basis of the mapping (1) as well as two checkbox controls.

Dither – For applying a Dither to the gradient to help smooth out changes in color and tone.

Reverse – Switches the mapping process so that dark tones are converted to light tones and light tones to dark.

Gradient mask

Menu: Enhance > Adjust Lighting > Levels
Shortcut: Ctrl/Cmd Alt/Opt Shft L   **See also:** Curves, Shadow/
Version: 6.0, 7.0, CS, CS2   Highlight

Adding a gradient mask to a layer makes the image take on the gradient when blending with other layers. This is useful for complex image creation and composition. The mask can then be edited to change the shape of the gradation by adding or subtracting from it.

To show how the Gradient Mask can be put to use I've merged three photographs – a portrait, sculpture and metal girder. The metal girder was first rotated to suit the angle of the neck on the sculpture, then a black to transparent mask was added to the sculpture layer so that the image fades to transparent. This was repeated on the girl layer and now you can't see the joins.

Linear

Gradients

Menu: –
Shortcut: G   **See also:** Gradient Editor
Version: 6.0, 7.0, CS, CS2

Photoshop has five different gradient types. All the options are used to gradually change color and tone from one point in the picture to another. The choices are:

Linear (1) – Changes color from starting to end point in a straight line.

Radial (2) – Radiates the gradient from the center outwards in a circular form.

Angle gradient (3) – Changes the color in a counter-clockwise direction around the starting point.

Reflection (4) – Mirrors a linear gradient on either side of the drawn line.

Diamond (5) – Changes color from the center outwards in a diamond shape.

To create a gradient start by selecting the tool and then adjusting the controls in the options palette. Choose the colors from the Gradient Picker drop-down menu (6) and the style from the five buttons to the right (1–5). Click and drag the mouse pointer on the canvas surface to stretch out a line that marks the start and end points of the gradient. Release the button to fill the layer with the selected gradient.

Grain filter

Menu: Filter > Texture > Grain
Shortcut: –   **See also:** Filters, Film Grain
Version: 6.0, 7.0, CS, CS2   filter,
                                                        Add Noise filter

The Grain filter, as one of the group of Texture filters, simulates the look of the grain of high-speed film.

The look of the effect is adjusted by three settings in the dialog. The Intensity slider (1) alters the density of the grain effect and the Contrast control (2) adjusts the underlying contrast of the whole picture. The Grain Type menu (3) provides a variety of texture options (4) that can be used for filtering. Film grain or Regular is one of the entries but the look of the end result differs greatly with different selections. With some grain types the current foreground and background colors are used for the grain and background hues. Changing these colors often results in dramatically different results.

Diamond

Reflected

Radial

Angle

Grayscale

Before

Monochrome

After

Graphic Pen filter

Menu: Filter > Sketch > Graphic Pen
Shortcut: –   **See also:** Filters
Version: 6.0, 7.0, CS, CS2

The Graphic Pen filter is one of the group of Sketch filters. The feature simulates the effect of making a drawing of the photograph with a thin graphic arts pen. Close, overlapping strokes are used for the shadow areas, midtones are represented by balancing strokes and with the paper color showing through, and highlight details are drawn with a few sparse strokes.

The filter dialog gives you control over the balance of light and dark – paper and stroke (2) and the length of the pen stroke (1) used to draw the picture. There is also a drop-down menu for selecting the direction of the pen strokes (3).

Grayscale images

Menu: –
Shortcut: –   **See also:** Channel Mixer
Version: 6.0, 7.0, CS, CS2

Grayscale images, in computer terms, are those photos that contain no color. These pictures contain a series of gray tones from pure black through to white. The more tones that exist between the black and white points the smoother any graduations in the picture will be. The photographic equivalent of a grayscale picture is a black and white photograph.

Sometimes the term monochrome is used to describe grayscale photos because they only contain a single (mono) color (chrome) – black on a white background. However, monochrome can also refer to photos that use a color other than black for the tones.

Grayscale mode

Menu: Image > Mode > Grayscale
Shortcut: –   **See also:** Color modes
Version: 6.0, 7.0, CS, CS2

It is possible to change the color mode of your picture by selecting a different mode from the Image > Mode menu (1).

A picture that is in Grayscale mode contains no color at all and supports a total of 256 levels of gray, with a value of 0 being black and 256 being white.

When converting a color photograph to Grayscale mode in Photoshop you may need to confirm that you wish to lose all the color in the photo. Clicking OK to this request will lose the picture's three color channels (RGB) and retain tone and detail in a single gray channel (2).

Graphics Tablet

Menu: –
Shortcut: –   **See also:** –
Version: 6.0, 7.0, CS, CS2

Many professionals prefer to work with a stylus and tablet when creating complex masks. The extra options provided by the pressure sensitivity of the stylus along with the familiar 'pencil and paper' feeling makes using this approach more intuitive and often faster than using a mouse.

Most drawing and painting tools in Photoshop have tablet or pen options (1) in the various characteristics section of the Brushes palette. Here you can select a range of settings that can be activated to or adjusted with the stylus or pen pressure.

NEW for CS2

Before

After

Grid

Menu: View > Show > Grid	
Shortcut: Ctrl/Cmd '	**See also:** Rulers, Guides,
Version: 6.0, 7.0, CS, CS2	Warp, Vanishing Point filter

A visual, non-printing grid is available for display in the Photoshop workspace. With the grid displayed and the Snap to Grid option (View > Snap to > Grid) selected objects will automatically align with grid lines and intersections when being moved or sized.

The grid is often used in conjunction with the Rulers (View > Rulers) feature to help align and size objects and picture parts.

The color, style and spacing of the grid can be adjusted via the Guides, Grids & Slices section of the Edit > Preferences dialog (1).

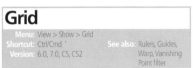

Group Layers

Menu: Layer > Group Layers	
Shortcut: Ctrl/Cmd G	**See also:** Layer Set
Version: CS2	

Grouping layers is a new way of combining individual layers into a common layer folder or Layer Set as it was known in CS.

In CS2 it is possible to multi-select layers and then create a new layer group (set) by choosing the Group Layers option (1) from the Layers menu or pressing Ctrl/Cmd G.

To remove layers from a group and restore their place in the Layers palette simply select Layer > Ungroup Layer.

To create an empty Layer Group click on the Create a new group button at the bottom of the Layers palette (2).

Before

After

Group with Previous – Create Clipping Mask

Menu: Layer > Create Clipping Mask	
Shortcut: Ctrl/Cmd Alt/Opt G	**See also:** –
Version: 6.0, 7.0, CS, CS2	

The Group with Previous command from CS becomes the Create Clipping Mask in CS2. The feature still combines the contents of two layers using a clipping group. The command is often used to insert the contents of one layer into the non-transparent areas of another. The example shows the winter image, top layer, being clipped by the letter shapes (non-transparent areas) of the bottom layer.

This occurs because all the layers in the clipping group have the opacity attributes and blend mode of the bottom-most layer.

You can create a clipping mask in two different ways:

1. Select the top layer and then choose Layer > Create Clipping Mask (previously Group with Previous).

2. Hold down the Alt/Opt key whilst you click on the boundaries between the two layers that you wish to group.

G

Before

After

NEW for CS2

Grow, selection

Menu: Select > Grow
Shortcut: –   **See also:** Modify Selections
Version: 6.0, 7.0, CS, CS2

As well as the options listed under the Select > Modify menu, an active selection can also be altered and adjusted using the Grow and Similar commands.

The Select > Grow feature increases the size of an existing selection by incorporating pixels of similar color and tone to those already in the selection. For a pixel to be included in the 'grown' selection it must be adjacent to the existing selection and fall within the current tolerance settings located in the options bar (1).

Guides

Menu: –
Shortcut: –   **See also:** Rulers, Grid,
Version: 6.0, 7.0, CS, CS2   Guides – Smart

These are horizontal or vertical lines that can be pulled out from the edge rulers to appear over the image. If the rulers aren't visible go to View > Rulers (Ctrl/Cmd R).

Guides can be used to align text or for laying out parts of the image in a symmetrical pattern. Go to Edit > Preferences > Guides, Grids & Slices (1) to choose the guides' color and style (straight or dotted line). The guides will not print and can be removed or repositioned using the Pointer tool.

As with the Grid, Paint tools will snap to the guides if the Snap to Guides option is selected from the View menu.

Pro's Tip

The new Vanishing Point filter provides the option of exporting the perspctive grids created in the feature as separate layers. The layers can then be dragged onto a new document and used as a set of custom perspective guides.

Guides, Smart

Menu: View > Show > Smart Guides
Shortcut: –   **See also:** Rulers, Guides,
Version: CS2   Grid

New for CS2 is the Smart Guides feature that automatically aligns different layer contents with other elements in a Photoshop document. When moving layer content Photoshop will automatically snap contents to align with edges or centers of other picture parts (1).

To display the Smart Guides as you arrange picture parts select Smart Guides from the View > Show menu (2).

The color of the Smart Guide display lines can be altered via the Edit > Preferences > Guides, Grid & Slices dialog (3).

Halftone Pattern filter

Menu: Filter > Sketch > Halftone Pattern
Shortcut: – **See also:** Filters, Color
Version: 6.0, 7.0, CS, CS2 Halftone filter

The Halftone Pattern filter, as one of the group of Sketch filters, simulates the look of a picture that has been printed using a halftone or screened pattern. The filter provides similar looking results to the Color Halftone feature except here the pattern is created in monochrome and is based on the current foreground and background colors. Another difference is that the filter contains a preview window and the ability to change the pattern type (3).

The size of the pattern element (1), dot or line, and the overall contrast of the effect (2) is controlled by the sliders in the dialog. The pattern type can be switched between dot (4), line (5) or circle (6) options.

Hand tool

Menu: –
Shortcut: H **See also:** Move tool
Version: 6.0, 7.0, CS, CS2

The Hand tool helps users navigate their way around images.

This is especially helpful when the image has been 'zoomed' beyond the confines of the screen. When a picture is enlarged to this extent it is not possible to view the whole image at one time; using the Hand tool the user can drag the photograph around within the window frame.

Hard Light blend mode

Menu: –
Shortcut: – **See also:** Blend modes
Version: 6.0, 7.0, CS, CS2

The Hard Light blending mode is one of the group of Overlay modes that base their effects on combining the two layers depending on the tonal value of their contents.

This option is similar to the Overlay mode but produces a more dramatic and sometimes more contrasty result. The content of the top layer is either Screened or Multiplied depending on its color and tonal value. If the tone in the top layer is lighter than 50% then this section of the bottom layer is screened (lightened); if the tone is darker, then it is multiplied (darkened). Blending with 50% gray produces no change. When combined with the High Pass filter this blend mode is used to create editable sharpening effects that don't use any of the sharpening filters.

Hard Mix blend mode

Menu: –
Shortcut: –   **See also:** Blend modes
Version: 6.0, 7.0, CS, CS2

The Hard Mix blending mode is one of the group of Overlay modes that base their effects on combining the two layers depending on the tonal value of their contents.

This option is similar to the Overlay mode but produces a more dramatic, contrasty and posterized result. The luminosity of the top layer is combined with the color of the bottom to produce a picture with large flat areas of dramatic color (maximum colors 8). Lowering the opacity of the top layer (Hard Mix layer) reduces the posterization effects. Blending with 50% gray produces no change.

The Hard Mix option can be used to add a high contrast sharpening effect to a picture. Blur a duplicate layer of the original and then change to Hard Mix and adjust the layer's opacity to control the degree of contrast and sharpening.

Hardness option

Menu: –
Shortcut: B
Version: 6.0, 7.0, CS, CS2   **See also:** Brush tool

Hardness (4) is one of the options from the Brush Preset Picker palette which is displayed when the down arrow button is pressed in the options bar. The slider controls the softness of the edge of the brush tip. A setting of 100% (1) produces a sharp edge brush stroke, 50% moderately soft (2) and 1% a very soft brush stroke (3).

HDR, capturing source images

Menu: –
Shortcut: –   **See also:** Merge to HDR
Version: CS2

To create a High Dynamic Range image in Photoshop you need to capture at least three separate pictures of the same subject with different exposures. Most digital cameras have a built-in option for exposure bracketing and using this feature will mean that you can photograph a sequence of pictures and the camera will alter the exposure settings to record over-, under- and correctly exposed frames automatically. Be sure that the camera is changing the shutter speed to alter the exposure as adjusting the aperture will cause changes in the depth of field of sharpness as well.

HDR, Exposure

Menu: Image > Adjustment > Exposure
Shortcut: –   **See also:** High Dynamic Range
Version: CS2

The Exposure feature is designed to adjust the contrast and brightness of the newly supported 32 bits per channel pictures. With this dialog you can make basic adjustments to image tones before converting the file to 16 or 8 bits per channel mode for further editing.

The Channel Mixer and Photo filter adjustment features can also be used in 32 bits per channel mode.

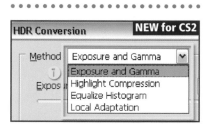

HDR, 32-bit to 8/16-bit

Menu: Image > Mode > 8 bits/channel
Shortcut: –   **See also:** Mode, Color depth
Version: CS2

Changing from 32 bits per channel mode to either 8 or 16 bits per channel displays the HDR Conversion dialog. In this feature it is possible to control how the many tones contained in the high-bit image are compressed into a lower-bit mode format. You can select from four conversion methods (1). The **Exposure and Gamma** option uses two slider controls to adjust the positioning of tones prior to conversion. **Highlight Compression** and **Equalize Histogram** selections both provide automatic tonal adjustment with no user controls.

In the final option, **Localized Adaptation**, a familiar curves feature can be used to determine which tones are compressed and by how much. A steep line indicates greater contrast and less compression of tones whereas a shallow part of the curve compresses the tones more radically and results in image areas of lower contrast.

Before

After

© www.ablestock.com 2005

Help

Menu:	Help > Photoshop Help
	Bridge: Help > Bridge Help
Shortcut: F1	**See also:** –
Version: CS2	

Though there has always been a great help system in Photoshop, CS2 introduces a completely revised version of the feature.

The newly named Help Center displays topics in a viewer palette that is independent of the main program. Other changes include the listing of topics in ways that provide quicker and easier access not just to information about a particular subject but also how to use the tool or feature in a fuller workflow.

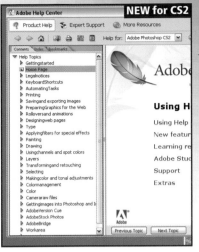

NEW for CS2

Healing Brush

Menu: Enhance > Adjust Lighting > Levels	
Shortcut: J	**See also:** Spot Healing Brush,
Version: 6.0, 7.0, CS, CS2	Patch tool,
	Vanishing Point filter

The Healing Brush is designed to work in a similar way to the Clone tool; the user selects the area (Alt/Option-click) to be sampled before painting and then proceeds to drag the brush tip over the area to be repaired.

The tool achieves such great results by merging background and source area details as you paint. Just as with the Clone Stamp tool, the size and edge hardness of the current brush determines the characteristics of the Healing Brush tool tip (1).

One of the best ways to demonstrate the sheer power of the Healing Brush is to remove the wrinkles from an aged face. In the example, the deep crevices of the fisherman's face have been easily removed with the tool. The texture, color and tone of the face remain even after the 'healing' work is completed because the tool merges the new areas with the detail of the picture beneath.

Shown

© www.ablestock.com 2005

Hidden

Hiding palettes

Menu: –	
Shortcut: Tab	**See also:** Full screen mode, Hiding/
Version: 6.0, 7.0, CS, CS2	Showing layers

Open palettes can be hidden and re-displayed by pressing the Tab key (1).

To close the palette altogether click the red 'X' in the top right corner of the palette window. Alternatively palettes open in the workspace can be dragged to the palette dock, where the palette is minimized and displayed as a single tab. Palettes can then be displayed by clicking on the tab or displayed and removed from the dock by double-clicking.

Text layer shown

Text layer hidden

Hiding/Showing layers

Menu: –	
Shortcut: –	**See also:** Full screen mode,
Version: 6.0, 7.0, CS, CS2	Hiding palettes

The Photoshop Layers palette displays all the layers in your picture and their settings in the one dialog box. Layers can be turned off by clicking the eye symbol on the far left of the layer so that it is no longer displayed. This action removes the layer from view but not from the stack. You can turn the layer back on again by clicking the eye space. You can Alt/Option-click on an eyeball icon to show all layers or just that layer.

NEW for CS2

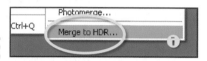

Photomerge...

Ctrl+Q   Merge to HDR...

High Dynamic Range (HDR)

Menu: File > Automate > Merge to HDR
Bridge: Tools > Photoshop > Merge to HDR
Shortcut: –   **See also:** HDR, 32- bit to 8/16-bit,
Version: CS2   HDR, capturing source images

A brand new feature in Photoshop CS2 is the ability to create and apply basic edits to 32 bits per channel digital photos. Most digital camera sensors are capable of capturing a brightness range of between 6 and 8 f-stops between deepest shadow and brightest highlights. For most shooting scenarios this range, often called the dynamic range of the sensor, equates to the contrast of the scene. So when photographing a scene with average brightness range the detail is captured and held throughout the whole file.

However, in particularly bright or contrasty environments (summer in the tropics) or when capturing a view that encompasses an inside space as well as a brightly lit exterior, the abilities of the sensor will be exceeded. This results in detail being lost in the highlight and/or the shadow area of the picture. To help solve this problem Adobe has created a new set of tools that can be used to combine the brightness range of several different pictures to create a High Dynamic Range or HDR picture.

To create an HDR picture start by shooting at least three pictures of the same scene with exposure differences of 2 f-stops or more. (See **HDR, capturing source images** entry for more details.) Next load the three files into the File > Automate > Merge to HDR feature (1). Photoshop will attempt to register the three pictures and determine the exposure difference between each using the metadata stored with the original camera file. If the exposure detail is not found or is stored in a format that isn't accessible by the feature then you will need to inform Photoshop of the exposure settings used to capture each photograph. This is entered via the Manually Set EV dialog (2). The Merge to HDR dialog (3) displays the combined image, thumbnails of the source pictures as well as a Set White Point preview option. The finalized HDR file can then be used as a basis for conversion to 8 or 16 bits per channel files.

In this release of Photoshop the following features and tools are 32-bit enabled: Crop, Image and Canvas Size, Trim, Free Transform, Selection (save and load), Clone Stamp, History Brush, Info palette, Channel Mixer, PhotoFilter and Exposure Adjustments as well as Add Noise, Unsharp Mask, Gaussian Blur, Motion Blur, Offset, High Pass, Lens Flare, Smart Sharpen, Average, Box Blur, Motion Blur, Radial Blur, Shape Blur, Surface Blur, De-Interlace, NTSC filters.

High Pass filter

Menu: Filter > Other > High Pass
Shortcut: –   **See also:** Filters
Version: 6.0, 7.0, CS, CS2

The High Pass filter, as one of the group of Other filters, isolates the edges in a picture and then converts the rest of the picture to mid gray. The filter locates the edge areas by searching for areas of high contrast or color change.

The filter contains a single slider, Radius (1), that controls the filtering effect. When the Radius value is set to low only the most prominent edge detail is retained and the remainder of the picture converted to gray. Higher values produce a result with less of the picture converted to gray.

The combination filter effects of edge finding and changing picture parts to gray makes this feature a tool that is often used for advanced sharpening techniques like the one detailed here.

Before High Pass Sharpening

After High Pass Sharpening

Highlights

Menu: –
Shortcut: – °   See also: Specular highlights
Version: 6.0, 7.0, CS, CS2

Highlights are the brightest parts of the image with detail that will still print (1).

These can be adjusted using the clear triangle on the slider control (white-point input slider) that appears on the right-hand side of the Levels graph (2).

The Shadow/Highlight feature provides another way of controlling the density (brightness) of the highlights in your pictures (3).

Histogram

Menu: Window > Histogram
Shortcut: –   See also: Levels command
Version: 6.0, 7.0, CS, CS2

The first step in taking charge of your pixels is to become aware of where they are situated in your image and how they are distributed between black and white points.

The Histogram palette displays a graph of all the pixels in your image. The left-hand side represents the black values (1), the right the white end of the spectrum (3) and the center section the midtone values (2). In a 24-bit image (8 bits per channel) there are a total of 256 levels of tone possible from black to white – each of these values is represented on the graph.

The number of pixels in the image with a particular brightness or tone value is displayed on the graph by height. The higher the spike at any point the more pixels of this value are present in the picture.

A low key image appears with most of the peaks concentrated in the shadow area at the left-hand side. A high key image has the peaks in the highlight area to the right. The average tone image should have a graph that rises from the far left, peaks across the middle section and falls to the far right.

Make a copy (Layer > Duplicate Layer) of the picture layer that you want to sharpen. Filter the copied layer with the High Pass filter (Filter > Other > High Pass) and press OK.

With the filtered layer still selected switch the blend mode to Hard Light. This mode blends both the dark and light parts of the filtered layer with the picture layer, causing an increase in contrast.

Adjust the opacity of this layer to govern the level of sharpening. Sharpening using this technique means that you can remove or adjust the strength of the effect later by manipulating the filtered layer.

History brush

Menu: –
Shortcut: Y   **See also:** History palette
Version: 6.0, 7.0, CS, CS2

Use this to paint in details from a previous stage of editing. Click on the box that appears in the History palette at the stage in the image editing process that you'd like to apply and paint onto the new level.

This is a great option if you're considering hand-coloring a black and white image. Cheat by starting off with a color image and convert it first to grayscale to discard all color information and then back to color. The black and white image can then be colored using the History brush.

Click on the left of the opening image to turn on the History brush icon. Then click on the latest stage and begin to paint.

The feature is also good for removing dust and scratches. Apply the Dust & Scratches filter and make the History brush active on that new layer. Then go back to a previous history level and paint with the History brush over dust and scratches to paint in the newer filtered layer.

History Log

Menu: Enhance > Adjust Lighting > Levels
Shortcut: Ctrl/Cmd Alt/Opt Shft L   **See also:** Curves, Shadow/
Version: 6.0, 7.0, CS, CS2   Highlight

First released in CS the History Log features is an option that records all actions that you perform in Photoshop.

The log can be saved as metadata that is attached to the picture or as a separated text file. When the History Log is saved as metadata the contents can be viewed via the File > Info palette (1).

Settings that govern the type of log created as well as where it is stored can be found in the Edit > Preferences > General dialog (2). Also located in this dialog is the option to turn the feature off and on.

History palette

Menu: Window > History
Shortcut: –   **See also:** History brush
Version: 6.0, 7.0, CS, CS2

Every task you perform in Photoshop is recorded as a step, or state, and then displayed as a list in the History palette.

Working like a multiple level undo feature this allows you to go back through previous stages of your image editing and correct changes that went wrong.

A slider on the left-hand side of the palette can be dragged slowly through the stages to help you find when things start to go wrong. Simply click on the last stage that you were happy with and start again to change history – if it was just that simple in life!

The number of states stored in the palette is controlled by the value set in the Edit > Preferences > General dialog. States are deleted by selecting the entry in the palette and then pressing the Dustbin button (1) at the bottom of the palette. A new document can be made from a state by clicking the new document button (2). A snapshot or temporary copy of any given state that is displayed at the top of the palette can be created with the Snapshot button (3).

History states

Menu: Window > History
Shortcut: –   **See also:** History palette,
Version: 6.0, 7.0, CS, CS2   History brush

Each editing or enhancement step that is performed on a picture in Photoshop is stored as a history state in the History palette.

The total number of states that can be stored is determined by the History States setting in the general area Preferences dialog. Once this number has been reached the oldest state is deleted to make way for the latest image change.

Clicking on an earlier state will restore the picture to the way it was when the state was first added to the palette.

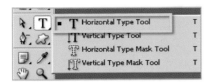

Horizontal Type tool

Menu: –
Shortcut: T   **See also:** Type
Version: 6.0, 7.0, CS, CS2

The Photoshop Type tool provides the option to apply text horizontally across the page, or vertically down the page.

To place text onto your picture, select the Horizontal Type tool from the toolbox. Next, click onto the canvas in the area where you want the text to appear.

Do not be too concerned if the letters are not positioned exactly, as the layer and text can be moved later.

Once you have finished entering text you need to commit the type to a layer. Until this is done you will be unable to access most other Photoshop functions.

To exit the text editor, either click the 'tick' button (1) in the options bar or press the Control + Enter keys in Windows (2) or Command + Return for a Macintosh system.

● ● ● ● ● ● ● ● ● ● ● ● ● ● ● ● ● ● ● ●

Hue/Saturation adjustment layer

Menu: Layer > New Adjustment Layer > Hue/Saturation
Shortcut: –   **See also:** Hue/Saturation
Version: 6.0, 7.0, CS, CS2

The Hue/Saturation adjustment layer provides the same functionality as the Adjust Hue/Saturation feature.

Manipulating the picture with an adjustment layer rather than directly means that the original picture is always kept intact and you can always change the settings of the adjustment later by double-clicking on the left-hand layer thumbnail.

Hue blend mode

Menu: –
Shortcut: –   **See also:** Blend modes
Version: 6.0, 7.0, CS, CS2

The Hue blending mode is one of the group of modes that base their effects on combining the hue (color), saturation (color strength) and luminance (tones and details) of the two layers in different ways.

This option combines the hue of the top layer with the saturation and luminance of the bottom.

● ●

Hue/Saturation

Menu: Window > History
Shortcut: Ctrl/Cmd U   **See also:** Hue/Saturation adjustment layer
Version: 6.0, 7.0, CS, CS2

To understand how this feature works you will need to think of the colors in your image in a slightly different way. Rather than using the three-color model (Red, Green, Blue) that we are familiar with, the Hue/Saturation control breaks the image into different components – Hue or color, Saturation or color strength, and Lightness (HSL).

The dialog itself displays slider controls for each component, allowing the user to change each factor independently of the others. Moving the Hue control (1) along the slider changes the dominant color of the image. From left to right, the hue's changes are represented in much the same way as colors in a rainbow. Alterations here will provide a variety of dramatic results, most of which are not realistic and should be used carefully.

Moving the Saturation slider (2) to the left gradually decreases the strength of the color until the image is converted to a grayscale. In contrast, adjusting the control to the right increases the purity of the hue and produces images that are vibrant and dramatic.

The Lightness slider (3) changes the density of the image and works the same way as the Brightness slider in the Brightness/Contrast feature.

The Colorize option (4) converts a colored image to a monochrome made up of a single dominant color and black and white.

If Master is selected in the Edit menu, changes will affect the entire image. You can also select different color ranges from the menu and changes will affect only the selected color range.

ijk

ICC profiles

Menu: –
Shortcut: –   **See also:** Color Settings
Version: 6.0, 7.0, CS, CS2

Essentially color management is concerned with describing the characteristics of each device in the editing chain. This includes cameras, scanners, screens, editing software and printers.

This description, often called an ICC profile, is then used to translate image detail and color from one device to another.

Pictures are tagged, when they are first created (via camera or scanner), with a profile and when downloaded to a computer, which has a profiled screen attached, the image is translated to suit the characteristics of the monitor.

With the corrections complete the tagged file is then sent to the printer, where the picture is translated again to suit the printer's profile.

Through the use of a color-managed, ICC profile-based system we can maintain predictable color throughout the editing process and from machine to machine.

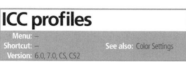

Image Interpolation

Menu: –
Shortcut: –   **See also:** Image Size
Version: 6.0, 7.0, CS, CS2   command, Bicubic
                                            interpolation

A file with the same pixel dimensions can have several different document sizes based on altering the spread of the pixels when the picture is printed (or displayed on screen). In this way you can adjust a high-resolution file to print the size of a postage stamp, postcard or a poster by only changing the dpi or resolution. This type of resizing has no detrimental quality effects on your pictures as the original pixel dimensions remain unchanged.

This said, in some circumstances it is necessary to increase or decrease the number of pixels in an image. Both these actions will produce results that have less quality than if the pictures were scanned or photographed at precisely the desired size at the time of capture.

As this isn't always possible, Photoshop can increase or decrease the image's pixel dimensions using tools such as the Image Size or the Scale features. Each of these steps requires the program to interpolate, or 'make up', the pixels that form the resized image.

Interpolation is a process by which the computer program reduces or increases the number of pixels in the picture. To achieve the color and brightness levels pixels are averaged and used as a basis for creating new pixels according to a specific algorithm. When resizing pictures in Photoshop you can select from several different interpolation algorithms (1). These options are available in the Image Size feature.

High resolution

Low resolution

NEW for CS2

Image resolution

Menu: –
Shortcut: – **See also:** Curves, Shadow/Highlight
Version: 6.0, 7.0, CS, CS2

One measure of digital image quality is the resolution of the picture which is usually stated in pixels per inch (ppi).

The more pixels per inch the higher the resolution. Not to be confused with sharpness, which is affected by a number of things, including lens quality. The resolution needs to be high enough to suit the viewing media and should not be confused with dpi (dots per inch).

If, for example, you only ever look at the images on a computer monitor for Web use you only need a resolution of 72 ppi for Macs and 96 ppi for a PC and each pixel will be displayed as a dot. If, on the other hand, you're wanting to send the images to a magazine or book publisher you'll need a resolution of at least 300 ppi, whilst most desktop inkjet printers require files with 150 to 240 ppi and lay down several dots per pixel to ensure accurate colors.

Image Processor

Menu: Bridge: Tools > Photoshop > Image Processor
File > Scripts > Image Processor
Shortcut: – **See also:** Camera Raw
Version: CS2

Russell Brown developed the Image Processor to demonstrate the power of the scripting engine within Photoshop and at the same time to provide a very handy image conversion utility. The feature is designed to quickly convert a range of Raw files into JPEG, PSD and TIFF versions. There are options to manually adjust the conversion settings for the first file and then apply these settings to the rest and the ability to apply an action during the process.

Image Size command

Menu: Image > Image Size
Shortcut: Ctrl/Cmd Alt/Opt I **See also:** Canvas Size
Version: 6.0, 7.0, CS, CS2

The Image Size dialog provides several options for manipulating the number of pixels in your photograph and how big it prints.

At first glance the settings displayed here may seem a little confusing, but if you can make the distinction between the Pixel Dimensions of the image (1) and the Document Size (2), it will be easier to understand.

Keep in mind:

Pixel Dimensions represent the true digital size of the file.

Document Size is the physical dimensions of the file represented in inches (or centimeters) based on using a specific number of pixels per inch (resolution or dpi).

To keep the ratio of width and height of the new image the same as the original, tick the Constrain Proportions checkbox (3).

To change resolution, open the Image Size dialog and uncheck the Resample Image option (4). Next, change either the resolution, width or height settings to suit your output.

To increase the pixels or upsize the image, tick the Resample Image checkbox (4) and then increase the value of any of the dimension settings in the dialog. To decrease the pixels or downsize the image, decrease the value of the dimension settings.

Image Space, color management

Menu: –
Shortcut: –   See also: Print options
Version: 6.0, 7.0, CS, CS2

The Image, or Source, Space refers to the ICC profile that a picture has been tagged with. The profile might have been attached at the time of capture or added later but it is this image space profile that allows the image to be correctly displayed and printed.

So when shooting make sure that any color management or ICC profile settings in the camera are always turned on (1). This will ensure that the pictures captured will be tagged with a profile. Those readers shooting film and converting to digital with scanners should search through the preference menus of their scanners to locate, and activate, any in-built color management systems here as well. This way scanned pictures will be tagged as well.

Next, to ensure that Photoshop is correctly using the image space, make sure that the most appropriate option (2) for your situation is selected in the Color Settings dialog of the program. This ensures that tagged pictures coming into the workspace are correctly interpreted and displayed ready for editing and enhancement. When it comes time to print select the File > Print with Preview option and then Let Photoshop Determine Colors and finally input your Printer Profile before pressing Print to finish (3).

ImageReady

Menu: –
Shortcut: –   See also: Jump to
Version: 6.0, 7.0, CS, CS2

ImageReady is a Web image editing program that's bundled with Photoshop. It has the same interface and allows seamless connection from within the program. We saw a jump from version 3.0 with Photoshop 6.0 to version 7.0 with Photoshop 7.0. Now it follows suit with ImageReady CS. The program allows you to slice a picture up so that it can be used more effectively on a Web page. You can also optimize pictures, create rollovers and edit animation. CS2 now includes features such as the Animation palette that started life as an ImageReady feature.

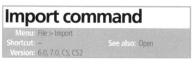

Import command

Menu: File > Import
Shortcut: –   See also: Open
Version: 6.0, 7.0, CS, CS2

The Import menu located under the File heading lists a range of sources for importing images into Photoshop. Acting much like the Import TWAIN feature found in older software, the feature links installed cameras and scanners with Photoshop and allows the user to control the driver software from inside the editing package.

The import sources listed under the menu normally include the following:

Installed scanners/cameras – Use the scanner driver or camera download software to import pictures from either of these device types.

WIA Support – Most cameras that are designed to connect to Windows computers are supplied with a WIA or Windows Image Acquisition driver that is used for downloading pictures from these devices.

Annotations – This option allows you to import annotations that have been saved in PDF or FDF file.

Variable Data Sets – Use this selection to import text-based data sets to be used when generating data driven graphics.

Note: The exact contents of the import menu list are determined by the scanners or cameras that you have installed on your computer.

Indexed Color mode

Menu: Image > Mode > Indexed Color
Shortcut: –   See also: Color modes
Version: 6.0, 7.0, CS, CS2

The Indexed Color mode can support up to 256 different colors and is the default color mode for the GIF file format.

When a full color picture is converted to the Index mode the colors used are drawn from a special palette (1). They are:

Exact – For pictures with 256 colors or less where the exact colors are used in the converted file.

System (Mac OS) and **System (Windows OS)** – Use the system palette.

Web – Uses a special set of 216 colors that can be displayed by all computer systems.

Uniform – Uses a palette of colors that have been evenly sampled from the RGB color space.

Perceptual – Uses a color set that gives priority to colors that the human eye is more sensitive to.

Selective – Similar to perceptual but also favors the web color set.

Adaptive – Builds a set of colors from those most present in the original picture.

Custom – Create your own palette of colors using the Color Table dialog box.

Previous – Uses the previous custom palette.

The dialog also has options to allow you to select the total number of colors to present in the final conversion, force specific colors to be included, add transparency, select a matte color and choose a dither type (2).

Info palette

Menu: Window > Info
Shortcut: F8   See also: –
Version: 6.0, 7.0, CS, CS2

The Info palette provides a variety of information about the open document. With the palette displayed, moving a tool pointer over the canvas surface will show details of the pixels beneath the tool tip. The details are displayed in five sections of the palette:

(1, 2) First and second color readouts displayed in Grayscale, RGB, WEB or HSB color.

(3) Mouse coordinates displayed in pixels, millimeters, centimeters, inches, points, picas or percent.

(4) Width and height of marquee displayed in pixels, millimeters, centimeters, inches, points, picas or percent.

(5) File information such as document size, profile or dimensions and scratch sizes, efficiency, timing and current tool.

The units used for each display section are set via the pop-out menu (6) displayed when the More button (top right) is pressed.

Ink Outlines filter

Menu: Filter > Brush Strokes > Ink Outlines
Shortcut: –   See also: Filters
Version: 6.0, 7.0, CS, CS2

The Ink Outlines filter, as one of the group of Brush Strokes filters, draws fine black ink lines over the edge details of the original picture.

Three controls in the filter's dialog allow adjustment of the filtering process and results.

The length of the stroke used in the outlining process can be varied with the Stroke Length slider (1).

The Dark Intensity (2) and Light Intensity (3) sliders provide control over the brightness and contrast of the final result. When low values are used for both sliders a low contrast picture results. Conversely higher settings produce a more contrasty result overall.

Input levels

Menu: Enhance > Adjust Lighting > Levels
Shortcut: Ctrl/Cmd Alt/Opt Shft L   See also: Levels command
Version: 6.0, 7.0, CS, CS2

The Levels feature controls image tones in two different ways. The upper sliders (the ones just below the histogram graph) alters the input levels (1) of the picture and are most often used to increase the contrast of low contrast picture. The example image shows the increase in contrast that is possible when you drag the black (left) and white (right) input sliders in towards the center of the graph until they reach the first groupings of pixels (3).

The slider at the bottom of the Levels dialog controls the output levels of the image (2).

Before

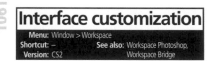

Interface customization

Menu: Window > Workspace
Shortcut: –   **See also:** Workspace Photoshop,
Version: CS2   Workspace Bridge

In Photoshop CS2 you can customize the user interface more than in any other version of Photoshop.

You can select, manage and save your own keyboard shortcut schema quickly and easily with the options in the new Keyboard Shortcuts and Menus dialog (1) located in the Window > Workspace menu. Apart from allocating specific keystroke combinations to particular tools, menus, features and actions, the options in the Menus tab control the color and visibility of different menu entries (3). After adjusting the settings the final workspace schema can be saved off and distributed to others to use. Customized workspaces can be imported and added to the list of presets that ship with Photoshop using options in the same dialog. You can then select from the schema that are installed via the entries in the Window > Workspace menu (2).

The size of the font used in the Photoshop Interface can also be changed using the setting in the General section of the Preferences dialog (4). Three sizes are available – small (5), medium (6) and large (7).

Interpolation

Menu: –
Shortcut: –   **See also:** Image Size
Version: 6.0, 7.0, CS, CS2   command

If you change the size of a digital file your software either adds pixels when increasing the size or removes them when making the image smaller.

This process is known as Interpolation and relies on Photoshop knowing which pixels to add or dump.

There are now five methods of interpolation in Photoshop – Nearest Neighbor, Bilinear and Bicubic, with Bicubic Smoother and Bicubic Sharper which were first added in Photoshop CS.

The default method used by Photoshop when changing image sizes can be set by going to Edit > Preferences > General.

Nearest Neighbor offers the fastest method by copying the adjacent pixels, but results are often poor. **Bilinear** looks at pixels above and below plus left and right and averages out the result to give an intermediate pixel and a smooth blend. It's slower than Nearest Neighbor, but not as slow as **Bicubic** which looks at all the pixels surrounding each pixel and averages them all out to create the new ones. It then boosts contrast between each pixel to reduce softness. **Bicubic Smoother** is used when you enlarge the image and **Bicubic Sharper** when you reduce the image.

The Image Size feature uses interpolation in the changes it makes to picture dimensions. The feature's dialog contains a drop-down menu where you can select the interpolation method used when processing the changes.

Nearest Neighbor

Bilinear

Bicubic

Bicubic – Smoother

Bicubic – Sharper

Before

After

Inverse, selection

Menu: Select > Inverse
Shortcut: Ctrl/Cmd Shft I   **See also:** Selections
Version: 6.0, 7.0, CS, CS2

This command makes a new selection by choosing all the pixels in the picture that are currently not selected.

When trying to select a subject that has a complex edge but a plain background, try selecting the background first (1) with a tool such as the Magic Wand or Color Range feature. Next swap the selection from the background to the foreground using the Select > Inverse option (2).

. . . .

Invert

Menu: Image > Adjustment > Invert
Shortcut: Ctrl/Cmd I   **See also:** –
Version: 6.0, 7.0, CS, CS2

The Invert adjustment reverses all the tones and colors in the picture, creating a negative effect.

No controls are available for the user to adjust the strength or style of the effect. The feature changes are applied immediately after the entry is selected from the menu.

Before

After

Invert adjustment layer

Menu: Layer > New Adjustment Layer > Invert
Shortcut: –   **See also:** Layers, Invert
Version: 6.0, 7.0, CS, CS2

The Invert adjustment layer produces a negative version of your image. The feature literally swaps the values of each of the image tones.

When used on a grayscale image the results are similar to a black and white negative. However, this is not true when applied to a color picture as the inverted image will not contain the typical orange 'mask' found in color negatives.

Manipulating the picture with an adjustment layer rather than directly means that the original picture is always kept intact and you can always remove the effect by deleting the adjustment layer.

UK

NEW for CS2

Preserve Details:

Reduce Color Noise: 45 %

Sharpen Details: 25 %

☑ Remove JPEG Artifact

Before

After

JPEG artifact removal

Menu: Filter > Noise > Reduce Noise
Shortcut: –   **See also:** Reduce Noise filter
Version: CS2

One feature of the new Reduce Noise filter is the option to smooth out the box-like appearance of JPEG artifacts.

One of the side effects of saving space by compressing files using the JPEG format is the creation of box-like patterns in your pictures. These patterns or artifacts are particularly noticeable in images that have been saved with maximum compression settings.

With the Remove JPEG Artifact option (1) selected in the Reduce Noise dialog, Photoshop smooths out the box-like pattern created by the overcompression.

JPEG Options

Matte: None

Image Options

Quality: 11 Maximum

small file   large file

Format Options
◉ Baseline ("Standard")
○ Baseline Optimized
○ Progressive

Scans: 3

Size
~1528.54K / 270.06s @ 56.6Kbps

OK
Cancel
☑ Preview

JPEG format

Menu: File > Save As, File Save for Web
Shortcut: Shft Ctrl/Cmd S   **See also:** Save for Web
            Alt/Opt Shft Ctrl/Cmd S
Version: 6.0, 7.0, CS, CS2

JPEG is a file format designed by the Joint Photographic Experts Group to use with pictures destined for the web or e-mail.

This format provides high levels of compression for photographic images. For instance, a 20 Mb digital file can be compressed in the JPEG format so that it can be e-mailed quickly and easily to anywhere in the world.

To achieve this level of compression the format uses a lossy compression system, which means that some of the image information is lost during the compression process.

In Photoshop, pictures can be saved in the JPEG format via dialogs in the Save As or Save for Web commands. The amount of compression is governed by a slider control (1) in the dialog box. The lower the number or the smaller the file, the higher the compression and more of the image will be lost in the process. You can also choose to save the image as a standard 'baseline', optimized or progressive image (2). This selection determines how the image will be drawn to screen when it is requested as part of a web page. The baseline image will draw one pixel line at a time, from top to bottom. The progressive image will show a fuzzy image to start with and then progressively improve as more information about the image comes down the line.

JPEG2000

Menu: File > Save As
Shortcut: Shft Ctrl/Cmd S   **See also:** JPEG format
Version: 6.0, 7.0, CS, CS2

The original JPEG format is more than a decade old and despite its popularity it is beginning to show its age. So in 2000 the specification for a new version of JPEG was released. The revision, called JPEG2000, uses wavelet technology to produce smaller (by up to 20%), sharper files with less artifacts than traditional JPEG. The standard also includes options to use different compression settings and color depths on selections within images, as well as making it possible to save images in lossless form.

Photoshop enables you to save in the JPEG2000 format via the Save As command. The feature's dialog contains a settings section (1), setting for the download preview (2) and a preview image (3). The format also supports layer transparency, saved selections, metadata, and 16-bit/channel images.

Jump to

Menu: –
Shortcut: –   **See also:** ImageReady
Version: 6.0, 7.0, CS, CS2

The 'Jump to' or 'Edit in' buttons at the bottom of the Photoshop and ImageReady toolbars allow you to switch programs dragging with you the currently selected open document.

No Knockout

Shallow Knockout

Deep Knockout

Keyboard Shortcuts

Menu: –
Shortcut: – **See also:** Keyboard Shortcuts
Version: 6.0, 7.0, CS, CS2 customize

Using combinations of keyboard keys you can quickly access commands, features and menu options. Learn ones you use regularly to speed up your work. When shortcuts are available they're listed in this book in the Entry heading with both Mac and Windows equivalents. The default shortcut for specific menu options are displayed on the right of the menu list (1).

From version CS Photoshop provided the ability to let you assign your own favorite shortcuts to regularly used features or actions.

• •

Keyboard Shortcuts, customize

Menu: Edit > Keyboard Shortcuts
Shortcut: Ctrl/Cmd Alt/Opt Shft K **See also:** Keyboard
Version: CS, CS2 Shortcuts

The shortcut keys associated with each menu and key options can be customized via the Keyboard Shortcuts dialog.

Here you can change the default stroke combinations (1), add your own or completely replace all the assigned shortcuts with a custom set designed around the way you work.

The completed set of shortcut keystrokes can then be output as a convenient HTML file by pressing the Summarize button at the bottom of the dialog.

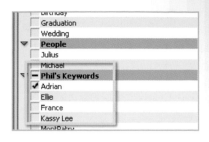

Keywords

Menu: File > File Info, Bridge: View > Keywords panel
Shortcut: – **See also:** Keywords Panel,
Version: 6.0, 7.0, CS, CS2 Bridge

Keywords are single word descriptions of the content of image files. Most photo libraries use keywords as part of the way they locate images with specific content.

The words are stored in the metadata associated with the picture. Users can allocate, edit and create new keywords (and keyword categories) using the File Info palette in Photoshop and Keywords panel in the Bridge browser.

To locate pictures with specific keywords input the text into the Find feature in Bridge setting Keywords as the location for the search.

• •

Keywords Panel, Bridge

Menu: Bridge: View > Keywords Panel
Shortcut: – **See also:** Keywords
Version: CS2

The Keyword panel displays the keyword options that are available for assigning to pictures in Bridge. New keywords and keyword categories (set) can be added to the panel by clicking the New Keyword Set (1) and New Keyword (2) buttons at the bottom of the panel. Unwanted sets or keywords can be removed by selecting first and then clicking the Deleted button (3). Unknown keywords imported with newly downloaded or edited pictures are stored in the panel under the Other Keywords set.

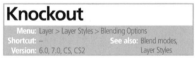

Knockout

Menu: Layer > Layer Styles > Blending Options
Shortcut: – **See also:** Blend modes,
Version: 6.0, 7.0, CS, CS2 Layer Styles

Knockout is a mode from the Blending Options palette (1) located in the Layer Style menu that allows you to be more creative with the ways layers interact with other layers.

It can be used with text and vector shapes to great effect. To illustrate how the feature works I've created a blue star layer on top that will be used as the Knockout layer. It's above four jigsaw piece layers and all five are grouped (placed in a layer set). The background is a photo of bananas and there's a yellow layer above that.

If the star is set to Shallow Knockout with opacity at 0% it would cut through the layer underneath and reveal the next layer. As the jigsaw pieces are in a group (set) it cuts through them too and reveals the yellow layer below. If the star is set to Deep Knockout with opacity at 0% it cuts through all the layers and reveals the background layer.

LAB color

Menu: Image > Mode > LAB		
Shortcut: –		**See also:** Color modes
Version: 6.0, 7.0, CS, CS2		

An international standard for color measurements developed by the Commission Internationale de L'Eclairage (CIE).

It's capable of reproducing all the colors of RGB and CMYK and uses three channels – one for luminosity and the other two for RGB type color ranges.

Some users prefer to work in this mode as it's device independent and colors that fall into the CMYK gamut aren't changed when you convert to CMYK.

Label files – Bridge

Menu: Bridge: Label		
Shortcut: Ctrl/Cmd 0-9		**See also:** Rate files
Version: CS2		

One of the many ways that you can organise the files that are displayed in the Bridge workspace is by attributing a label to the picture.

In CS2 the labels option is supplied in two forms – a color tag, called Label (2) or star rating, called Rating (4). Either or both (3) label types can be applied to any picture.

Labels are attached by selecting the thumbnail(s) in the workspace and then choosing the desired label from the list under the Label menu (1). Keyboard shortcuts are also provided for each label option making it possible to quickly apply a label to a thumbnail or group of thumbnails. The label tag can then be used to sort or locate individual pictures from groups of photos.

Lasso tools

Menu: –
Shortcut: L
Version: 6.0, 7.0, CS, CS2
See also: Polygonal Lasso tool
Magnetic Lasso tool

As the name suggests, the Lasso tools are designed to capture picture parts by surrounding them with a drawn selection marquee (1).

The standard Lasso tool (2) works like a pencil, allowing the user to draw freehand shapes for selections. In contrast, the Polygonal Lasso tool draws straight edge lines between mouse-click points. Either of these features can be used to outline and select irregular-shaped image parts.

A third version of the tool, the Magnetic Lasso, helps with the drawing process by aligning the outline with the edge of objects automatically.

For most tasks, the Magnetic Lasso is a quick way to obtain accurate selections, so it is good practice to try this tool first when you want to isolate specific image parts.

Last filter, reapply

Menu: Filter > (last filter name)
Shortcut: Ctrl/Cmd F
Ctrl/Cmd Alt/Opt F
Version: 6.0, 7.0, CS, CS2
See also: Filters

Once a filter has been used to change the appearance of a picture, it can be reapplied using the same settings by selecting the filter's name from the top of the Filter menu. As a shortcut alternative the Alt and F keys can be pressed (Command F for Macintosh).

To reapply the last filter but allow for the settings to be changed via the filter's dialog use the Ctrl Alt F keystroke combination (Command Option F for Macintosh).

. . . .

Layer based slice

Menu: Layer > New Layer Based Slice
Shortcut: –
Version: 6.0, 7.0, CS, CS2
See also: Slice tool

This feature, introduced with version 6.0, lets you cut up, or slice, your picture into several pieces. Then when the image is used in a Web page each slice is saved as an independent file with a piece of HTML code containing instructions for recombining the photo so that it appears as a single image. The HTML code contains color palette info and links, rollover effects, and animations can be added in ImageReady. Slices help you gain faster download speeds and increased image quality. Apply a layer based slice on a layer with a selection and the slice will be positioned around it. This can then be moved and scaled using the Move tool. In the example a selection was made around the fishing reel and this was copied and pasted onto a new layer. Now when you request a New Layer Slice it appears around the selection and can be set to be used as a hot link on a Web page.

Without clipping mask

With clipping mask

Layer clipping mask

Menu: Layer > Create Clipping Mask
Shortcut: Alt/Opt Ctrl/Cmd G
Version: 6.0, 7.0, CS, CS2
See also: –

A layer clipping mask is used to control what section of lower layers are hidden and what parts are displayed. The bottom-most layer is used as the mask with solid areas, picture parts, displaying the contents of the grouped layers above and the transparent areas letting the layers beneath show through.

In this way the feature is often used to insert the contents of one layer into the nontransparent areas of another. The example shows the flag image, top layer, being clipped by the flower shape layer (non-transparent areas) of the middle layer with the bottom gradient layer showing through.

Only the flag and the flower layers are part of the clipping mask. The effect occurs because all the layers in the clipping group have the opacity attributes and blend mode of the bottom-most layer in the group (1).

You can create a clipping mask in two different ways:

1. Select the top layer and then choose Layer > Create Clipping Mask.

2. Hold down the Alt/Opt key whilst you click on the boundaries between the two layers you wish to group.

To unclip a set of layers, select the bottom layer in the group (name underlined) and then choose Layer > Release Clipping Mask.

Layer, Group Layers

Menu: Layer > Group Layers
Shortcut: Ctrl/Cmd G   **See also:** Layer Set
Version: CS2

After multi-selecting at least two layers in the Layers palette (1) you can move these layers into a new Layer Group (2) by selecting Group Layers from the Layer menu. To ungroup a set of layers select the group first and then choose Layer > Ungroup Layers.

Layer From Background

Menu: Layer > New > Layer From Background
Shortcut: –   **See also:** Background layer
Version: 6.0, 7.0, CS, CS2

The bottom-most layer of any layer stack is called the background layer.

By default this layer is locked, which means that you cannot change its position in the layer stack, its opacity or the blend mode. In order to make these type of changes to the background layer it must be first converted to a standard image layer. This can be achieved by making the background layer active (click on the layer) and then choosing the Layer From Background option from the Layer > New menu (1).

Alternatively, double-clicking the background layer in the Layers palette will perform the same function.

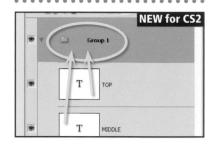

Layer Comps

Menu: Window > Layer Comps
Shortcut: –   **See also:** Snapshot
Version: 6.0, 7.0, CS, CS2

Layer Comps is a feature that first appeared in CS. It lets you create a snapshot of a state of the Layers palette.

Layer Comps records a layer's position in the Layers palette and whether it's showing or hidden. It also records whether layer styles are applied. This is a useful feature if you want to try different effects to show a client. You can then turn each version on or off in the Layer Comps palette and view the differences with speed.

To make a new layer comp arrange the layer content, styles and opacity and then click the Create New Layer Comp button at the bottom of the palette. Insert a name for the comp in the dialog that is displayed and click OK. The new comp appears in the palette.

To display a comp click on the empty box at the left of the comp name. To cycle through all comp options (from top to bottom) press the Apply Next Selected Layer Comp button (right arrow) at the bottom of the palette.

Layer Groups

Menu: –
Shortcut: –   **See also:** Layer Set
Version: CS2

Layer Groups are a collection of layers that have been moved into a single layer folder. When working with a complex picture that contains many layers grouping layers into logical folders makes their management easier and the Layers palette less crowded. Layers can be dragged into an existing folder from elsewhere in the palette or placed into a newly created group folder by multi-selecting and then pressing the Create New Group button at the bottom of the palette. In previous versions this feature is referred to as Layer Sets.

Before

100% opacity

After

50% opacity

Layer mask

Menu: –
Shortcut: –   **See also:** Adjustment layers,
Version: 6.0, 7.0, CS, CS2   Brush tool

Each time you add a fill or adjustment layer to an image two thumbnails are created in the Layers palette. The one on the left controls the settings for the adjustment layer (1). The thumbnail on the right represents the layer's mask that controls how the adjustment is applied to the picture (2).

The mask is a grayscale image. When it's colored white no part of the layer's effects are masked or held back from the picture below. Conversely if the mask thumbnail is totally black then none of the layer's effects are applied to the picture. Shades of gray equate to various levels of transparency. In this way the adjustment or fill layer can be selectively merged with the picture beneath by painting (in black and white and gray) directly on the layer mask thumbnail.

0% opacity

Layer opacity

Menu: –
Shortcut: –   **See also:** Layers
Version: 6.0, 7.0, CS, CS2

The opacity or transparency of each layer in Photoshop can be changed independently. Depending on the level of opacity the parts of the layer beneath will become visible. Change the opacity of each layer by moving the slider in the Layers palette. A value of 100% means the layer is completely opaque, 50% translates to half transparent and 0% means that it is fully transparent.

Layer Set

Menu: –
Shortcut: –   **See also:** Layer Groups
Version: 6.0, 7.0, CS, CS2

Just like the new Layer Groups in Photoshop CS2, the Layer Sets used in previous versions of the program are designed to help organize the many layers that combine to form a complex Photoshop document.

Whilst the layers reside in the Layer Set they can be hidden, modified, moved and locked as a single entity.

To create a Layer Set in Photoshop CS click on the Create New Layer Set button at the bottom of Layers palette. Click and drag layers from the palette into the new set. The layers that reside inside a set are indented in the palette.

Pro's Tip
Sets can also be nested inside other sets creating a hierarchy of layers.

1

Change how adjustment layers merge with the image layer beneath by editing the layer mask. Start by creating a fill layer such as Pattern to the image. Then check to see that the default colors (white and black) are selected for the Photoshop foreground and background colors.

2

Select the Brush tool with black as the foreground color, click onto the layer mask thumbnail and paint onto the patterned surface. The pattern is removed, the picture beneath shows through and a black mark now appears in the layer thumbnail corresponding to your painting actions.

3

Painting with white as your foreground color restores the mask and paints back the pattern. You can experiment with transparent effects by painting on the mask with gray. The lighter the gray the more the pattern will dominate, the darker the gray the less the pattern will be seen.

LAYER STYLES

Layer Styles

Menu: Window > Styles, Layer > Layer Styles
Shortcut: –   See also: –
Version: 6.0, 7.0, CS, CS2

Layer Styles, sometimes referred to as layer effects, are a set of preset effects that can be applied to the contents of a layer by simply clicking a thumbnail in the Layer Styles palette.

When a style is applied to the contents of a layer a small 'f' appears to the right end of the layer in the palette (1). The style effects are now linked with the layer and will move and change as the content is edited.

Multiple styles can be applied to a single layer and their effects can be cleared or hidden using the options in the Layer > Layer Styles menu. The individual settings used for the style can be adjusted by double-clicking the Effects area (2) of the palette and then changing the settings in the Layer Style dialog (3).

Layer via Copy

Menu: Layer > New > Layer via Copy
Shortcut: Ctrl/Cmd J   See also: Layers, Layer via Cut
Version: 6.0, 7.0, CS, CS2

The Layer via Copy command creates a new layer and copies the contents of the current selection onto it.

Layer via Cut

Menu: Layer > New > Layer via Cut
Shortcut: Shft Ctrl/Cmd J   See also: Layers, Layer via Copy
Version: 6.0, 7.0, CS, CS2

The Layer via Cut command cuts the contents of a selection, creates a new layer and pastes it into the layer.

If the detail is cut from a background layer then the empty space is filled with the background color. When the detail is cut from a layer the space is left transparent.

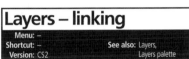

115

Layers

Menu: Window > Layers	
Shortcut: F7	**See also:** Background layer
Version: 6.0, 7.0, CS, CS2	

Digital photographs are flat files with all the picture parts contained in a single document. Unless you are undertaking complex editing and enhancement tasks many pictures remain this way until they are printed, but Photoshop also contains the ability to use layers with your pictures.

This feature releases your images from having to keep all their information in a flat file. Different image parts, added text and certain enhancement tasks can all be kept on separate layers. The layers are kept in a stack and the image you see on screen in the work area is a composite of all the layers.

Sound confusing? Well try imagining, for example, that each of the image parts of a simple portrait photograph are stored on separate plastic sheets. These are your layers. The background sits at the bottom. The portrait is laid on top of the background and the text is placed on top. When viewed from above the solid part of each layer obscures the picture beneath. Whilst the picture parts are based on separate layers they can be moved, edited or enhanced independently of each other.

When layered files are saved in the PSD or Photoshop file format all the layers will be preserved and present the next time the file is opened.

Photoshop supports the following layer types:

Image layers – This is the most basic and common layer type and contains any picture parts or image details. Background is a special type of image layer (3).

Text layers – Designed solely for text, these layers allow the user to edit and enhance the text after the layer has been made (1). They are vector-based layers and must be simplified (rasterized) to apply a filter or to paint on.

Adjustment layers – These layers alter the layers that are arranged below them in the stack. They act as a filter through which the lower layers are viewed (2). You can use adjustment layers to perform many of the enhancement tasks that you would normally apply directly to an image layer without changing the image itself.

Fill layers – Users can also apply a Solid Color, Gradient or Pattern to an image as a separate layer. These three selections are available as a separate item (Layer > New Fill Layer) under the Layer menu or grouped with the adjustment layer options via the quick button at the bottom of the Layers palette.

Shape layers – Drawing with any of the shape tools creates a new vector-based shape layer. The layer contains a thumbnail for the shape as well as the color of the layer.

Background layers – An image can only have one background layer. It is the bottom-most layer in the stack. No other layers can be moved beneath this layer and you cannot adjust this layer's opacity or its blending mode (4).

By default Photoshop classifies a newly downloaded picture as a background layer. You can add extra 'empty' layers to your picture by clicking the new layer button at the bottom of the Layers palette. The new layer is positioned above your currently selected layer. Actions, such as adding text with the Type tool, automatically create a new layer for the content. When selecting, copying and pasting image parts, Photoshop also creates a new layer for the copied portion of the picture.

Layers – linking

Menu: –	
Shortcut: –	**See also:** Layers,
Version: CS2	Layers palette

Another layer feature that has changed slightly in CS2 is the way that layers are linked.

In previous versions of Photoshop layers were linked by clicking in the link box on the left of the layer but now linking several layers is a simple matter of multi-selecting the candidate layers and then pressing the Link button (1) at the bottom of the Layers palette.

A Link or Chain icon is then displayed on the right of the individual layers that are linked together (2).

Once layers are linked the relationship of the content of each layer is fixed and all picture parts move together when one layer is repositioned.

To unlink a group of layers select any layer in the linked set and click on the Link button at the bottom of the Layers palette.

Layers – multi-selecting

Menu: –
Shortcut: – **See also:** Layers, Layers palette
Version: CS2

In CS2 layers can be more easily grouped, moved and managed than in previous releases of the program. It is now possible to multi-select layers inside the Layers palette using the same keystrokes employed for selecting thumbnails in Bridge.

Select a group of layers – Click on the top-most layer and then hold down the Shift key and click on the bottom-most layer in the group. All layers between these layers and the layers themselves will be selected (1).

Select individual layers – Select the first layer and hold down the Control key (Command – Mac) and select the other individual layers (2).

In addition to selecting layers in the Layers palette you can also select groups of layers that combine to make up an image part by dragging a Move tool marquee around the image area. For this feature to work the Auto Select Layer and Auto Select Groups options must be selected in the Move tool's options bar (3).

Layers palette

Menu: Window > Layers
Shortcut: F7 **See also:** Layers
Version: 6.0, 7.0, CS, CS2

The Layers palette displays all your layers and their settings in the one place. Display the palette by selecting Window > Layers.

Individual layers are displayed, one on top of the other, in a 'layer stack'. The composite image you see in the workspace is viewed from the top down through the layers. Each layer is represented by a thumbnail on the left and a name on the right.

You can edit or enhance only one layer at a time. To select the layer that you want to change you need to click on the layer. At this point the layer will change to a different color from the rest in the stack and is now called the active layer (3).

Layers can be hidden from display in the workspace by clicking the eye symbol (4) on the far left of the layer so that it is no longer showing. This action removes the layer from view but not from the stack. You can redisplay the layer by clicking the eye space again.

The blend mode (1) and opacity (2) of individual layers can be altered using the controls at the top of the palette. New layers (5) as well as new adjustment layers (6) can be created by clicking the buttons just below the blend and opacity controls. The dustbin button (7) is used to delete unwanted layers and the lock transparency (8) and lock all (9) buttons are used to restrict layer changes.

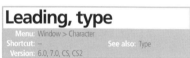

Leading, type

Menu: Window > Character
Shortcut: – **See also:** Type
Version: 6.0, 7.0, CS, CS2

Originally referring to the small pieces of lead that were placed in between lines of metal type used in old printing processes, nowadays it is easier to think of the term referring to the space between lines of text.

Smaller values reduce the space between lines (1) and larger numbers increase this space (2).

Photoshop includes the ability to alter the leading of the type input in your documents. The leading control can be found in the Character dialog (3).

Start with the Auto setting or a value equal to the font size you are using and increase or decrease from here according to your requirements.

www.Photoshop-A-Z.com

Lens Correction filter

Menu: Filter > Distort > Lens Correction
Shortcut: –   **See also:** –
Version: CS2

New to Photoshop CS2 is the sophisticated Lens Correction filter (Filter > Distort > Lens Correction).

The feature is specifically designed to correct the imaging problems that can occur when shooting with different lenses. Apart from correcting Barrel and Pincushion distortion, the filter can also fix chromatic aberration or color fringing (color outlines around subject edges) and vignetting (darkening of the corners) problems that can also occur as a result of poor lens construction. Controls for changing the perspective of the picture (great for eliminating the issue of converging verticals) as well as how to handle the vacant areas of the canvas that are created after distortion correction are also included.

The example image, photographed with a wide angle auxiliary lens, displays both Barrel distortion and converging verticals that are in need of correction.

1. With a suitable image open select Filter > Distort > Lens Correction. Adjust the zoom control and drag the grid with the Move Grid tool, so that it aligns with a straight edge in the photo. Adjust the Remove Distortion slider to the right to correct the barrel effects in the picture. Your aim is to straighten the curve edges of what should be straight picture parts.

2. Now concentrate on correcting the converging verticals. Move the Vertical

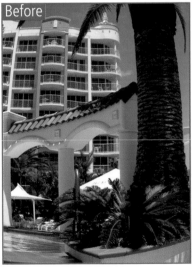
Before

Perspective option to the left to stretch the details at the top of the photo apart and condense the lower sections. Again aim to align straight and parallel picture parts with the grid lines.

3. If necessary, lighten the edges of the image by moving the Amount slider to the right and adjusting the percentage of the picture that this control affects with the Midpoint control.

4. Zoom in to at least 600% to check for chromatic aberration problems and use the Fix Red/Cyan Fringe or Fix Blue/Yellow Fringe controls to reduce the appearance of color edges. Click OK to apply the correction settings. Crop the 'fish tail' edges of the corrected photo to complete.

Lens Flare filter

Menu: Filter > Render > Lens Flare
Shortcut: –   **See also:** Filters
Version: 6.0, 7.0, CS, CS2

The Lens Flare filter, as one of the group of Render filters, adds a bright white spot to the surface of photos in a way that resembles the flare from light falling on a camera lens.

This filter is often used when light sources such as the sun, a street lamp or car headlights are part of the picture.

The filter dialog contains a preview thumbnail on which you can position the center of the flare by click-dragging the cross hairs (1). Also in the dialog is a brightness or strength slider (2) and a selection of lens types to choose from (3).

The filter has been revamped for CS2 so that it can also be used in 16 bits/channel mode.

Pro's Tip

You can set the Lens Flare center precisely by Alt/Opt-clicking on the preview image and then inputting the X and Y coordinates for the center of the effect.

Contrast increase

To increase contrast – Move the input black and white controls to meet the first group of pixels.

Contrast decrease

To decrease contrast – Move the output black and white points towards the center of the slider.

Darken midtones

To make middle values darker – Move the input midtone control to the right.

Lighten midtones

To make middle values lighter – Move the input midtone control to the left.

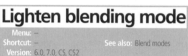

Lighten blending mode

Menu: –	
Shortcut: –	**See also:** Blend modes
Version: 6.0, 7.0, CS, CS2	

The Lighten blending mode is one of the group of Lighten modes that base their effects on combining the light tones of the two layers.

Both top and bottom layers are examined and the lightest tones of either layer are kept whilst the darker values are replaced. This mode always produces a lighter result.

Levels command

Menu: Enhance > Adjust Lighting > Levels	
Shortcut: Ctrl/Cmd L	**See also:** Curves, Shadow/
Version: 6.0, 7.0, CS, CS2	Highlight

Looking very similar to the Histogram, this feature allows you to interact directly with the pixels in your image.

As well as a graph (1), the dialog contains two slider bars. The one directly beneath the graph has three triangle controls for black (2), midtones (3) and white (4), and represents the input values of the picture.

The slider at the bottom of the box shows output settings, and contains black (5) and white (6) controls only.

To distribute the picture tones across the whole of the spectrum, drag the input shadow (left end) and highlight (right end) controls until they meet the first set of pixels at either end of the graph. When you click OK, the pixels in the original image are redistributed using the new white and black points.

Altering the midtone control will change the brightness of the middle values of the image, and moving the output black and white points will flatten, or decrease, the contrast.

Clicking the Auto button is like selecting Image > Adjustment > Auto Levels from the menu bar.

Use the following guide to help you make tonal adjustments to your images using the Levels feature.

Pro's Tip

To help you gauge the darkest and lightest points hold down the Alt key (Option on a Mac) whilst you click on the white or black triangle.

This creates a posterized image showing the lightest point as white and the darkest point as black. As you drag the markers inwards you will see the white or black areas increase over the picture. This will give you an indication of how far to drag the sliders to make effective use of clipping the image. Use the values displayed as your highlight and shadow points.

Five down lights

Before

Before

Spotlight

After

After

Lighting Effects filter

Menu: Filter > Render > Lighting Effects
Shortcut: –   **See also:** Filters
Version: 6.0, 7.0, CS, CS2

The Lighting Effects filter, as one of the group of Render filters, simulates the look of various light sources shining onto the picture surface. Single or multiple light sources can be added to the photo.

The filter dialog contains a preview thumbnail that is used to adjust the position, shape and size of the projected light (1). The rest of the dialog is broken into four different control sections:

Style (2) – Provides a drop-down menu of pre-designed light styles along with any customized styles you have created and saved.

Light Type (3) – Alters the color, intensity and focus of the selected light.

Properties (4) – Contains controls for how the subject reacts to the light.

Texture Channel (5) – Has options for creating texture with the light shining onto the photo.

This feature is often used for creating, or enhancing existing, lighting type effects on the main subject in a picture.

Linear Burn blending mode

Menu: –
Shortcut: –   **See also:** Blend modes
Version: 6.0, 7.0, CS, CS2

The Linear Burn blending mode is one of the group of Darken modes that base their effects on darkening the picture by adjusting the brightness of the blended image.

This option analyzes the brightness of the details in the top and bottom layers and darkens the bottom layer to reflect the tone of the top layer.

The filter always produces a darker effect and blending with a white top layer produces no change.

Linear Dodge blending mode

Menu: –
Shortcut: –   **See also:** Blend modes
Version: 6.0, 7.0, CS, CS2

The Linear Dodge blending mode is one of the group of Lighten modes that base their effects on lightening the picture by adjusting the brightness of the blended image.

This option analyzes the brightness of the details in the top and bottom layers and brightens the bottom layer to reflect the tone of the top layer.

The filter always produces a lighter effect and blending with a black top layer produces no change.

Linear Gradient tool

Menu: –
Shortcut: G
Version: 6.0, 7.0, CS, CS2
See also: Gradients

Photoshop has five different gradient types. All the options gradually change color and tone from one point in the picture to another.

The linear gradient (1) changes color from start to end point in a straight line.

To create a gradient start by selecting the tool and the linear gradient type (2). Then adjust the controls in the options palette.

Choose the colors from the Gradient Picker drop-down menu and the style from the five buttons to the right.

Click and drag the mouse pointer on the canvas surface to stretch out a line that marks the start and end points of the gradient. Release the button to fill the layer with the selected gradient.

Linear Light blending mode

Menu: –
Shortcut: –
Version: 6.0, 7.0, CS, CS2
See also: Blend modes

The Linear Light blending mode is one of the group of Overlay modes that base their effects on combining the two layers depending on the tonal value of their contents.

This option combines both burning and dodging of the picture in the one action.

If the tone in the top layer is lighter than 50% then this section of the bottom layer is lightened; if the tone is darker, then it is darkened.

Blending with 50% gray produces no change.

Lines

Menu: –
Shortcut: U
Version: 6.0, 7.0, CS, CS2
See also: Arrowhead options
Shape tools

The Line tool is one of the vector-based shape tools. Unlike the Brush or Pencil tool, which draws with pixels, the lines created with this tool are always sharp edged and high quality.

To create a line with the tool click and drag on the canvas surface. Holding down Shift when drawing restricts the tool to drawing straight lines at intervals of 45°.

The options bar for the tool contains the following settings:

Arrowhead start and end – Determines which end of the line an arrowhead will be added. Leaving the boxes unchecked creates a line with no arrowheads.

Arrowhead width and length – Sets the width of the arrowhead at the base and the overall length of the head based on a percentage of the line weight.

Concavity – Determines the degree to which the arrowhead is concaved as a percentage of the total length of the head.

Weight – Controls the thickness of the line in pixels.

Color – Sets the line color.

Style – Determines if a layer style is automatically added to the line as it is drawn.

(1) 3 pixels weight, black.
(2) 10 pixels weight, gray.
(3) 20 pixels weight, red, arrowheads start and end.
(4) 20 pixels weight, chrome style, arrowheads start and end.

Before

After

Line art

Menu:	–		
Shortcut:	–	See also:	–
Version:	6.0, 7.0, CS, CS2		

An image that's drawn using one color on a background color with no midtones.

Line art is a popular giveaway on royalty-free CDs and websites. This frog was found on www.free-graphics.com, a website with over 130,000 free graphics for use when downloaded.

I've picked a small sized one to show you what happens to line art if the file size is too small. It looked sharp on screen, but here in print it looks smudged so choose with care.

Liquify filter

Menu:	Filter > Liquify		
Shortcut:	–	See also:	Filters
Version:	6.0, 7.0, CS, CS2		

The Liquify filter is a very powerful tool for warping and transforming your pictures. The feature contains its own sophisticated dialog box complete with a preview area and no less than ten different tools that can be used to twist, warp, push, pull and reflect your pictures with such ease that it is almost as if they were made of silly putty. In CS2 the filter now also works with 16-bit images. The effects obtained with this feature can be subtle or extreme depending on how the changes are applied. Stylus and tablet users have extra options and control based on pen pressure (in Photoshop only).

Liquify works by projecting the picture onto a grid or mesh (1). In an unaltered state, the grid is completely regular, when liquifying a photo the grid lines and spaces are intentionally distorted, which in turn

causes the picture to distort. As the mesh used to liquify a photo can be saved and reloaded, the distortion effects created in one picture can also be applied to an entirely different image.

The tools contained in the filter's toolbox are used to manipulate the underlying mesh and therefore distort the picture. Areas of the picture can be isolated from changes by applying a Freeze Mask to the picture part with the Freeze Mask tool.

Whilst working inside the filter dialog it is possible to selectively reverse any changes made to the photo by applying the Reconstruct tool. When applied to the surface of the image the distorted picture parts are gradually altered back to their original state (the mesh is returned to its regular form). Like the other tool options in the filter, the size of the area affected by the tool is based on the Brush Size setting and the strength of the change is determined by the Brush Pressure value.

Loading Brushes

Menu: Edit > Preset Manager
Shortcut: –   **See also:** Brush tool,
Version: 6.0, 7.0, CS, CS2   Define Brush

New brushes can be added into the Brush Preset palette (Brush tool options bar) by pressing the sideways button at the top of the dialog and then selecting the Load Brushes item from the pop-up menu.

The feature opens a file browser dialog so that you can search for ABR or Adobe Brush files to load. Photoshop includes a range of predefined brush sets, or ABR files, that can be loaded from the Photoshop/Presets/Brushes folder.

Alternatively you can download and install extra brush tips from resource sites on the internet or create and save your own brush sets using the Edit > Define Brush from Selection feature and the settings in the tool's option bar.

Loading Patterns

Menu: Edit > Preset Manager
Shortcut: –   **See also:** Pattern Stamp,
Version: 6.0, 7.0, CS, CS2   Define Pattern

A variety of patterns are preloaded in the Photoshop program when it is shipped. New options can be added into the Pattern Preset palette (Pattern Stamp tool options bar) by pressing the sideways button at the top of the dialog and then selecting the Load Patterns item from the pop-up menu.

The feature opens a file browser dialog so that you can search for PAT or Adobe Pattern files to load. Those PAT files included in Photoshop can be loaded from the Photoshop/Presets/Patterns folder.

Alternatively you can create and save your own patterns using the Edit > Define Pattern from a selection feature.

Patterns can be used with the Paint Bucket tool and are also located as an option in the Fill Layer dialog box.

Load Selection

Menu: Select > Load Selection
Shortcut: –   **See also:** Save Selection
Version: 6.0, 7.0, CS, CS2

Photoshop thankfully gives you the option to save complex selections so that they can be used again later.

With your selection active choose the Save Selection option (1) from the Select menu. Your selection will now be saved as part of the file.

When you close your file and then open it again later you can retrieve the selection by choosing Load Selection from the same menu.

This feature is particularly useful when making sophisticated multi-step selections, as you can make sequential saves, marking your progress and ensuring that you never lose your work.

The Save Selection dialog also provides you with another way to modify your selections. Here you will find the option to save a newly created selection in any of the four selection modes (2). This provides you with an alternative method for building complex selections which is based on making a selection and then saving it as an addition. In this way you can create a sophisticated selection one step at a time.

Loading Gradients

Menu: Edit > Preset Manager
Shortcut: –   **See also:** Gradients,
Version: 6.0, 7.0, CS, CS2   Gradient Editor

Photoshop is shipped with a variety of gradient styles which are displayed in the Gradient Preset palette (Gradient tool options bar). New gradients can be added into the preset palette by pressing the sideways button at the top of the dialog and then selecting the Load Gradients item from the pop-up menu.

The feature opens a file browser dialog so that you can search for GRD or Adobe Gradient files to load. Those GRD files included in Photoshop can be loaded from the Photoshop/Presets/Gradients folder.

Alternatively you can create and save your own gradients using the Gradient Editor.

Load Swatches

Menu: Window > Swatches
Shortcut: –   **See also:** Swatches palette
Version: 6.0, 7.0, CS, CS2

A variety of color swatch palettes are supplied with Photoshop. A default set is the preloaded Swatches palette. Other swatch options, custom colors you have created or downloaded from the Web, can be loaded into the palette by pressing the sideways button at the top of the dialog and then selecting the Load Swatches item (1) from the pop-up menu. The feature opens a file browser dialog so that you can search for ACO (Swatch) or ACT (Color Table) files to load. Swatch files are generally stored in the Photoshop/Presets/Color Swatches folder.

Other industry-based color swatch sets (2) are also listed in the menu and can be added to the current list by selecting and appending the swatch list.

Lock All

Menu: –
Shortcut: –   **See also:** Layers palette
Version: 6.0, 7.0, CS, CS2

Photoshop provides the option to lock layers so that their transparency, pixels or position cannot be changed.

This option is great for fixing the current editing state of a layer so that neither its content nor its position are changed by subsequent enhancement steps.

The Lock All button located at the top of the Layers palette locks and unlocks selected layers (1). A locked padlock icon is displayed on the right-hand end of all locked layers (2). A dark shaded padlock indicates that the layer has been locked with the Lock All button.

To lock a layer, select the layer and click on the Lock All button at the top of the Layers palette. The shaded padlock will be displayed.

To unlock a locked layer, select the layer and then press the Lock All button. The shaded padlock will be removed from the right end of the selected layer.

Lossless compression

Menu: –
Shortcut: –   **See also:** Lossy
Version: 6.0, 7.0, CS, CS2   compression, TIFF

Lossless compression is an approach to reducing the size of picture files that does not lose any image details or quality in the process. The same details are present in pictures after compressing and decompressing as there were in the original file.

At best the lossless approach produces compressed files that are half their original size. Some file formats such as JPEG2000 have options for both lossless and lossy compression (1).

A lossless file format should always be used to save original photos and artwork.

Common file formats that use lossless compression are:

- **TIFF** (available in uncompressed and compressed lossless forms)
- **PNG**
- **GIF** (only supports 256 colors)
- **JPEG2000** (has lossy and lossless options)

123

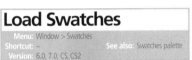

Lock options

Menu: Enhance > Adjust Lighting > Levels
Shortcut: Ctrl/Cmd Alt/Opt Shft L   **See also:** Lock All, Layers
Version: 6.0, 7.0, CS, CS2   palette

As well as the option to lock all the attributes of a layer, Photoshop also provides an option to lock the transparent parts (1), pixels (2) and/or position (3) of a layer.

Use the **Lock Transparent** option to ensure that editing changes do not alter, or impinge upon, the transparent part of the layer.

The **Lock Image Pixels** feature ensures that no editing can take place in the image

parts of a layer. Using this lock to protect layer content from inadvertent changes during the editing process.

The third option, **Lock Position**, stops the layer content from being moved. This option doesn't protect the layer from being edited.

To lock the transparency of a layer, select the layer and click on the Lock button of your choice at the top of the Layers palette. The lightly shaded padlock will be displayed (4). To unlock a layer with its transparency locked, select the layer and then press the same lock button. The lightly shaded padlock will be removed from the right end of the selected layer.

Example

JPEG Options

Matte: None

Image Options

Quality: 10 Maximum

small file   large file

☑ P

Format Options

○ Baseline ("Standard")

Original file – 2.6 Mb

© www.ablestock.com 2005

TIFF compressed – 1.6 Mb

GIF comp. 256 col. -– 0.3 Mb

JPEG2000 lossless

JPEG2000 max.comp. – 0.02 Mb

JPEG max.comp. – 0.02 Mb

Before BLEND MODES

BLEND MODES Top

Bottom

After BLEND MODES

Lossy compression

Menu: –
Shortcut: –   See also: Lossless compression,
Version: 6.0, 7.0, CS, CS2   JPEG format, JPEG2000,
                                 Save for Web

Lossy compression is an approach to reducing the size of picture files that discards image details and reduces photo quality in the process of creating smaller files.

The save dialogs for file formats that use this method of compression generally contain a slider control that adjusts picture quality and file compression (1).

In general terms the better the picture quality the larger the files (less compression) will be and conversely the smaller the file size (most compression) the worse the resultant image quality.

The Photoshop Save for Web feature contains a visual before and after preview of the results of differing levels of lossy JPEG compression. This provides the opportunity to preview the visual results of the compression to ensure that the degree of quality loss is acceptable.

Picture files can be dramatically reduced in size using lossy compression algorithms, which makes this approach most suitable for shrinking files for internet work or file transmission. Lossy file formats should not be used as primary archival format.

Common file formats that use lossy compression are:

- **JPEG**
- **JPEG2000** (has lossy and lossless options)
- **Photoshop PDF** (JPEG option)
- **Photoshop TIFF** (JPEG option)

Luminosity blending mode

Menu: –
Shortcut: –   See also: Blend modes
Version: 6.0, 7.0, CS, CS2

The Luminosity blending mode is one of the group of Hue modes that base their effects on combining the hue, saturation and luminosity of the two layers.

This option creates the result by combining the hue and saturation of the bottom layer with the luminosity of the top layer.

The final image is the inverse of the results obtained when the Color mode is selected.

• •

TIFF Options

Image Compression
○ NONE
⊙ LZW
○ ZIP
○ JPEG

OK
Cancel

LZW compression

Menu: –
Shortcut: –   See also: Lossy compression,
Version: 6.0, 7.0, CS, CS2   Lossless compression,
                                 JPEG format

LZW or Lempel-Ziv-Welch compression is a lossless compression algorithm used to shrink the size of picture files by recognizing repeating patterns in the picture and only storing these once.

The algorithm is commonly used in the GIF format and is an option when saving TIFF files (1). Though LZW doesn't reduce file sizes as small as JPEG it does have the advantage of not losing any of the original data in the compression process.

Before

After

Tolerance – 30

© www.ablestock.com 2005

Tolerance – 10

© www.ablestock.com 2005

mM
U
WXYZABCDEFGHIJKLM

Magic Eraser tool

Menu: –
Shortcut: E
Version: 6.0, 7.0, CS, CS2
See also: Eraser tool, Background Eraser tool

The Magic Eraser selects and then erases pixels of similar tone and color. The tool is great for removing unwanted backgrounds when making composite or montage pictures.

The Tolerance setting determines how alike the pixels need to be before they are erased. High settings will include more pixels of varying shades and colors.

Select the Contiguous option to force the tool to select pixels that are adjacent to each other and choose Sample All Layers if you want to sample the color to be erased from a mixture of all visible layers.

Select the tool from the toolbox. Click the side arrow to reveal hidden tools if the standard eraser is showing. Set the Tolerance, Contiguous and Use Sample Layers settings.

Magic Wand tool

Menu: –
Shortcut: W
Version: 6.0, 7.0, CS, CS2
See also: Color Range

The Magic Wand makes selections based on color and tone. When the user clicks on an image with the Magic Wand tool Photoshop searches the picture for pixels that have a similar color and tone.

How identical a pixel has to be to the original hue selected is determined by the Tolerance value (1) in the options bar. The higher the value, the less alike the two pixels need to be, whereas a lower setting will require a more exact match before a pixel is added to the selection.

Turning on the Contiguous option will only include the pixels that are similar and are adjacent to the original pixel in the selection.

M

Select the Opacity value: 100% removes all pixels, lower values make the erased area semi-transparent. Click on the layer part you wish to erase.

Magnetic Lasso tool

Menu: –	
Shortcut: L	**See also:** Lasso tools,
Version: 6.0, 7.0, CS, CS2	Magnetic Pen tool

The Magnetic Lasso is one of three Lasso tools available in Photoshop. Lasso tools make selections by drawing a marquee around the picture part to be selected. The Magnetic Lasso helps with the drawing process by aligning the selection outline with the edge of objects automatically.

The tool uses contrast of color and tone as a basis for determining the edge of an object. The accuracy of the 'magnetic' features of this tool is determined by three settings in the tool's options bar.

Edge Contrast is the value that a pixel has to differ from its neighbor to be considered an edge.

Width is the number of pixels either side of the pointer that are sampled in the edge determination process.

Frequency is the distance between fastening points in the outline.

For most tasks, the Magnetic Lasso is a quick way to obtain accurate selections, so it is good practice to try this tool first when you want to isolate specific image parts.

Magnetic Pen tool

Menu: –	
Shortcut: P	**See also:** Magnetic Lasso
Version: 6.0, 7.0, CS, CS2	tool

The Free Form Pen tool is used for creating vector-based paths in Photoshop documents. Magnetic is one of the tools options located on the options bar (1).

With the magnetic feature turned on the pen tool aligns the path with the edges of contrasty picture parts automatically. Like the Magnetic Lasso tool the Magnetic Pen uses contrast of color and tone as a basis for determining the edge of an object. The accuracy of the 'magnetic' features of this tool is determined by the Width, Contrast and Frequency settings in the drop-down dialog of the tool's options bar (2).

After selecting the Magnetic Lasso tool, click and release the mouse button to mark the first fastening point. Trace the outline of the object with the mouse pointer. Extra fastening points will be added to the edge of the object automatically.

If the tool doesn't snap to the edge automatically, click the mouse button to add a fastening point manually. Adjust settings in the options bar to vary the tool's magnetic function. To close the outline, either double-click or drag the pointer over the first fastening point.

Magnifying pictures

Menu: –	
Shortcut: –	**See also:** Zoom tool, Zoom
Version: 6.0, 7.0, CS, CS2	In/Zoom Out

To magnify a specific area of a picture select the Zoom tool and click and drag a marquee over the area to be magnified. When you release the mouse button the picture zooms into the area you selected.

Before

After

Marquee tools

Menu: –
Shortcut: M   See also: Lasso tools, Magic
Version: 6.0, 7.0, CS, CS2   Wand tool, Selections

Photoshop has four different marquee tools – Rectangular (1), Elliptical (2), Single Row Marquee Tool and Single Column Marquee Tool. The Rectangular and Elliptical tools are designed to draw regular shapes around the picture parts to be selected and the Single Row/Column options are used for selecting a solitary line of pixels.

By clicking and dragging the Rectangular or Elliptical Marquees, it is possible to draw rectangular and oval-shaped selections.

Holding down the Shift key whilst using these tools will restrict the selection to square or circular shapes, whilst using the Alt (Windows) or Options (Mac) keys will draw the selections from their centers.

Before

After Match Location

Masks

Menu: –
Shortcut: –   See also: Alpha Channel, Quick
Version: 6.0, 7.0, CS, CS2   Mask mode, Layer mask

The masks in Photoshop provide a way of protecting areas of a picture from enhancement or editing changes. Used in this way, masks are the opposite to selections, which are designed to restrict the changes to only the area selected.

Masks are standard grayscale images and because of this fact they can painted, edited, filtered and erased just like other pictures. Masks are displayed as a separate thumbnail to the right of the main layer thumbnail in the Layers palette (1).

The black portion of the mask thumbnail is the protected area (2) and the white section shows the area where the image is not masked and therefore can be edited and enhanced.

Photoshop uses masks as part of the application of adjustment and fill layers, as well as providing a specialized Quick Mask mode in which masks can be interactively painted onto a canvas.

Match Location

Menu: Window > Arrange > Match Location
Shortcut: –   See also: Zoom tool,
Version: 6.0, 7.0, CS, CS2   Magnifying pictures

The Match Location feature adjusts all open pictures so that the same view (middle, upper right, lower left, etc.) of each photo is displayed for all photos.

The location setting that is matched is based on the setting of the currently selected document.

Match color

Menu: Image > Adjustments > Match Color
Shortcut: –   See also: –
Version: 6.0, 7.0, CS, CS2

The Match Color command is designed to allow users to match the colors from one picture (called the source) to another (the target). The feature is a great way of bringing a consistent coloring to a series of pictures by using one picture's colours as the source for all others. The matching can also be applied from layer to layer in a single image or, as we see below, from a selection in one picture to selection in another.

In the example the aim is to change the color of the shirt on the little girl from its original orange to something that is more like the blue of the beads (1) in the source image. To make the change we need to isolate the part of the target image that we want to change, that is the shirt, and also be selective about the area of the source image that we will draw our color matching from.

The first step is to select the girl's shirt and then add a little feather to the selection to soften the edge. Next a selection was made of the area of the beads picture that most represented the colors that will be used as a substitute. After switching back to the Target image the Match Color feature was opened. Using the settings in the dialog the bead image was chosen as the source and the checkboxes for using the selections for both target and source were ticked. And 'Hey presto!' we have a new color for the shirt based on the color in a separate image.

M

Match Zoom

Menu: Window > Arrange > Match Zoom	
Shortcut: –	**See also:** Zoom tool, Magnifying
Version: 6.0, 7.0, CS, CS2	pictures, Match Location

Photoshop provides a range of ways to view several images when they are all open in the workspace at the same time.

Added to the viewing modes that were available in version CS of the program is the Match Zoom and Location options.

The Match Zoom feature displays all open pictures at the same magnification. The zoom setting that is matched is based on the setting of the currently selected document (1).

Maximize mode

Menu: –	
Shortcut: –	**See also:** Tile
Version: 6.0, 7.0, CS, CS2	

The Maximize mode is one of the many ways that open pictures can be viewed in the Photoshop workspace. By clicking the Maximize button (1) in the top right of the document window, you can switch the view from tiled mode to a single image surrounded by the gray work area background. The style of buttons that are used in this part of the screen change depending on whether they are controlled by Photoshop or the operating system.

The same option is available for the window that contains the Photoshop program.

Other options for displaying open documents include:

Minimize (2) – Reduces an open window to just a title bar but keeps the document in the workspace.

Close (3) – Closes the document.

Multi-window mode (4) – Displays the document in its own smaller, movable window in the workspace.

The Minimize and Maximize options are also available from the pop-up menu that is displayed by clicking the Photoshop features icon at the top left of the document windows (5).

Maximum filter

Menu: Filter > Other > Maximum	
Shortcut: –	**See also:** Filters
Version: 6.0, 7.0, CS, CS2	

The Maximum filter, as one of the Other group of filters, grows or bleeds the lighter areas of the picture whilst reducing the size of the darker toned parts.

In making these changes, the filter analyzes the brightness of the pixels in a given area (radius) and increases the brightness to the level of the darkest pixel in the area.

The filter contains a single slider control that adjusts the radius (1) or size of the area used to determine the pixel brightness value.

Measure tool

Menu: –
Shortcut: **See also:** Info palette
Version: 6.0, 7.0, CS, CS2

The Measure tool reports on the distance between two points on the Photoshop canvas. After selecting the tool you click and drag the cursor to create a non-printing line from the starting point to the finishing point. The Info palette displays the position of the line's starting and ending points, the distance between these points and the angle of the line created (1). The measure tool is located in a pop-up tool menu with the Eyedropper and Color Sampler tools. This tool is very useful in establishing a blur angle for the motion blur target in Smart Sharpen filter.

- -

Median filter

Menu: Filter > Noise > Median
Shortcut: – **See also:** Filters
Version: 6.0, 7.0, CS, CS2

The Median filter, as one of the Noise group of filters, reduces the speckle type noise in a picture by finding the middle pixel brightness across the selected radius and removing pixels that deviate greatly from this brightness.

The filter contains a single slider control that adjusts the radius (1) or size of the area used to determine the median, or middle, pixel brightness value.

The filter has a blur effect as well as a reduction in local contrast.

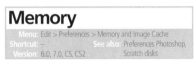

Memory

Menu: Edit > Preferences > Memory and Image Cache
Shortcut: – **See also:** Preferences Photoshop,
Version: 6.0, 7.0, CS, CS2 Scratch disks

Photoshop uses three types of memory in the process of editing and enhancing your pictures.

RAM (Random Access Memory) – Temporarily stores program information and the details of any pictures you have open. This type of memory is extremely fast and is the memory most preferred by the program. Typical figures for the RAM size are 256 Mb, 512 Mb and 1024 Mb. You can allocate how much of your computer's RAM is used by Photoshop by adjusting the Memory and Image Cache settings in the Edit > Preferences dialog (1). Photoshop CS2 can address up to 3.5 Gb of RAM.

Hard drive memory – As the information is stored in RAM only whilst the computer is turned on, there is also a need for a permanent memory storage option as well. A hard drive is used for this type of long-term storage. Although much slower than RAM, it is the hard drive that we 'Save' our pictures to and 'Open' them from. Most computers these days have hard drives of between 80 and 200 Gb (80,000 and 200,000 Mb) on which to store your pictures.

Virtual memory – For those occasions when the Photoshop project you are working on requires more RAM than you have available you can allocate part of your hard drive as extra 'Virtual' RAM or in Photoshop speak – a 'Scratch Disk'. Set the location of your scratch disk via the Plug-ins and Scratch disks option of the Edit > Preferences dialog (2).

Note: Memory settings changes only take effect after restarting Photoshop.

Menu bar

Menu: –
Shortcut: – **See also:** Options bar,
Version: 6.0, 7.0, CS, CS2 Shortcuts buttons
– Bridge

The Photoshop menu bar contains five specialist menus of Image, Enhance, Layer, Select and Filter as well as the usual File, Edit, View, Window and Help headings common to most programs (1). Grouped under these special menu headings are the various editing and enhancement commands that are the real power of the program. Selecting a menu item is as simple as moving your mouse over the menu heading, clicking to show the list of items or menu (2) and then moving the mouse pointer over the option you wish to use. With some selections a second menu (submenu) appears (3), from which you can make further selections.

- -

M

Menus, customize

Menu: Window > Workspace > Keyboard Shortcuts & Menus
Shortcut: – **See also:** Keyboard Shortcuts
Version: CS2

CS2 provides the capability of customizing the visibility and color of the menu options in Photoshop. The customized interface can then be saved and loaded at any time or even distributed to other Photoshop users. To customize the menus in the workspace adjust the visibility and color settings (1) (for each menu item) in the Keyboard Shortcuts & Menus dialog and save the final interface. This option will become an entry on the Set menu of the dialog and when selected will display the interface that you have designed (2).

A-Z

M

Before Merge Down

After Merge Down

NEW for CS2

Merge Down

Menu: Layers > Merge Down
Shortcut: Ctrl/Cmd E   **See also:** Merge Layers,
Version: 6.0, 7.0, CS, CS2   Merge Visible

The Merge Down command combines the contents of the selected layer with the one directly beneath it in the layer stack. In the example, the Brightness/Contrast adjustment layer was selected (1) and merged down into the picture layer (2). Merging options can be selected from the pop-out menu in the Layers palette as well as the options in the Layers menu.

Multiple layers add to the overall file size and memory usage when editing. Merging layers reduces file size and hence memory usage. Be careful though as merging layers also reduces the ability to edit the content of the individual layers later. For this reason, pros often make a copy of the layered file first before flattening the picture.

Merge to HDR

Menu: File > Automate > Merge to HDR
         Bridge: Tools > Photoshop > Merge to HDR
Shortcut: –   **See also:** High Dynamic Range
Version: CS2

The Merge to HDR feature combines three or more source images of the same subject that have been photographed with differing exposures. In the case of a three exposure sequence the underexposed frame captures the highlights, the metered exposure, the mid-tones and the overexposed frame the shadow details. Typically the exposure difference between frames equates to 2 f-stops or EV settings. The Merge to HDR feature imports and arranges the pictures to create a High Dynamic Range (HDR) document that contains 32 bits per channel. If the feature can't automatically detect the exposure difference between source images from the camera's EXIF data you will need to supply the details manually via the pop-up dialog.

Merge Layers

Menu: Layer > Merge Layers
Shortcut: Ctrl/Cmd E   **See also:** Merge Down,
Version: 6.0, 7.0, CS, CS2   Merge Visible

The Merge Layers command combines the content of layers that have been multi-selected in the Layers palette. This command largely replaces the Merge Linked command that was used to perform the same function in previous versions of Photoshop. To multi-select several layers click on the first layer and then Shift-click the last layer in the group. Multi-selecting layers and then applying the Merge Layers command is a good way to flatten a selected subset of all the layers that make up the document. The Merge Layers option is only available in the Layers menu when multiple layers are selected.

Original layered image

After Merge Visible

Merge Visible

Menu: Layers > Merge Visible
Shortcut: Shft Ctrl/Cmd E   **See also:** Merge Down,
Version: 6.0, 7.0, CS, CS2   Merge Layers

The Merge Visible command combines the content of all visible layers within the document into a single image layer. Layers can be hidden from view (made not visible) by clicking the eye icon on the left of the layer in the Layers palette. In the example the visible type (1), adjustment (2), picture (3) and background layers (4) were all merged (5).

To make a copy of the merged visible layers, create a new layer and then hold down the Alt (Option for Mac) key whilst selecting the Merge Visible option.

Merging any layer with the background yields the background; merging with another layer creates a single layer.

Metadata, Append/Replace

Menu: File > File Info
Bridge: View > Metadata Panel
Shortcut: –   **See also:** Metadata Panel,
Version: CS2   Metadata Templates

The Metadata associated with a single image or a group of multi-selected images can be appended (added to) or replaced using the options listed in the menu that appears after pressing the side-arrow (1) in the top left of the metadata panel in Bridge.

The content of the data that is amended or replaced is contained in a metadata template. The template is created by editing the metadata details displayed in the File > File Info dialog and then saving these changes as a new template (2) using the side-arrow menu located in the top right. The newly created template is added to this menu and can be applied to other images by selecting it here or in Bridge.

Metadata Panel, Bridge

Menu: File > File Info
Bridge: View > Metadata Panel
Shortcut: –   **See also:** Metadata Append/Replace,
Version: CS2   Metadata Templates

The Metadata panel in Bridge displays a variety of information about your picture. Some of this detail is created at time of capture or creation and other parts are added as the file is edited.

The metadata that can be displayed (1) includes File Properties, IPTC (copyright and caption details), EXIF (camera data), GPS (navigational data from a global positioning system), Camera Raw and Edit History. To display the contents of each metadata category click on the side-arrow to the left of the category heading (2).

The data displayed in this palette, such as the copyright, description, author and caption information, can be edited here or via the File > File Info dialog.

The range of content types that is displayed in the palette is controlled by the selections in the Metadata Preferences for Bridge (3).

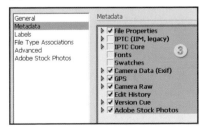

Metadata Templates

Menu: File > File Info
Bridge: View > Metadata Panel
Shortcut: –   **See also:** Metadata Panel,
Version: CS2   Metadata Append/Replace

The metadata options in CS2 allow users to create and apply groups of metadata settings to individual or groups of files. The settings are created, saved and applied as a metadata template.

To create a template open an example image in Photoshop and then display the File Info dialog. Add your own details and information into the editable areas of the various data sections in the dialog (1). Next select the Save Metadata Template option from the pop-up menu that appears after pressing the sideways arrow at the top right of the dialog (2).

The new template will be added to this menu allowing you to easily append existing details in Photoshop by opening the picture's File Info dialog and selecting the template from the pop-up menu. The same template can be applied to several by multi-selecting thumbnails first and then selecting the desired template from the list available in the pop-up menu in the Metadata Panel in Bridge.

The template files that you create are stored in XML format and are saved to a Metadata Templates folder in Documents and Settings\User\Application Data\Adobe\ XMP for Windows machines (3).

Mezzotint filter

Menu: Filter > Pixelate > Mezzotint
Shortcut: –   **See also:** Filters
Version: 6.0, 7.0, CS, CS2

The Mezzotint filter, as one of the Pixelate group of filters, recreates tone and color in a similar way to the way it is produced with etched printing plates. A series of strokes, dots or lines are used in a pattern to create detail and tone. Grayscale pictures are recreated in black and white strokes, and colored photos remade with a fully saturated pattern of colored texture.

The filter contains no single slider control to adjust the strength or positioning of the effect, rather a drop-down menu of texture types is provided (1). Each type (stroke, line, dot) creates a different pattern of texture and tone.

Minimize mode

Menu: Window > Arrange > Minimize Mode
Shortcut: –   **See also:** Tile
Version: 6.0, 7.0, CS, CS2

The Minimize mode is one of the many ways that open pictures can be viewed in Photoshop. Selecting this option from the pop-up menu (4) that appears after clicking on the feathers icon in the top left of a document window by clicking the minimize button (1) in the opposite corner of the window will display the picture as a title bar at the bottom of the workspace.

Other options for displaying open documents include:

Maximize (2) – Displays the picture the maximum size in the workspace.

Close (3) – Closes the document.

Multi-window mode (5) – Displays the document in its own smaller, movable window in the workspace.

Missing Profile

Menu: –
Shortcut: –   **See also:** Color Settings
Version: 6.0, 7.0, CS, CS2

After opting for a fully managed system in the Edit > Color Settings of Photoshop, opening a picture that doesn't have an attached ICC profile will display a Missing Profile dialog. Here you have three choices about how to proceed, and more importantly, how Photoshop will deal with the colors in the file:

Leave as is – This option keeps the file free of a color profile. Not a preferred option.

Assign working RGB – Attaches the profile that has been set as the default working profile in the Edit > Color Settings dialog.

Assign Profile – Assigns a profile from the list of those installed in your machine. Select the option that most suits your output needs and then click OK. Many photographers use the AdobeRGB profile for working with images destined for publishing and sRGB for those pictures that are to be used on screen.

Minimum filter

Menu: Filter > Other > Minimum
Shortcut: –   **See also:** Filters
Version: 6.0, 7.0, CS, CS2

The Minimum filter, as one of the Other group of filters, grows or bleeds the darker areas of the picture whilst at the same time reducing the size of the lighter toned parts. In making these changes, the filter analyzes the brightness of the pixels in a given area (radius) and reduces the

brightness to the level of the darkest pixel in the area.

The filter contains a single slider control that adjusts the radius (1) or size of the area used to determine the pixel brightness value.

Before

After

© www.ablestol.com 2005

Mode

Menu: Image > Mode
Shortcut: –   **See also:** Color modes,
Version: 6.0, 7.0, CS, CS2   Color depth

Photoshop can create, edit and convert images to and from several different color modes. The mode of a picture document determines the maximum number of colors that can be stored in the file, the way that color is constructed within the file (color channels) and this in turn affects the size of the file. Generally speaking more colors and more channels mean a larger file size.

The mode options available in Photoshop are listed under the Image > Mode menu (1). They are Bitmap, Grayscale, Duotone, Indexed Color, RGB Color, CMYK Color, LAB Color and Multichannel.

The same menu also contains options for altering the color depth or Bits/Channel of your pictures (2).

Modify range of Hue sliders

Menu: Image > Adjustments > Hue/Saturation
Shortcut: Ctrl/Cmd U   **See also:** Hue/Saturation
Version: 6.0, 7.0, CS, CS2

The Hue/Saturation control adjusts the color and vibrancy of color in a picture. In the default mode, Edit Master (1), these changes are applied to all the colors in the picture. The drop-down Edit menu allows the user to select a different range of colors to apply the changes to. In the example, the hue of the blue colors in the picture were altered to green.

In addition to selecting a specific color to edit, the Hue/Saturation dialog also provides the ability to fine-tune the range of tones included in the selection.

Two color bars are displayed at the bottom of the dialog when a color range is selected in the Edit menu. The top bar shows the color currently selected; the bottom bar indicates the colors that the selected hues will be converted to. Between the two bars are four slider controls. The vertical white bars (2) define the edges of the color range and the triangles (3) are the edges of the fall-off from the color range. By click-dragging the white bars the size and scope of the selected range can be altered. This allows fine-tuning of the colors selected and substituted.

Modify selections

Menu: Select > Modify
Shortcut: –   **See also:** Smooth, Expand
Version: 6.0, 7.0, CS, CS2   Selection,
                 Contract –
                 selection

Existing selections can be modified in the following ways:

Border – Choosing the Border option from the Modify menu displays a dialog where you can enter the width of the border in pixels (between 1 and 200). Clicking OK creates a border selection that frames the original selection.

Smooth – This option cleans up stray pixels that are left unselected after using the Magic Wand tool. After choosing Modify enter a radius value to use for searching for stray pixels and then click OK.

Expand – After selecting Expand enter the number of pixels that you want to increase the selection by and click OK. The original selection is increased in size. You can enter a pixel value between 1 and 100.

Contract – Selecting this option will reduce the size of the selection by the number of pixels entered into the dialog. You can enter a pixel value between 1 and 100.

Moiré

Moiré reduced

Moiré patterns

Menu: –
Shortcut: –   See also: –
Version: 6.0, 7.0, CS, CS2

A mottled pattern caused when a patterned material is converted to digital using a scanner or camera. The problem can occur when scanning photographs that are printed in a magazine or book or shooting images that contain fabrics that have a definite woven appearance.

Some scan software has a descreening feature that eliminates the pattern but this can soften the image.

You can also rotate the material to be scanned slightly in the scanner and straighten it up once scanned, which sometimes helps.

Cell Size: 25 square

Mosaic filter

Menu: Filter > Pixelate > Mosaic
Shortcut: –   See also: Filters
Version: 6.0, 7.0, CS, CS2

The Mosaic filter, as one of the Pixelate group of filters, simulates the look of a pixel-based picture that has been enlarged greatly. The photo is recreated in large single colored blocks. The filter contains a single slider control that adjusts the Cell Size (1) or 'pixel' block size. The higher the value entered here the larger the blocks used to recreate the photo.

• •

Mosaic Tile filter

Menu: Filter > Texture > Mosaic Tiles
Shortcut: –   See also: Filters
Version: 6.0, 7.0, CS, CS2

The Mosaic filter, as one of the Texture group of filters, simulates the look of a picture that is constructed of small pieces of broken tiles. True to the tile idea, each tile is surrounded by an area of grout.

The filter contains three slider controls. The Tile Size slider (1) adjusts the size of each tile fragment. The Grout Width (2) setting determines the size of the grout in relationship to the tiles and the Lighten Grout option (3) controls the brightness of the grout area.

Angle: 0
Distance: 37 pixels

Motion Blur filter

Menu: Filter > Blur > Motion Blur
Shortcut: –   See also: Filters,
Version: 6.0, 7.0, CS, CS2   Smart Sharpen
                                              filter

The Motion Blur filter is one of several blur options that can be found in the Blur section of the Filter menu. This feature is great for putting back a sense of movement into action pictures that have been frozen by being photographed with a fast shutter speed. Used by itself, the filter produces pictures that are very blurred and often lack any recognizable detail. For more realistic results apply this filter via a feathered selection to help retain sharpness in some picture parts whilst blurring others.

The filter dialog contains a single slider, a preview window and a motion direction (angle) dial. The Angle dial (1) determines the direction of the blur and should be set to simulate the natural direction of the subject. The Distance slider (2) controls the amount of blur added to the picture.

• •

Mosaic Tiles
Tile Size   12
Grout Width   3
Lighten Grout   9

Move tool

Menu: –
Shortcut: V   **See also:** –
Version: 6.0, 7.0, CS, CS2

The Move tool is used to change the position of layer content within the confines of the image window.

The Move tool has two extended features in the options bar that change the way that the tool works:

Auto Select Layer – Allows the tool to automatically select the uppermost layer when the mouse cursor clicks on it.

Auto Select Groups – New for CS2, this option allows the user to select all layers in a specific area of a picture by click-dragging a marquee around a canvas part that is common to the layers.

Show Transformation Controls – Automatically shows the bounding box (1) of the layer content that is currently selected. In this mode the corner and side handles of the bounding box can be moved to transform the layer contents.

Multiply blending mode

Menu: –
Shortcut: –   **See also:** Blend modes
Version: 6.0, 7.0, CS, CS2

The Multiply blending mode is one of the group of Darken modes that multiplies the color of the bottom layer with the top producing an overall darker result.

When the top layer is black the resultant blended layer is also black. There is no change when the bottom layer is blended with a white top layer.

This blend mode is often used for creating fancy edge effects on photos (see below) and it's also very handy for 'washed out' or overexposed images. Simply duplicate the layer and set it to Multiply mode.

Multi-Page PDF to PSD

Menu: File > Automate > Multi-page PDF to PSD
Shortcut: –   **See also:** –
Version: 6.0, 7.0, CS

In Photoshop versions up to CS2 the Multi-Page PDF to PSD option that was located in the File > Automate menu was used to convert individual pages of a PDF document to separate Photoshop PSD files.

In the dialog of this version of the feature you could input the name and location of the source PDF document (1), the destination directory for the converted files (4), page range (2), output resolution and color mode (3) as well as the base name (4) for the newly created documents.

In CS2 you can convert several PDF pages by simply opening the PDF file and then multi-selecting the pages to convert using the PDF Import dialog (5). This feature contains options that control the Resolution, Color Mode, Bit Depth and Crop area used in the conversion and a choice between displaying whole pages or just the images they contain (6).

Create an edge picture with a black surround and a completely white interior. Layer this image on top of a picture and resize to suit the image.

With the edge layer selected, change the blend mode to Multiply to allow the picture beneath to show through the white sections of the edge layer.

nN

Nearest Neighbor 500% upsize

Original

Navigator

Menu:	Window > Navigator		
Shortcut:	–	**See also:**	Zoom In/Zoom
Version:	6.0, 7.0, CS, CS2		Out

The Navigator palette is a small scalable preview palette that shows the entire image together with a highlighted rectangle (1) the size, scale and shape of the area currently displayed in the document window (2).

A new frame can be drawn (scaling the Image window with it) by holding the Command/Ctrl keys and making a new marquee. The frame can be dragged around the entire image with the Hand tool.

The Zoom tools (3) at each end of the slider can be clicked, the slider can be dragged, or a figure can be entered as a percentage to change view size.

Nearest Neighbor interpolation

Menu:	–		
Shortcut:	–	**See also:**	Interpolation, Image Size
Version:	6.0, 7.0, CS, CS2		command,
			Bicubic interpolation

Nearest Neighbor is one of the interpolation methods that is available when resizing pictures using the Image Size feature (1).

This option provides the fastest and coarsest results and is only recommended for use with screen grabs or hard-edged illustrations.

It is not a method that works well with photographs. Instead, one of the bicubic options should be used to resize these image types.

Neon Glow filter

Menu: Filter > Artistic > Neon Glow
Shortcut: –   **See also:** Filters
Version: 6.0, 7.0, CS, CS2

The Neon Glow filter, as one of the Artistic group of filters, colors the image with foreground and background hues, adds a glow color and then softens the image.

The filter contains two sliders and a color selection box.

The Glow Size setting (1) adjusts the position of the glow in the tonal range of the picture. Low values place the glow in the shadow areas, higher settings move the glow to the highlights.

The Glow Brightness slider (2) oscillates the picture's tinting between foreground, background and glow colors.

The Glow Color (3) can be selected by double-clicking (single-click) the color box and selecting a new hue from the Color Picker dialog.

Changing the foreground and background colors greatly alters the nature of the filtered results (4).

New command

Menu: File > New
Shortcut: Ctrl/Cmd N   **See also:** –
Version: 6.0, 7.0, CS, CS2

The File > New option in both the Photoshop and ImageReady workspaces provides the user with a new blank document.

The option creates a Photoshop/ImageReady document from the settings selected in the New dialog box.

In Photoshop the dialog (1) has sections for the image's name, width, height, resolution, mode and background content. You can also choose an existing template from a range of document types from the drop-down Preset menu.

The Advanced section (2) contains options for selecting the color profile that will be attached to the document as well as for choosing the pixel shape or aspect ratio that will be the basis of the picture.

Changes made in the New dialog can be saved as a new document preset using the Save Preset button (3) on the right of the window. The new preset is added to the menu listings and can be used to quickly create documents with the same characteristics in the future.

The New dialog in ImageReady (4) is a little more simplified contain document size and content options only.

New Brush

Menu: –
Shortcut: B   **See also:** Brush tool
Version: 6.0, 7.0, CS, CS2

To add a new brush to those listed in the Brush Preset palette display the pop-up palette from the options by pressing the downwards arrow (1). Select a brush from those listed and modify using the various settings in the options bar. Press the New Preset button (2) in the top right of the palette. Enter the new brush name in the Brush Name pop-up dialog (3) and click OK. The new brush will be added to the bottom of the list in the palette.

• •

New Layer button

Menu: –
Shortcut: –   **See also:** Layers palette
Version: 6.0, 7.0, CS, CS2

The New Layer button located at the bottom of the Layers palette (1) creates a new blank layer above the currently selected layer when pressed. The new layer is transparent by default. The results are the same as if the Layer > New > Layer menu item is selected.

New Window

Menu: Window > Arrange > New Window for
Shortcut: –   See also: –
Version: 6.0, 7.0, CS, CS2

The New Window command creates another image window for the current document. The two windows can be sized, zoomed and moved independent of each other but changes made to one image are reflected in the other.

This feature is most often used to help see the effects of fine detail editing. The view in one window is magnified (1) whilst the other is kept so that the whole picture is displayed (2). Enhancing or editing activities are performed in the zoomed-in window and the changes checked in the whole display view.

Normal blending mode

Menu: –
Shortcut: –   See also: Blend modes
Version: 6.0, 7.0, CS, CS2

The Normal blending mode is the default mode of newly created layers and newly selected brush tools.

When the top layer's blend mode is set to Normal and set to 100% opacity, no part of the bottom layer is visible and no blending of the two layers takes place. The picture parts of the top layer are treated as opaque and therefore cover and obscure all image detail beneath.

• •

Note Paper filter

Menu: Filter > Sketch > Note Paper
Shortcut: –   See also: Filters
Version: 6.0, 7.0, CS, CS2

The Note Paper, as one of the Sketch group of filters, redraws the photo as textured light and dark tones based on the current selection of fore- and background colors.

The filter dialog contains three sliders that control the look and strength of the effect.

The Image Balance setting (1) adjusts which areas are toned the foreground color and which are converted to the background hue. Low values favor the background color and high settings color more of the picture with the foreground color. The Graininess slider (2) determines the amount of grain that is added to the picture. The Relief slider (3) adjusts the strength of the simulated side lighting falling on the paper surface. With higher values the texture is more pronounced. Changing the foreground and background colors away from their defaults greatly alters the nature of the filtered results.

• •

Notes

Menu: –
Shortcut: –   See also: –
Version: 6.0, 7.0, CS, CS2

A feature introduced on version 6.0 that allows you to leave messages around the picture.

These appear as little notes on the image which, when clicked open, reveal the message you've left. Useful if you're working with a designer who needs to do something with the picture before it goes to print.

Ocean Ripple filter

Menu: Filter > Distort > Ocean Ripple
Shortcut: –　　　　　　　　　**See also:** Filters
Version: 6.0, 7.0, CS, CS2

The Ocean Ripple filter, as one of the Distort group of filters, applies a rippled distortion to the whole of the picture surface. In this way it can create similar looking results to those obtained with the Glass or Ripple filters.

The filter contains two slider controls.

The Ripple Size setting (1) adjusts the scale of the wave-like ripples that are added to the picture. Low values create smaller, less dramatic ripples.

The Ripple Magnitude slider (2) determines how far each ripple is distorted. High settings create a greater level of distortion in the final result.

. . . .

Set to Background

Repeat Edge Pixels

Offset filter

Menu: Filter > Other > Offset
Shortcut: –　　　　　　　　　**See also:** Filters
Version: 6.0, 7.0, CS, CS2

The Offset filter, as one of the Other group of filters, displaces the picture within the image window.

The filter contains two slider controls plus several options that determine how the offset areas are dealt with.

The Horizontal and Vertical sliders (1) adjust how offset the picture is from its original position. The greater the values the larger the offset will be.

The Undefined Area options (2) determine how the space left in the image window when the picture is repositioned will be treated.

Set to Background – This options fills the gap left in the image window with the current background color.

Repeat Edge Pixels – The pixels at the edge of the repositioned picture are repeated to the edge of the image window.

Wrap Around – The picture is wrapped around the image window so that the edges that are cropped due to the repositioning are added back into the picture on the opposite side.

Wrap Around

139

Omni Lighting Effects

Menu: Filter > Render > Lighting Effects
Shortcut: –   **See also:** Lighting Effects
Version: 6.0, 7.0, CS, CS2   filter

Omni is one of the lighting types featured in the Lighting Effects filter. The Omni style shines light in all directions, creating a bright center and then a sharp fall-off of light intensity.

This light type is great for highlighting a specific part of a scene whilst reducing the brightness of the rest of the picture.

Move the light by click-dragging the light's center. You can decrease or increase the size of the Omni light source by click-dragging one of the light handles.

Adjust the characteristics of the light source by changing its properties. The brightness of the light is determined by the Exposure and Intensity sliders.

Online Help

Menu: Help > Photoshop Online
Shortcut: F1   **See also:** –
Version: 6.0, 7.0, CS, CS2

As well as the extensive help and tutorial resources that are contained within the Photoshop program itself, extra tutorials, hints, tips and tricks can be found online. Select the Help > Photoshop Online menu item (1) to take you to the Adobe web pages dedicated to your favorite photo editing program (2). Alternatively you can click onto the colored feathers icon (3) at the top of the toolbar. This will take you to the same web pages.

Online Printing

Menu: File > Online Prints
Bridge: Tools > Photoshop Services > Photo Prints
Shortcut: Ctrl/Cmd Alt/Opt Shft L   **See also:** Print options
Version: CS2

Although many images you make, or enhance, with Photoshop will be printed right at your desktop, occasionally you might want the option to output some prints on high quality photographic paper. The File > Online Prints option in Photoshop (1) and the Tools > Photoshop Services > Photo Prints in Bridge (2) provides just this ability.

Using the resources of Kodak's Easy Share Gallery (previously ofoto.com) in the USA, Europe and the UK, Photoshop users can upload copies of their favorite images to the company's site and have them photographically printed in a range of sizes (3). The finished prints are sent to you via the mail.

This service provides the convenience of printing from your desktop with the image and tactile qualities of having your digital pictures output using a photographic rather than inkjet process.

Before

After Omni Lighting Effects

Opacity

Menu: –
Shortcut: –   See also: Layer opacity
Version: 6.0, 7.0, CS, CS2

The opacity setting can be adjusted for a range of tools and features in Photoshop. It is a setting that controls the transparency of an object or layer.

A value of 100% is completely opaque (not transparent at all), whereas a setting of 0% means that the layer or object is completely transparent. Brush opacity slider (1). Layer opacity control (2).

Opacity 100%

Opacity 50%

Opacity 20%

Open

Menu: File > Open
Shortcut: Ctrl/Cmd O   See also: Open As,
Version: 6.0, 7.0, CS, CS2   Open Recent

The File > Open option presents you with the standard Windows (1) or Macintosh (2) file browser. From here you can navigate from drive to drive on your machine before locating and opening the folder that contains your pictures. You can refine the display options by selecting the specific file type (file ending) to be displayed (3) and as we have already noted you can also choose the way to view the files.

In the Windows example, the thumbnail view was selected so that it is possible to quickly flick through a folder full of pictures to locate the specific image you are after. In CS2 it is also possible to switch to the new Adobe Dialog (3) for opening and saving actions.

Open As

Menu: File > Open As
Shortcut: Alt Shft Ctrl O   See also: Open,
Version: 6.0, 7.0, CS, CS2   Open Recent

On the odd occasion that a specific Windows file won't open using the File > Open command you can try to open the file in a different format. Do this by selecting the File > Open As option and then choosing the file you want to open (1). The feature is used if a file has an incorrect file extension or no file extension at all.

After making this selection pick the desired format (2) from the Open As pop-up menu, and click the Open button. This action forces the program to ignore the file format it has assumed the picture is saved in and treat the image as if it is saved as the file type you have selected.

If the picture still refuses to open, then you may have selected a format that does not match the file's true format, or the file itself may have been damaged when being saved.

O

Open in Camera Raw

Menu: Bridge: Open on Camera Raw
Shortcut: Ctrl/Cmd R   **See also:** Camera Raw
Version: CS2

New for CS2 is the ability to convert Raw files to other formats using a stand-alone version of Camera Raw. No longer is this utility merely part of the process of opening a Raw file in Photoshop.

It is now possible to open candidate files directly into Camera Raw from inside the Bridge workspace. The files are first selected in the browser and then the Open in Camera Raw option is selected from the File menu (1) or by right-clicking the thumbnail and then choosing the same option from the pop-up menu (2). The file is then opened in the Camera Raw dialog and is ready for processing.

In addition to using this option for processing individual files, multiple pictures can be added to the Camera Raw dialog (3) by firstly selecting the thumbnails and then choosing File > Open in Camera Raw.

Open Recent

Menu: File > Open Recent
Shortcut: –   **See also:** Open, Open As
Version: 6.0, 7.0, CS, CS2

As you browse, open and edit various pictures from your folders Photoshop keeps track of the last few files and lists them under the File > Open Recently Edited Files menu item (1).

This is a very handy feature as it means that you can return quickly to pictures that you are working on without having to navigate back to the specific folder where they are stored.

By default Photoshop lists the last 10 files edited. You can change the number of files kept on this menu via the 'Recent file list' setting in the Edit > Preferences > File Handling window (2). Don't be tempted to list too many files as each additional listing uses more memory.

Optimization, web

Menu: File > Save for Web
Shortcut: Alt/Opt Shft Ctrl/Cmd S   **See also:** JPEG format,
Version: 6.0, 7.0, CS, CS2   GIF format

The skill of making a highly visual site that downloads quickly is largely based on how well you optimize the pictures contained on the pages of the site.

The process of shrinking your pictures for web use involves two steps:

• Firstly, the pixel dimensions of the image need to be reduced so that the image can be viewed without scrolling on a standard screen. This usually means ensuring that the image will fit within a 600 × 480 pixel space.

• Secondly, the picture is compressed and saved in a web-ready file format. There are two main choices here, GIF and JPEG.

The best way to optimize your pictures for web use is via the Save for Web (File > Save for Web) option in Photoshop.

This feature provides before and after previews of the compression process as well as options for compression (1) and reducing the pixel dimensions of your pictures (2), all in the one dialog.

Using the feature you can select the file format, adjust compression settings, examine the predicted file size and preview the results live on screen.

Options bar

Menu: –
Shortcut: –   **See also:** Menu bar
Version: 6.0, 7.0, CS, CS2

Long bar beneath the menu bar, which displays the various settings and options available for the tool that is currently selected. The bar also contains the palette well (1) and go to Bridge button (2).

• • • • • • • • • • • • • • • • • •

Output Levels

Menu: Enhance > Adjust Lighting > Levels
Shortcut: Ctrl/Cmd L   **See also:** Levels command
Version: 6.0, 7.0, CS, CS2

The Output Levels controls (1) in the Levels dialog sit at the very bottom of the feature.

By moving these black and white point sliders inwards, you are compressing the full tonal range of the picture.

The result is a less contrasty photo. Such a change may be necessary to suit the requirements of a particular printer, or just to reduce the contrast of a picture taken on a sunny day.

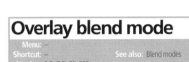

Overlay blend mode

Menu: –
Shortcut: –   **See also:** Blend modes
Version: 6.0, 7.0, CS, CS2

The Overlay blending mode is one of the group of Overlay modes which combines the effects of both the Multiply and Screen modes. Colors of the top layer overlay the bottom layer's pixels but the highlight and shadow tones of the bottom layer are preserved.

There is no change when the bottom layer is blended with a 50% gray top layer.

PQ

Page Setup

Menu: File > Page Setup
Shortcut: Ctrl/Cmd Shft P   **See also:** Print options
Version: 6.0, 7.0, CS, CS2

The Page Setup dialog, in conjunction with the Print and the Print Multiple Photos dialogs, controls all the printing options from Photoshop.

Here you can change the orientation of the paper that you are printing on – Portrait is vertical and Landscape is horizontal (1).

Page Setup also provides options to input values for the paper Size (2) and paper Source (3), which are both determined by the printer that is currently selected.

If you wish to change printers, then clicking the Printer button (4) will take you to a second dialog, where you can select another printer that is installed and connected to your computer.

The Page Setup dialog can also be accessed via the button at the top right of the Print dialog (5) that is displayed when selecting File > Print with Preview.

Paint Bucket tool

Menu: –
Shortcut: G   **See also:** Magic Wand tool
Version: 6.0, 7.0, CS, CS2

The Paint Bucket tool is grouped with the Gradient tool in the Photoshop toolbar (4).

The feature combines the selecting prowess of the Magic Wand and the coloring abilities of the Fill command to create a tool that fills all pixels of a similar color (1) with the current foreground color (2).

If the Contiguous option is selected then the pixels that will be filled must be adjacent to one another. How similar in color and tone the pixels have to be before being filled is based on the Tolerance setting.

To ensure a realistic substitution of color try using the tool in the Color mode (3) as this will maintain the texture, shadow and details of the original picture.

Paint Daubs filter

Menu: Filter > Artistic > Paint Daubs
Shortcut: –   **See also:** Filters
Version: 6.0, 7.0, CS, CS2

The Paint Daubs filter, as one of the Artistic group of filters, applies a painterly effect to the whole of the picture surface. In the process the fine detail of the photo is eclipsed by large areas of painted color.

The filter contains two slider controls and a Brush Type menu. The Brush Size setting (1) adjusts the scale of the painted areas. Low values create smaller areas with finer detail. The Sharpness slider (2) determines how much of the original detail is maintained in the painting process. High settings create a greater level of detail and low values create broad areas of smooth color.

The Brush Type menu (3) contains a list of different styles of brushes. Changing brush types can alter the final filter result greatly.

Paintbrush

Menu: –
Shortcut: B   **See also:** Brush tool
Version: 6.0, 7.0, CS, CS2

The Paintbrush or Brush tool (1) allows the user to draw onto the picture's surface with the currently selected foreground color.

The basic characteristics of the brush such as size and hardness of edge can be adjusted with the slider controls in the Brush Preset Picker accessed via the down-arrow button in the tool's option bar.

Many more characteristics can be altered with the controls in the Brushes palette (Window > Brushes).

Painting tools

Menu: –
Shortcut: –   **See also:** Brush tool,
Pencil tool
Paint Bucket tool
Version: 6.0, 7.0, CS, CS2

Although many people will employ Photoshop to enhance images captured using a digital camera, some users make pictures from scratch using the program's painting and drawing tools.

Illustrators, in particular, generate their images with the aid of tools such as the Brush, Paint Bucket, Airbrush and Pencil.

This is not to say that it is not possible to use drawing or painting tools on digital photographs. In fact, the judicious use of tools like the Brush can enhance detail and provide a real sense of drama in your images.

All the painting and drawing tools are grouped in the one section of the program's toolbar for easy access.

Palette Knife filter

Menu: Filter > Artistic > Palette Knife
Shortcut: –   **See also:** Filters
Version: 6.0, 7.0, CS, CS2

The Palette Knife filter, as one of the Artistic group of filters, simulates the look of a picture created by applying thick broad areas of paint with a palette knife.

The filter contains three slider controls.

The Stroke Size setting (1) adjusts the strength of the effect and the size of the broad areas of paint. Low values retain more of the detail of the original picture.

The Stroke Detail slider (2) determines how coarsely the color is applied. Low values create a more broken-up result.

The Softness control (3) alters the sharpness of the stroke's edge. A high setting produces strokes with a softer edge.

P9

Palette Well

Menu: –
Shortcut: –   **See also:** Palettes
Version: 6.0, 7.0, CS, CS2

In Photoshop open palettes could be dragged to, or 'docked' in the Palette Well space at the right end of the options bar to save workspace area.

This action reduces the palette to a tab in the well. To view the full palette again click onto the tab heading, to reinstate the palette to the workspace click and drag the tab out of the well.

Palettes

Menu: Window >
Shortcut: –   **See also:** Palette Well
Version: 6.0, 7.0, CS, CS2

A palette is a window that contains details and information that are used for the alteration of image characteristics. Photoshop contains the following palettes: Actions, Animation, Brushes, Channels, Character, Color, Histogram, History, Info, Layer Comps, Navigator, Paragraph, Paths, Styles, Swatches and Tool Presets.

The palettes are displayed and hidden by selecting them from the Window menu (1) or by pressing associated shortcut keys.

They can be hidden but kept active by dragging them into the Palette Well (2), or grouped together into a palette set by dragging palettes onto other palettes (3).

Panoramas, creating

Menu: –
Shortcut: –   **See also:** Photomerge
Version: 6.0, 7.0, CS, CS2

The process of creating a wide-angle picture, or panorama, using the Photoshop Photomerge feature is broken into three different stages:

1. **Capturing the source photos** – Shoot a range of images whilst gradually rotating the camera so that each photograph overlaps the next.

2. **Stitching images using Photomerge** – Import the pictures into Photomerge and use its automated process to position, match and stitch the edge details of the separate image files to create a new single panoramic picture.

3. **Producing the panorama** – Make final editing and enhancement changes on the finished panoramic photo before printing the picture.

Capture source images

Stitch photos

Produce panorama

Before

After

Paste command

Menu: Edit > Paste
Shortcut: Ctrl/Cmd V
Version: 6.0, 7.0, CS, CS2
See also: Paste Into
Selections

The Edit > Paste command pastes the current contents of the computer's clipboard as a new layer in the open Photoshop document.

This menu option is grayed out (not available) if there is currently nothing copied to the clipboard.

• •

Before sky change

After sky change

To replace the sky in a picture start by making a selection of just the sky. Here the Magic Wand was used to select the predominantly blue sky region.

Paste Into

Menu: Edit > Paste Into
Shortcut: Shft Ctrl/Cmd V
Version: 6.0, 7.0, CS, CS2
See also: Paste command

The Edit > Paste Into command pastes the contents of the clipboard into the active selection of the current Photoshop document.

The pasted picture part is inserted into the selected area and the boundaries of the inserted picture are highlighted by a selection marquee (marching ants). The selection can be moved and transformed within the boundaries of the insertion area whilst the selection remains active.

This process creates a new layer that holds the pasted selection and uses a layer mask to shield it from areas that were not initially selected.

Now open a substitute sky picture and make a selection of the sky. Copy the selection (Edit > Copy) and then switch back to the original picture and choose Edit > Paste Into.

Immediately after pasting, press the Ctrl/Cmd T keystrokes combination and use the Free Transform feature to resize and adjust the proportions of the new sky to fit the area of the old.

Patch tool

Menu: –
Shortcut: J
Version: 6.0, 7.0, CS, CS2
See also: Healing Brush,
Spot Healing brush

The Patch tool breaks the limitations of the Healing Brush by providing users with the ability to apply the repairing power of the tool to whole sections of their pictures in one step.

Using the tool involves a simple three step process – 'select, drag the selection and patch'. When first selected the Patch tool works like the Lasso tool allowing you to draw a selection around a specific area of the picture. Just like Photoshop's other selection tools you can add to, subtract from or even use the intersection of multiple selections to refine your selected picture part.

After making the selection the Patch tool provides you with two very different ways of using the feature to repair your pictures. If Source is selected, in the tool's options bar, then you can drag the selection to the area that you want to use as a patch. Letting go of the mouse button will use this area to patch the original selection. If Destination is chosen, then the area you selected will become a patch that you can drag over the part of your picture that needs repairing.

See over page for an example of how to use the Patch tool

PQ

PD

Patchwork filter

Menu: Filter > Texture > Patchwork
Shortcut: –   **See also:** Filters
Version: 6.0, 7.0, CS, CS2

The Patchwork filter, as one of the Texture group of filters, simulates the look of the surface of a patchwork quilt. In the process the picture is broken up into a series of squares.

The filter contains two slider controls. The Square Size setting (1) adjusts the size of each square. The Relief slider (2) determines the degree of shadow that is applied to the texture squares. Low values have less shadow and therefore the appearance of lower relief.

Select the Patch tool from Photoshop's toolbar. Using the tool like you would the lasso, click and drag the cursor to draw a selection around the area that you want to use as the 'source' of your patch.

Select the 'Source' option in the options bar. Click inside the selection and drag it to the repair. When you let go of the mouse button the selected area's detail, color and tone will merge with the image.

Paths

Menu: –
Shortcut: –   **See also:** Pen tool
Version: 6.0, 7.0, CS, CS2

Paths are another way to select objects or parts of pictures in Photoshop (1). Unlike the selection tools which work on the pixels in the picture the Path tools are vector based.

The Shape tool uses paths technology to outline the shapes it draws. This means that no matter what size they are scaled to the edges will always remain sharp. Paths are made up of segments held in place by anchor points and are drawn and modified with the Pen tools.

Once created a thumbnail of the path can be viewed in the Paths palette (2), and from here you can select a number of options to apply to the active layer from a row of icons along the base or from the arrow's drop-down menu (3). These options include: Filling the path with the foreground color;

Path Selection tools

Menu: Enhance > Adjust Lighting > Levels
Shortcut: Ctrl/Cmd Alt/Opt Shift L   **See also:** Curves, Shadow/
Version: 6.0, 7.0, CS, CS2   Highlight

producing a Stroke to add the foreground color along the selected path and making a Selection from the path.

A path can be moved to a new image by dragging the original path icon from the palette and pulling it over a new image. You can also copy paths from one location and paste them into another using the normal copy and paste option.

Paths are also used by designers who turn the selection into a clipping path and import it into a page layout. The clipping path ensures everything outside the frame appears as transparent on the layout. This ensures text wraps around the subject and the subject blends well with the layout.

To create a path quickly with using the Pen tool use the Quick Mask mode to paint a mask around the subject. Magnify an area and use the Eraser and Airbrush to remove or add to the mask, then convert the masked selection into a path. Paths can be converted quickly into selections and selections can be turned into paths.

To edit a path you must first select it. Photoshop provides several options for this task.

To select a path component, choose the Path Selection tool and click on the path. To select several components or segments, choose the Direct Selection tool and drag a marquee over the area. To add extra path segments to those currently selected hold down the Shift key whilst using the Direct Select tool to pick more segments.

After Fill Layer

After Fill Selection

Pattern, Fill Layers

Menu: Edit > Fill
Shortcut: –   **See also:** Fill command,
Version: 6.0, 7.0, CS, CS2   Define Pattern

The Edit > Fill command is generally used for filling layers, or active selections, with solid colors, but the feature can also be used for applying patterns to layers or selections.

After selecting Edit > Fill, choose Pattern as the option from the Use menu (1) and then select a pattern from the Custom Pattern palette (2). To fill a layer, select the layer first and then choose Edit > Fill Layer. To restrict the pattern fill to the extent of a selection, create the selection first and then choose Edit > Fill.

Photoshop also contains a Pattern adjustment layer which can be used to fill individual layers with patterns. Create a Pattern adjustment layer by selecting the option from the Layer > New Fill layer menu or by pressing the Create a New Fill layer button at the bottom of the Layers palette.

Use the Define Pattern feature to produce custom patterns to use with the Fill command.

Pattern Maker filter

Menu: Filter > Pattern Maker
Shortcut: Ctrl/Cmd Alt/Opt Shft X **See also:** Filters
Version: 6.0, 7.0, CS, CS2

The Pattern Maker feature creates tiled patterns from selected image areas. The tiles are not just created from the repetition of the selected area but rather the sampled picture part is used as a basis for the tile.

The filter features a dialog with full preview and adjustment controls. The finished tiles can even be saved as a patterns preset for use later with tools like the Pattern Stamp tool.

Pattern Stamp

Menu: –
Shortcut: S   **See also:** Define Pattern
Version: 6.0, 7.0, CS, CS2

The Pattern Stamp tool (1) is nestled in the toolbar with the Clone Stamp tool. The feature works like the Brush tool except that, instead of laying down color, the stamp paints with a pattern.

The specific pattern used is selected from the tool's options bar (2). A range of preset patterns are included with Elements or you can create your own from a selection with the Edit > Define Pattern.

PDF format

Menu: –
Shortcut: –   **See also:** PDF, Save As
Version: 6.0, 7.0, CS, CS2

PDF or Portable Document Format (sometimes saved with a PDP extension) is an Adobe multi-use file format that can be read equally as well by Windows-, Macintosh- and Linux-based machines.

The format correctly displays images, text and formatting on the different systems and is fast becoming a standard for press- and web-based document delivery. Photoshop can read PDF files and also provides an option for output of image files in the format. When opened, multi-page PDF documents are displayed in the Import PDF dialog, where individual pages are previewed and can be selected for opening (1).

PDF, Save As

Menu: File > Save As
Shortcut: Ctrl/Cmd Shft S   **See also:** PDF format,
Version: CS2   PDF Presets

Though saving a Photoshop document in the PDF format is nothing new CS2 includes a new Save Adobe PDF dialog which provides more choice and control than previously offered.

Here you can select from one of range of pre-installed PDF Presets or even create, customize and save your own options.

Standard and Capatibility options ensure that the PDF files that you write will suit the requirements of your customers or co-workers and the individual preference areas (1) allow you to customise the quality and security of your output.

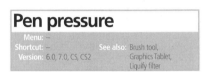

PDF Presentation

Menu: File > Automate > PDF Presentation
Bridge: Tools > Photoshop > PDF Presentation
Shortcut: –   **See also:** PDF format
Version: CS, CS2

The PDF Presentation option creates a slide-show saved in the PDF format. The dialog for the feature provides controls for adding pictures (1), ordering their display (change the position in the file list) and applying transitions (2) and timing (3) between individual slides. With the options selected the whole sequence is then saved as a self-running slideshow.

In CS2 the Save Adobe PDF dialog is displayed as part of the process for creating the presentation. At this stage you can alter the quality of the pictures that are included in the slideshow and the compatibility of the PDF file.

The resultant PDF file can be saved to disk or CD or even uploaded to the web ready for online viewing.

By creating PDF-based slideshows, digital image makers can put together a showcase of their work, which can be shared with a range of viewers, irrespective of the computer system they use.

Pictures can be included in the presentation in three ways:

1. By multi-selecting their thumbnails in the Bridge and then choosing the feature from the Tools > Photoshop menu,

2. Opening the feature from the File > Automate menu in Photoshop and then Browsing for the images to be included, or

3. Opening all images to be included in the show in Photoshop first and then choosing the Add Open Files option in the feature.

PDF Presets

Menu: Edit > Adobe PDF Presets
Shortcut: –   **See also:** PDF format
Version: CS2

CS2 includes a completely new PDF engine that ships with a range of very usable generic PDF presets (1) and also includes the ability to create, customize and save your own specific PDF output styles or presets (2). A preset is essentially a collection of settings that determine the characteristics of the PDF file that you create.

The presets are used and managed through two new dialogs:

Edit Adobe PDF (Edit > Adobe PDF Presets) – This dialog is used for managing your presets. Here you can copy existing, create new, load supplied, delete old and save modified PDF presets (3).

Save Adobe PDF (File > Save As) – The save dialog is displayed any time that you have elected to output your current file as a PDF. The dialog lists the presets that are currently loaded in Photoshop and also provides the option to alter any specific characteristics via a series of settings tabs (4).

Photoshop ships with the following PDF presets: High Quality Print, Press Quality, Smallest File Size and the industry standard options of PDF/X-1a and PDF/X-1.

Pen pressure

Menu: –
Shortcut: –   **See also:** Brush tool,
Version: 6.0, 7.0, CS, CS2   Graphics Tablet,
Liquify filter

The stylus, or pen, which is used in conjunction with a graphics tablet, has the ability to alter the way a tool functions according to the amount of pressure being applied to the stylus tip. The Brush tool is one such tool in Photoshop that is especially designed to take advantage of this function.

For example, the tool can be set to change the amount of color (opacity) laid down by the brush with the pressure applied to the pen. Light pressure produces lightly colored areas whereas heavy pressure paints with the full strength of the current foreground color.

Using a stylus and graphic tablet, along with Photoshop's pen pressure features and some skillful manipulation of the pen, will enable users to produce very subtle hand-drawn gradient (1) and shading effects.

You can attribute which characteristics are controlled via pen pressure via the various settings in the Brushes palette (2).

Pen tool

Menu:	–	
Shortcut:	P	See also: Paths
Version:	6.0, 7.0, CS, CS2	

Creates a path that can be turned into a selection. It's unusual to use at first, but spend some time getting familiar with it and your drawing and selection skills will improve tenfold.

The Pen Tool icon on the toolbar has several options. The first is Pen Tool which you use to add points, known as anchor points, around the subject. Points are automatically linked to make a path. This is ideal when you want to draw straight lines and smooth curves. You can have as many anchor points as you like and they can be removed by clicking on them.

To draw a straight line, click at a start point then move to the finish point and click again. To complete a straight path click the Pen Tool icon in the toolbox when you reach the end. To complete a round path click on the original start point to complete the shape.

The Freeform Pen Tool is like the normal Lasso Tool and creates a path wherever you draw. It's like using a normal pen and is very accurate, providing you are! Anchor points are added along the path, and their positions can be changed when the path is complete. The Magnetic Pen tool works like the Magnetic Lasso and automatically locates high contrast differences between pixels and lays the path along the edge.

1. When using the Magnetic Pen tool move slowly so the Pen locates the edge you're drawing along.

2. Hold down the Shift key to create a straight line running at a 45° angle.

3. Click the Rubber Band box in the Pen Options palette to see the curve of the path you're about to create as you move the Pen tool.

Pencil tool

Menu:	–	
Shortcut:	B	See also: Brush tool,
Version:	6.0, 7.0, CS, CS2	Auto Erase
		– pencil

The Pencil tool is a pixel-based tool that uses the foreground color to paint with. It works in much the same way as the Brush tool, with the one difference that the pencil can only draw lines that have hard edges.

Freehand lines are drawn by click-dragging the mouse. Straight lines are drawn by holding down the Shift key whilst click-dragging.

The thickness or size (1), mode and opacity of the line can be altered via the tool's options bar. Also any brush that has a hard edge can be selected for use with the Pencil tool from the Brushes Preset palette section of the options bar (2).

Perceptual rendering intent

Menu:	–	
Shortcut:	–	See also: Color management
Version:	6.0, 7.0, CS, CS2	

At various points in the digital photography process it is necessary to change or alter the spread of colors in a picture so that they fit the characteristics of an output device, such as a screen or printer, more fully. Perceptual is one of the four different approaches that Photoshop can use in this conversion process. The other choices are Saturation, Relative Colorimetric and Absolute Colorimetric.

Each approach produces different results and is based on a specific conversion or 'rendering intent'. The **Perceptual** setting puts conversion emphasis on ensuring that the adjusted picture, when viewed on the new output device, appears to the human eye to be very similar to the original photo. So this is a good choice for photo conversions.

The **Saturation** option tries to maintain the strength of colors during the conversion process (even if color accuracy is the cost). The **Relative Colorimetric** setting squashes or stretches the range of colors in the original so that they fit the range of possible colors that the new device can display. The **Absolute Colorimetric** option translates colors exactly from the original photo to the range of colors for the new device. Those colors that can't be displayed are clipped.

Specific Intents can be selected as part of the printing process via the color management controls in the Show More Options section of the Print Preview dialog (1).

Before

After

Perspective, changing

Menu: Filter > Distort > Lens Correction
Shortcut: – **See also:** Perspective options,
Version: CS2   Lens Correction filter,
                          Vanishing Point filter

The new Lens Correction filter in CS2 doesn't just correct Barrel and Pincushion distortion, the filter also contains controls for changing the perspective of the picture. This option is particularly useful for eliminating the problem of converging verticals that plagues pictures photographed with wide angle lenses and the camera pointing upwards.

To correct the problem using the new filter move the Vertical Perspective slider (1) to the left to stretch the details at the top of the photo apart. This change also condenses the lower sections of the picture and in so doing corrects the image.

 Switch on the Grid display and use these lines as a guide when adjusting the picture. Your aim is to align straight and parallel picture parts with the grid lines.

Perspective options

Menu: Edit > Transform > Perspective
Shortcut: – **See also:** Lens Correction
Version: 6.0, 7.0, CS, CS2   filter

Prior to the all conquering Lens Correction filter released in Photoshop CS2 the perspective of a picture was manipulated in one of two ways.

When cropping by selecting the Perspective option (1) in the Crop tool's option bar and then dragging the corner handles to make the adjustment. The option only appears after the cropping marquee has been drawn on the canvas surface.

The second method is to select the object or picture part to adjust and then use the Edit > Transform > Perspective command. Again adjustments are made by dragging the corner handles of the selection (2).

 These options are still one of the best ways for altering the perspective of illustrations or Web graphics but the Lens Correction filter offers more power and control when applying these changes to photographic images.

Photo Filter

Menu: Image > Adjustments > Photo Filter
Shortcut: – **See also:** Color temperature
Version: 6.0, 7.0, CS, CS2

The Photo Filter is one of the enhancement options available from the Image > Adjustments menu. The feature simulates the color changes that are made to a picture when it is photographed through a color correction filter.

The filter contains three controls.

In the Use section (1) you can select the type of filter from the drop-down list provided or create your own by double-clicking the color swatch and selecting a new hue.

The Density slider (2) determines the strength of the filters and the Preserve Luminosity (3) option adjusts the filtered photo to account for the density of the filter with the aim of maintaining the picture's original brightness.

The filter is also available as an adjustment layer.

Photocopy filter

Menu: Filter > Sketch > Photocopy
Shortcut: –   See also: Filters
Version: 6.0, 7.0, CS, CS2

The Photocopy filter, as one of the Sketch group of filters, simulates the look of a picture that has been photocopied several times. The main highlight and shadow areas are represented as light and dark but there is very little middle tone retained in the filtered picture.

The filter contains two slider controls.

The Detail control (1) adjusts the level of original detail that is retained in the picture.

The Darkness slider (2) determines the overall brightness of the result.

The hues of the filtered picture are based on the current foreground and background colors.

Photomerge

Menu: File > Automate > Photomerge
         Bridge: Tools > Photoshop > Photomerge
Shortcut: –   See also: Panoramas
Version: 6.0, 7.0, CS, CS2   – creating

Photomerge (1) is included free within Photoshop and is Adobe's stitching technology that enables photographers to join overlapping photos to create wide-angle pictures.

In this release of Photoshop Photomerge has been updated to include enhanced support for larger file sizes and better fine-tuning controls as well as the ability to produce the final composition as a document with separate layers.

The source files are added to the feature by multi-selecting in the Bridge, being open in the Photoshop at the time of selecting the feature or via the Browse button within the dialog.

Start the Photomerge feature. Click the Browse button in the dialog box. Search for the pictures for your panorama. Click Open to add the files to the Source Files section of the dialog.

Select OK to open the Photomerge main workspace. The feature will automatically position the source files. If need be, click-drag photos to change position or add from the light box (top of window).

With the Snap to Image function turned on, Photomerge will match like details of different images when they are dragged over each other.

Use the Advanced Blending option to smooth out uneven exposure or tonal difference between stitched pictures. Click Preview to see the blending before clicking OK to produce the panorama.

P9

Photoshop format (PSD and PSB)

Menu: –	
Shortcut: –	**See also:** Save As,
Version: 6.0, 7.0, CS, CS2	PDF format

The Photoshop file format (PSD) is the native format of both Photoshop and Photoshop Elements programs. The format is capable of supporting layers, editable text, adjustment layers and millions of colors.

You should choose this format for all manipulation of your photographic images. The format contains no compression features but should still be used to archive complex images with multiple layers and sophisticated selections or paths as other format options remove the ability to edit these characteristics later.

The PSB extension is used for Photoshop documents that are bigger then 2 Gb. In all other respects this file format is the same as PSD.

PICT format

Menu: –	
Shortcut: –	**See also:** Photoshop format,
Version: 6.0, 7.0, CS, CS2	DNG

The PICT file format is an Apple-based picture format that can support both vector- and pixel-based graphics.

The format is widely employed by Mac operators for use in graphics and page layout programs, and is ideal for transferring between the two.

It supports RGB and allows a single Alpha channel, Index colors and Grayscale. Latest versions of the format can even support a color depth of up to 32 bits per pixel.

Picture Package

Menu: File > Automate > Picture Package	
Bridge: Tools > Photoshop > Picture Package	
Shortcut: –	**See also:** Print options,
Version: 6.0, 7.0, CS, CS2	Picture Package –
	customization

The feature allows you to select one of a series of predesigned, multi-print layouts that have been carefully created to fit many images neatly onto a single sheet of standard paper.

You can select the images to include in the feature via the Bridge workspace, opt to use those images that are already open in Photoshop or browse for individual pictures(1). Double-clicking in the layout space will also allow you to choose the image to place in this part of the design and this approach is often the quickest way to work (2).

The preset layout designs for different page sizes can be selected from the Document section for the dialog (3). There are designs that place multiples of the same size pictures together and those that surround one or two larger images with many smaller versions.

The feature provides a preview of the pictures in the layout (2). In the bottom section of the dialog there is an option to add labels to the pictures included in the composition.

Picture Package, customization

Menu: File > Automate > Picture Package	
Bridge: Tools > Photoshop > Picture Package	
Shortcut: –	**See also:** Picture Package
Version: 6.0, 7.0, CS, CS2	

The Picture Package feature is a special layout tool that sizes, rotates and positions a series of images on a single page ready for printing. The pictures can be completely different or copies of the same original.

The CS version of the feature included a layout editor so that you can customize the preset layouts to suit your own needs.

To create your own layout templates press the Edit Layout button at the bottom of the Picture Package dialog. This displays a new dialog that contains a section for inputting the settings for the new layout (1), some input boxes and buttons used to add, size and delete picture zones or boxes (2) and an interactive preview of the zones as they appear on the page (3).

Zones are added by pressing the Add Zone button. They can be sized and positioned by either inputting the dimensions and location in the boxes provided or by click-dragging the boxes (and their sizing handles) in the preview.

Clicking the save buttons adds the newly designed template to the list available in drop-down menu in the Picture Package dialog.

Pin Light blend mode

Menu: –
Shortcut: –　　　　　　　　**See also:** Blend modes
Version: 6.0, 7.0, CS, CS2

The Pin Light blending mode is one of the group of Overlay modes which replaces colors based on the tone of the pixels in the top layer.

If the pixels in the top layer are lighter than 50% gray then all pixels in the bottom layer that are darker are replaced with the upper layer's colors. Pixels lighter than the upper layer are not changed.

If the pixels in the top layer are darker than 50% gray then all pixels in the bottom layer that are lighter are replaced and those darker are left unchanged.

Pinch filter

Menu: Filter > Distort > Pinch
Shortcut: –　　　　　　　　**See also:** Filters
Version: 6.0, 7.0, CS, CS2

The Pinch filter, as one of the Distort group of filters, bloats or squeezes in a picture according to the setting selected.

The filter contains a single slider control, Amount (1), that varies both the strength of the effect and whether the filter bloats or squeezes the picture.

Also included in the dialog is a wire frame representation of the type and strength of the changes (2) and a preview window.

Pixel, aspect ratio

Menu: –
Shortcut: –　　　　　　　　**See also:** –
Version: 6.0, 7.0, CS, CS2

A feature that first appeared in CS that enables either DV or D1 video format files which are composed of rectangular (non-square) pixels to be viewed accurately on screen.

DV is a digital video standard with a 4:3 frame aspect ratio and a screen resolution of either 720×480 (NTSC) or 720×576 (PAL). D1 is also known as CCIR-601 and has a screen resolution of either 720×486 (NTSC) or 720×576 (PAL). If you were to view files created in these formats in a workspace that is based on square pixels the image would look squashed. By selecting the correct non-square format you can view the files as they will appear on a video display or in video editing software such as Premier or Premier Elements.

The range of choices of non-square pixel types has been increased in CS2 and now includes an option for customizing the pixel aspect ratio (1).

The pixel aspect ratio that is being used to view an open document can be changed by selecting a new option from those listed under the Image > Pixel Aspect Ratio menu (1). A similar option is also available in the Advanced section of the New document dialog where it is possible to create a new document with non-square pixels (2).

Pixel dimensions

Menu: –	
Shortcut: –	**See also:** Pixels
Version: 6.0, 7.0, CS, CS2	

Digital files have no real physical dimensions (inches or cm) until they are printed.

The true dimensions of a digital file are based on the picture's width and height in pixels. It is only when the file is printed or displayed on screen that a set number of pixels are used to print a square inch of the photograph that the file has physical dimensions. The pixel dimensions of a photo can be viewed via the Image > Image Size dialog (1).

In previous versions of Photoshop you could also click on the document info area of the image window (Mac) or status bar (Windows) and get a quick glimpse of this info, plus channels and resolution. In CS2 this detail is now displayed as one of the options in the Info palette (2).

Pixels

Menu: –	
Shortcut: –	**See also:** Pixel dimensions
Version: 6.0, 7.0, CS, CS2	

Short for picture element, refers to the smallest image part of a digital photograph. From a distance, or with high resolution pictures, the pixel-based nature of digital photographs is not obvious, but when overly enlarged the blocky structure of the picture becomes noticeable.

Place

Menu: File > Place	
Shortcut: –	**See also:** Vector graphics
Version: 6.0, 7.0, CS, CS2	

The File > Place command is used for importing and creating a new layer for documents created in vector file formats.

In Photoshop you can place PDF (Acrobat files), AI (Illustrator files) and EPS (Encapsulated PostScript files).

After choosing the option (1), select the picture to place from the file browser dialog that appears and then size the graphic by click-dragging the corner handles of the bounding box (2). Complete the placement by double-clicking inside the bounding box, or clicking the tick mark in the options bar, or hitting Enter/Return keys.

During the placing process the vector information is converted to pixels (bitmap).

Plaster filter

Menu: Filter > Sketch > Plaster	
Shortcut: –	**See also:** Filters
Version: 6.0, 7.0, CS, CS2	

The Plaster filter, as one of the Sketch group of filters, colors and shadows broad areas of the photo in textureless shapes. Some picture parts are raised and flattened, the rest is made to look hollow and low lying. The colors in the filtered picture are based on the current foreground and background colors.

The filter contains two slider controls and a drop-down menu for selecting the direction of the light (3) used for creating depth, shadow and highlight effects.

The Image Balance control (1) adjusts the amount of the image that is converted to a raised flat surface and that which is changed to receding areas. The Smoothness slider (2) determines how much detail is retained in the raised areas.

Plastic Wrap filter

Menu: Filter > Artistic > Plastic Wrap	
Shortcut: –	**See also:** Filters
Version: 6.0, 7.0, CS, CS2	

The Plastic Wrap filter, as one of the Artistic group of filters, simulates the look of wrapping the photograph in a sheet of close-fitting plastic or cling film.

The filter contains three controls. The Highlight Strength (1) controls the size, amount and dominance of the highlight areas.

The Detail slider (2) determines how broad the highlight areas are and the Smoothness (3) option adjusts the sharpness of the edge of the highlight.

Plug-in options:

Flaming Pear – *Super Blade Pro*

Effect: This plug-in provides the most sophisticated control over surface and texture characteristics of text and objects available.
OS: Mac, Windows   **Cost:** US$30.00
Website: www.flamingpear.com

Extensis – *Intellihance Pro 4*

Effect: Capable of comparing and applying up to 25 different enhancement options at one time, Intellihance Pro is the master of the quick fix.
OS: Mac, Windows   **Cost:** US$199.00
Website: www.extensis.com

Alien Skin – *Eye Candy 4000*

Effect: Eye Candy 4000 is a collection of 23 different creative filters used for creating effects such as shadows, bevels, chrome, smoke, wood and even fur.
OS: Mac, Windows   **Cost:** US$169.00
Website: www.alienskin.com

Digital Film – *Ozone 2*

Effect: Simulates the same tonal control available when using the film-based Zone System (created by Ansel Adams) with your digital photographs.
OS: Mac, Windows   **Cost:** US$50.00
Website: www.digitalfilmtools.com

Harry's – *Filters 3.0*

Effect: A free collection of filters that can be used for creating up to 69 different imaging effects. Also contains the option to encrypt your photos.
OS: Mac, Windows   **Cost:** FREE
Website: www.thepluginsite.com

Photowiz – *Color Washer*

Effect: The Color Washer plug-in is used for the correction and enhancement of colors in your pictures. Great for restoring faded colors in old photos.
OS: Windows   **Cost:** US$49.95
Website: www.thepluginsite.com

PhotoTune – *20/20 Color MD*

Effect: Using a side-by-side comparison approach this PhotoTune plug-in takes the guesswork out of correcting the colors in your photos.
OS: Mac, Windows   **Cost:** US$49.95
Website: www.phototune.com

AutoFX – *Photo/Graphic Edges*

Effect: Photo/Graphic Edges provides 14 photographic effects that are used to create an astonishing array of edges and borders for your images.
OS: Mac, Windows   **Cost:** US$179.00
Website: www.autofx.com

Before

After

© www.ablestock.com 2005

Plug-ins

Menu: –
Shortcut: –   **See also:** Filters
Version: 6.0, 7.0, CS, CS2

Ever since the early days of Photoshop Adobe has provided the opportunity for third party developers to create small pieces of specialist software that could plug into the program. These extra features extend the capabilities of the program and some of them have become so popular that they find themselves added into the program proper in the next release of the software. Most plug-ins register themselves as extra options in the Filter menu, where they can be accessed just like any other Elements feature.

The Delta100 filter (1) from www.silveroxide.com is a great example of plug-in technology. Designed to reproduce the look of particular types of black and white film stock, the installed filter can be selected from the Silver Oxide group (2) of products in the Filter menu.

Power Retouche – *Black & White Studio*

Effect: This plug-in replicates many of the effects of a traditional darkroom including specific film looks.
OS: Mac, Windows   **Cost:** US$75.00 £45.00
Website: www.powerretouche.com

VanDerLee – *Old Movie*

Effect: Create the look and feel of an old photo or movie frame with this plug-in. Includes controls for film type, scratches, camera, dust, fat and hair.
OS: Windows   **Cost:** US$19.95
Website: www.v-d-l.com

Andromeda – *Shadow Filter*

Effect: Billed as the 'most advanced shadowing plug-in available' this filter really lives up to the hype. Master the controls and any shadows are possible.
OS: Mac, Windows   **Cost:** US$109.00
Website: www.andromeda.com

Richard Roseman – *Vignette Corrector*

Effect: The plug-in removes or adds the darkened edges that are produced by low quality wide-angle lenses.
OS: Windows   **Cost:** Free
Website: www.richardroseman.com

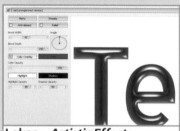

Lokas – *Artistic Effects*

Effect: The Artistic Effects collection is a series of customized filters that add surface effects to text and shapes. The options include gel, ice, metal, smoke and snow.
OS: Windows   **Cost:** US$59.95
Website: www.artistic-effects.com

NIK – *Sharpener Pro Inkjet*

Effect: The range of NIK sharpening plug-ins are designed to sharpen your pictures to clarify output to a variety of print devices.
OS: Mac, Windows   **Cost:** US$79.95
Website: www.nikmultimedia.com

AV Bros – *Puzzle Pro*

Effect: Although at first this seems like a simple jigsaw puzzle maker the ability to customize and add extra shapes really extends the options for this plug-in.
OS: Mac, Windows   **Cost:** US$49.95
Website: www.avbros.com

ASF – *Digital GEM Airbrush*

Effect: Provides glamor photo type results by automatically smoothing skin whilst retaining details in the areas like eyelashes and hair.
OS: Mac, Windows   **Cost:** US$99.95
Website: www.asf.com

Digital Element – *Aurora*

Effect: The Aurora plug-in is an advanced world creator that produces highly sophisticated water, sky and lighting elements.
OS: Mac, Windows   **Cost:** US$199.00
Website: www.digi-element.com

Andrew's Plugins – *V8*

Effect: There is plenty of creative choice here with nearly 20 different plug-in sets providing thousands of different effects and only costing $10.00 each.
OS: Mac, Windows   **Cost:** US$10.00
Website: www.graphicxtras.com

The Imaging Factory – *Convert to B&W*

Effect: Powerful and customizable conversion plug-in designed for the dedicated monochrome enthusiast.
OS: Mac, Windows   **Cost:** US$99.00
Website: www.theimagingfactory.com

PictureCode – *Noise Ninja*

Effect: Noise Ninja is a very sophisticated noise reduction plug-in that works extremely well with photographs taken using high ISO settings.
OS: Mac, Windows   **Cost:** US$44.95
Website: www.picturecode.com

PNG format

Menu: File > Save As
Shortcut: –   **See also:** JPEG format,
Version: 6.0, 7.0, CS, CS2   GIF format

A comparatively new web graphics format that is very flexible and has a lot of great features. Like TIFF and GIF the format uses a lossless compression algorithm that ensures what you put in is what you get out. It also supports partial transparency (unlike GIF's transparency off/on system) and color depths ups to 64 bit. Add to this the built-in color and gamma correction features and you start to see why this format is a popular choice with web producers.

Images can be saved in this format using the File > Save As command or the File > Save for Web feature.

Pointers

Menu: –
Shortcut: –   **See also:** Cursors – tool
Version: 6.0, 7.0, CS, CS2   pointer

The terms pointers and mouse cursors are often used interchangeably to represent the shape or icon that is displayed on screen at the mouse position.

The default pointer styles for different tools can be selected from the Edit > Preferences > Displays & Cursors dialog (1).

• •

Pointillize filter

Menu: Filter > Pixelate > Pointillize
Shortcut: –   **See also:** Filters
Version: 6.0, 7.0, CS, CS2

The Pointillize filter, as one of the Pixelate group of filters, recreates the picture in a series of colored dots on a background the color of the current background color. The end result simulates the look of a pointillist painting.

The filter contains a single slider control, Cell Size (1), that varies the size of the dots used to create the effect.

Points, type size

Menu: –
Shortcut: –   **See also:** Type
Version: 6.0, 7.0, CS, CS2

The size of the text you place in your image files can be measured as pixels, millimeters or points.

Most photographers find the pixel setting most useful when working with digital files, as it indicates to me the precise size of the text in relationship to the whole image.

Millimeter and points values, on the other hand, vary depending on the resolution of the picture and the resolution of the output device.

It is true that there are approximately 72 points to 1 inch, but this only remains true if the picture's resolution is 72 dpi. At higher resolutions the pixels are packed more closely together and therefore the same 72 point type is displayed smaller in size.

The default unit of measurement for type in Photoshop can be altered in the Edit > Preferences > Units & Rulers dialog (1).

P

160

Polygonal Lasso tool

Menu: –
Shortcut: L
Version: 6.0, 7.0, CS, CS2

See also: Lasso tools,
Magnetic Lasso
tool

The Polygonal Lasso is one of three Lasso tools available in Photoshop.

Lasso tools make selections by drawing a marquee around the picture part to be selected. Unlike the other options the Polygonal Lasso draws in straight lines and is particularly good at selecting regular-shaped objects.

To start a new selection choose the tool from the toolbar and click on the canvas at the picture part that will mark the beginning of the selection marquee. Now move the tool to a new position and notice that the marquee line stretches out from the first click position to follow the cursor. Move the cursor around until the stretched marquee aligns itself with the edge of the picture you are selecting and then click again. This marks another anchor point for the lasso line. Continue around the area to be selected, clicking the mouse at points where you wish to change direction until you reach your starting point, where you can double-click the tool to join up the two ends of the selection.

Pop-up palettes

Menu: –
Shortcut: –
Version: 6.0, 7.0, CS, CS2

See also: Options bar

Pop-up palettes are located in the options bar of selected tools in the Photoshop workspace. The palette is displayed or 'popped up' by clicking the down-arrow (1) on the right of the preview thumbnail of the current selected option. The example shows the brush options bar with the pop-up palette displayed containing a library of preset brush shapes. Pop-up palettes are also available with the gradient, swatch, patterns, layer styles and custom shapes tools.

Unlike normal palettes, they are not meant to persist and they disappear from view when you click off them or hit Enter/Return.

Poster Edges filter

Menu: Filter > Artistic > Poster Edges
Shortcut: –
Version: 6.0, 7.0, CS, CS2

See also: Filters

The Poster Edges filter, as one of the Artistic group of filters, posterizes the colors in a picture whilst surrounding the edges with a dark border. The filter also adds some simple stippled shading to the picture.

The filter contains three controls. The Edge Thickness setting (1) adjusts the weight of the line and the heaviness of the shading.

The Edge Intensity slider (2) controls the darkness of the border and shading, and the Posterization setting (3) alters the number of colors used in the final result.

Posterize adjustment layer

Menu: Layer > New Adjustment Layer > Posterize
Shortcut: –   **See also:** Posterize filter,
Version: 6.0, 7.0, CS, CS2   Adjustment layers

The Posterize adjustment layer produces the same effect as the Posterize filter but adds the benefits of maintaining the original picture and being able to edit the Posterize settings at a later date.

· · · · · · · · · · · · · · · · · ·

Posterize filter

Menu: Filter > Adjustments > Posterize
Shortcut: –   **See also:** Filters, Posterize
Version: 6.0, 7.0, CS, CS2   adjustment layer

The Posterize filter, as one of the Adjustments group of filters, reduces the total number of colors in an image by letting you set the number of brightness levels per channel.

A setting of 3 will produce three levels of tone for each of the red, green and blue channels, giving a nine-color result.

Preferences, Photoshop

Menu: Edit > Preferences
Shortcut: Ctrl/Cmd K   **See also:** Preferences
Version: 6.0, 7.0, CS, CS2   – Bridge

The Preferences dialog for the Photoshop workspace contains a range of settings that control the way that the program looks, displays pictures and processes your files. The settings are grouped in nine separate but housed together dialogs. When the Preferences option (1) is selected from the Edit menu the General dialog is displayed first with the other options accessed via the Next and Previous buttons (or by selecting the precise dialog from the Preferences menu). Each Preferences dialog is displayed below and on the facing page.

Grid – Settings for the spacing, style and color of the grid, guide and slice lines that are displayed via the options in the View menu.

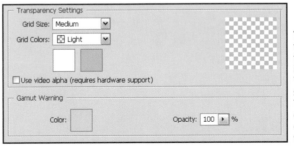

Transparency – Options to alter the way that the transparent part of image layers is displayed. You can change the grid size and the colors used. This section also contains options for the color and opacity of the gamut warning.

P9

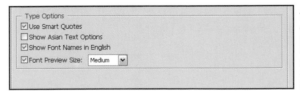

Type – The settings here govern text options in Photoshop including the language that the font names are displayed in and the size of the font preview.

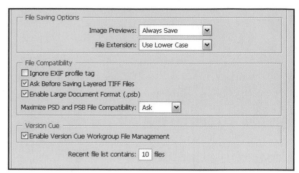

Plug-Ins & Scratch Disks – Sets the location of the virtual memory or scratch disks that Photoshop uses when it runs out of RAM memory whilst processing your files. Make sure that the system drive is not selected as a scratch disk location as most operating systems run their own disk-based memory system on these drives. Also included here is the ability to identify an additional plug-ins folder. This plug-ins location is separate and extra to the default/Photoshop/Plug-Ins/directory.

General – The General options here control the day-to-day functioning of Photoshop. The most important settings are the number of History States (high values really chew up memory resources), the UI font size, Save Palette Locations, Show Tool Tips, if and where to save a History Log and the default image interpolation method but the specifics of your setup will depend largely on the way that you prefer to work.

Memory & Image Cache – Use the Memory Usage setting here to ensure that as much RAM as possible is allocated exclusively to Photoshop. In this example, other programs will be run alongside Photoshop so 55% of the total RAM is earmarked for the program, but more memory would mean faster processing.

File Handling – Preferences for ensuring that an image preview is always stored with newly saved files and that all file extensions added are in the same case (upper or lower). Other options include the number of files in the File > Open Recently Edited list and ensuring compatibility of PSD and PSB file formats.

Units & Rulers – Use the settings in this dialog to alter the base units of measurement for rulers, type and print sizes that are displayed throughout the program. Though these preferences set the global units for all dialogs and tools in Photoshop, most features also contain drop-down menus that allow on-the-fly changes to units of measure. Default column sizes and gutters along with resolution settings for new documents are also stored in this location.

Display & Cursors – Use this dialog to alter the default cursor or tool pointers used for painting, drawing and selection tools. Selecting the Use Pixel Doubling option speeds up the display of the results of editing changes by temporarily halving the resolution of the photo.

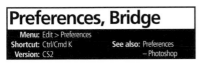

Preferences, Bridge

Menu: Edit > Preferences
Shortcut: Ctrl/Cmd K **See also:** Preferences
Version: CS2 – Photoshop

As the Bridge application is a completely separate entity and sits apart from Photoshop CS2 (and the other Creative Suite applications) it contains its own set of preferences that control the way the program behaves.

General – Settings for the general display options used for the browser workspace and specifically for thumbnails and the metadata that is shown with the pictures.

Adobe Stock Photos – Options that control the management of stock photos from inside Bridge. This includes storing and billing details and the settings used for the purchase process.

Advanced – This section is used to adjust the settings for the thumbnail cache that speeds up the Bridge display process as well as number of Recently Visited Folders, Double-click actions and the maximum file size of images that will be displayed.

File Type Associations – This is a central location for controlling the file types that are associated with different programs.

Metadata – Use this dialog to adjust the type of metadata that is displayed for a given photo. The Hide Empty Fields option keeps empty data types from being displayed.

Labels – Change the label names (not their colors) and the shortcut keys used to attach them using the settings in this section.

Preserve Transparency

Menu: –
Shortcut: – **See also:** Lock Options
Version: 6.0, 7.0, CS, CS2

The preserve transparency option in features like Fill Layer (1) shields the transparent area of a layer from any editing or enhancement changes.

An alternative to selecting this option when using a tool is to lock the layer's transparency in the Layers palette.

• •

Preset Manager

Menu: Edit > Preset Manager
Shortcut: – **See also:** Brush tool,
Version: 6.0, 7.0, CS, CS2 Swatches palette

The Edit > Preset Manager is a central location for the organization, saving and loading of Photoshop resources (or Preset Libraries) such as brushes, swatches, gradients, styles, contours, custom shapes, tools and patterns (1) used in the Editor.

The side-arrow button (top right of the dialog) displays a pop-up palette with view choices and extra resource libraries.

The dialog also provides the ability to load, save, rename and delete individual resource items (e.g. brushes) or whole libraries (e.g. Faux Finish Brushes). Extra resources libraries downloaded from the web can be loaded and managed from this dialog.

163

P•Q

Print Online

Menu: File > Print Online
Bridge: Tools > Photoshop Services > Photo Prints
Shortcut: –   **See also:** Print options
Version: CS2

New for CS2 is the ability to print and share images online from inside Photoshop and Bridge.

These features are made possible by the new Photoshop Services technology which seamlessly links your desktop to an external online provider such as KodakGallery.com (formerly ofoto.com).

After an initial registration process is completed Photoshop users can upload copies of their favorite images to the company's site and have them photographically printed in a range of sizes (3). The finished prints are sent to you via the mail.

This print option is available either from within Photoshop by selecting File > Print Online (1) or by choosing the Photoshop Services option from the Tools menu in Bridge (2).

Print options

Menu: File > Print
File > Print with Preview
File > Page Setup
Shortcut: Ctrl/Cmd P   **See also:** Print Online,
Ctrl/Cmd Alt/Opt P   Print One Copy
Ctrl/Cmd Shft P
Version: 6.0, 7.0, CS, CS2

When printing in Photoshop you have five choices that you can select (1) from the file menu. The Print One Copy and Print Online options are new for CS2.

Print One Copy bypasses all print settings dialogs and outputs a print using the current default settings for page and printer.

Print Online links to an internet print provider giving the user the option of uploading and printing using this third party.

The other three options containing all the Photoshop print settings.

The **Print with Preview** dialog (2) is the first stop for most users. Here you can interactively scale your image to fit the page size currently selected for your printer. By deselecting the Center Image option and ticking the Show Bounding Box feature, it is possible to 'click and drag' the image to a new position on the page surface. Pressing the More Options button provides further settings for color management and output control.

The **Page Setup** dialog contains the settings for the printer, such as paper type, size and orientation, printing resolution and color control, or enhancement.

The **Print** option (3) takes you directly to the control for your printing hardware. Only use this command if you are sure that the paper orientation and print size are correctly set. If in doubt use the Print with Preview option instead.

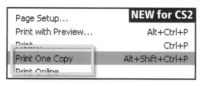

Print One copy

Menu: File > Print One Copy
Shortcut: Ctrl/Cmd Alt/Opt Shft P   **See also:** Print options
Version: CS2

The File > Print One Copy option is a one button express print feature that bypasses all print dialogs and simply outputs the current picture to the default printer using the saved settings.

Print resolution

Menu: –
Shortcut: –   **See also:** Curves, Shadow/
Version: 6.0, 7.0, CS, CS2   Highlight

The number of dots along the length and width of a print, measured in dots per inch.

Generally the more dots per inch the higher the resolution. Most inkjet printers print out at between 600 dpi and 1440 dpi, but these are slightly misleading as the figures allow for between three and six ink color droplets which are used to make up each dot.

A 1440 dpi printer that uses six individual ink colors actually means the print resolution is more like 240 dpi. The highest true resolution is around 400 dpi for dye-sub printers and most books and magazines print at around 300 dpi.

Print Space

Menu: File > Print with Preview
Shortcut: Ctrl/Cmd Alt/Opt P   **See also:** Image Space –
Version: 7.0, CS, CS2   color management

The Print Space refers to an ICC profile that has been specially created to characterize they way that your printer works.

Generally printer companies supply profiles with their hardware. The installation programs that provide drivers for the printers also install the Print Space profiles into the main system color folder. From here the profiles can be accessed by a range of programs including Photoshop.

When Photoshop is aware of the Print Space it can more easily translate the picture's tones and colors to suit the abilities of the printer.

To ensure that Photoshop uses your printer's profile select the More Options button (1) of the Print with Preview dialog and then choose Color Management from the drop-down menu at the top of the newly displayed section (2).

From the Color Handling menu choose the Let Photoshop Determine Colors and then select the profile from the Printer Profile drop-down menu (3).

Profile to profile conversions

Menu: Edit > Assign Profile
           Edit > Convert to Profile
Shortcut: –   **See also:** Color Settings
Version: 6.0, 7.0, CS, CS2   ICC profiles

Photoshop provides two different options for altering, removing or converting the color profiles that are attached to photographs – Assign Profile and Convert to Profile (1) located in the Edit menu.

Assign Profile – This option maps the color numbers (without changing them) directly to the newly selected color space. Using this approach you may notice color shift in the picture as it changes from one profile to the other. The Assign Profile dialog provides three choices (2):

1. Don't Color Manage This Document which removes the existing ICC profile and leaves the document untagged,

2. Working Space tags the photo with the current working space profile, and

3. Profile is used to tag the picture with the selected color space without converting the colors or the underlying numbers.

Convert to Profile – Changes the actual or original color numbers of the picture before mapping them to the new profile space. The Change to Profile dialog (3) contains settings for selecting the destination space as well as the conversion options used in the mapping process.

Progressive JPEG

Menu: File > Save As (JPEG)
Shortcut: Shft Ctrl/Cmd S   **See also:** JPEG format
Version: 6.0, 7.0, CS, CS2

Selecting the Progressive option (1) in the Save for Web dialog, or Save As JPEG feature creates a JPEG file that downloads in several separate passes rather than line by line. The initial pass displays a coarse blurry image which sharpens and becomes clearer with each successive pass.

Proof Colors

Menu: View > Proof Colors
Shortcut: Ctrl/Cmd Y   See also: Proof Setup
Version: 6.0, 7.0, CS, CS2

The View > Proof Colors command simulates how the current document will appear when output using the settings in the Proof Setup.

Using this feature you can preview how a picture will look after printing or displaying on a range of devices.

• •

Proof Setup

Menu: View > Proof Setup
Shortcut: –   See also: Proof Colors
Version: 6.0, 7.0, CS, CS2

Lets you view the image on the monitor as it will appear when reproduced on a specific output device. This is known as soft-proofing and saves you printing a hard copy of your document to preview how the colors will look.

Select the space to be proofed from the menu (1) or create a specific proofing option via the Custom selection (2) and its associated dialog.

It is only any use when you have calibrated your monitor and also have an ICC profile installed for the device you are proofing.

PSB format

Menu: File > Save As
Shortcut: Ctrl/Cmd Shft S   See also: Photoshop format
Version: CS, CS2

PSB is a format for huge documents that was introduced in CS (1). It is designed to get around the file size limitations of Photoshop's native PSD format.

In the same way PSD stands for Photoshop Document format PSB is short for Photoshop Big document. The format allows you to work on files with up to 300,000 pixels in any dimension.

When creating documents larger than 30,000 pixels in either dimension or bigger than 2 Gb Photoshop displays a compatibility warning dialog and automatically uses the PSB format.

Purge

Menu: Edit > Purge
Shortcut: –   See also: Memory
Version: 6.0, 7.0, CS, CS2

The Purge command frees up Photoshop's memory from storing temporary items such as copies of pictures stored in the clipboard, the record of changes made to the image kept for use by the Edit > Undo command and the History palette.

You'd use the Purge command when the computer is starting to run slowly or can't finish an action due to a lack of memory.

Several options are available from the Purge drop-down menu including Undo, Clipboard, History and All (all stored items).

Before

After

Quadtones

Menu: Image > Mode > Duotone
Shortcut: –   **See also:** Duotone
Version: 6.0, 7.0, CS, CS2

Quadtones, like Duotones and Tritones, are grayscale images that use process or Pantone colors to give a subtle color tint to monochrome pictures.

The results are almost like the sepia, blue and gold toning of the conventional darkroom but with much more control and repeatability.

Photoshop has a selection of preset Quadtones in the Duotone folder found in the Preset folder.

· ·

To mask an area start by selecting the Quick Mask mode button at the bottom of the toolbox. The foreground and background colors will automatically change to black and white.

Select the Paintbrush tool and paint out the area that you want to be shielded from changes. The area you brush will be colored semi-transparent red to indicate the mask.

Quick Mask mode

Menu: –
Shortcut: Q   **See also:** Masks
Version: 6.0, 7.0, CS, CS2

The Quick Mask mode is a great way for isolating areas that you don't want to be altered with editing and enhancement activities. Enter this mode by clicking on the icon near the bottom of the toolbar (1). It's a quick way to create a mask around a section. The mask can be increased using one of the Painting tools or decreased using the Eraser.

When you've made all your adjustments to the mask, click the off icon at the base of the toolbar to return to the standard editing mode and a selection will appear on the edges where the mask meets the unmasked area.

Switch back to the Standard Mode (selection mode) by clicking the button at the bottom of the toolbox (2). The non-masked areas will now be selected ready for adjustments.

Use the Eraser tool to remove any overpainting of the mask edges.

Switch back to the Standard Mode (selection mode) by clicking the button at the bottom of the toolbox. The non-masked areas will now be selected ready for adjustments.

167

PQ

Radial Blur filter

Menu: Filter > Blur Radial Blur
Shortcut: –   See also: Filters
Version: 6.0, 7.0, CS, CS2

The Radial Blur filter, as one of the group of Blur filters, applies a directional blur to pictures to simulate either spinning or zooming the camera whilst the picture is being taken.

The dialog contains four controls. The Amount slider (1) determines the strength of the effect or the level of blur in the final result.

The Blur Method options (2) allow the user to select between Spin (5) or Zoom (6) type blurs.

The Quality options (3) determine the length of time taken to apply the effect and the level of quality in the final result. The Draft setting produces rough results quickly whereas the Best option creates a higher quality end product but takes more time.

The Blur Center preview (4) not only provides a wire frame preview of the settings, but allows the user to reposition the center of the blur.

Radial Gradient tool

Menu: –
Shortcut: G   See also: Gradients
Version: 6.0, 7.0, CS, CS2

Photoshop has five different gradient types. All the options gradually change color and tone from one point in the picture to another.

The Radial Gradient (1) changes color from the center of a circle outwards.

To create a gradient start by selecting the tool and the Radial Gradient type (2). Then adjust the controls in the options palette.

Choose the colors from the Gradient Picker and then click and drag the mouse pointer on the canvas surface to stretch out a line that marks the start and end points of the gradient. Release the button to fill the layer with the selected gradient.

• •

Raster image

Menu: –
Shortcut: –   See also: Bitmap image,
Version: 6.0, 7.0, CS, CS2   Vector graphics

A Raster image is one that is created from a grid of pixels. Each pixel represents the color and tone of the area sampled from the original scene.

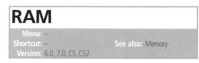

RAM

Menu:	–	
Shortcut:	–	See also: Memory
Version:	6.0, 7.0, CS, CS2	

RAM is short for Random Access Memory which is the part of the computer that runs programs. Photoshop CS2 needs a minimum of 192 Mb to run, 256 Mb for anything more than basic manipulation and as much as you can install in your machine to do complex multi-layer picture editing of large files.

Most computers can be upgraded and RAM, while fragile, is comparatively easy to install. Installing more RAM is a surefire method for increasing the efficiency of your machine when it is running Photoshop.

Photoshop CS2 can now address up to 3.5 Gb of RAM on Windows machines and 4 Gb on Mac systems both of which need to be running 64-bit hardware in conjunction with a 64-bit enabled operating system.

• •

Rasterizing

Menu:	–	
Shortcut:	–	See also: Bitmap image,
Version:	6.0, 7.0, CS, CS2	Vector image

Rasterizing is the process by which vector-based graphics, such as shapes, text, solid color layers, patterns and gradients are converted to pixel-based pictures.

Converting a layer containing vector graphics to bitmap artwork is a necessary step if any of the filters are to be applied to the layer's content or if you want to edit the layer using the painting tools. The vector contents in Illustrator (.AI, .EPS) or Acrobat (.PDF) files are also rasterized when opened in Photoshop. However, vector art that is embedded as a Smart Object in CS2 maintains its vector base and can be edited at any time with Illustrator CS2.

Rate files

Menu:	Bridge: Label	
Shortcut:	Ctrl/Cmd 0-5	See also: Label files – Bridge
Version:	CS2	

The rating system is a Bridge feature that allows users to attribute a set number of stars (1–5) individually to photographs and then use this rating as a basis for searches and filtering which thumbnails are displayed in the workspace.

Ratings can be applied in Bridge (1) by selecting the thumbnail and then choosing a rating level from the Label menu or by using the associated shortcut keys. Ratings can also be attached to pictures in Camera Raw (2).

To form a search based on a rating level select the Edit > Find feature and choose Rating, equal to, greater than, less than and the star value as the criteria (4).

Filter the current view based on ratings values, click the filtering button at the top right of the bridge window and select the filter option to suit (3).

Raw file camera support

Menu:	–	
Shortcut:	–	See also: Raw files
Version:	CS2	

The Adobe Camera Raw feature supports a range of Raw file formats. The current version of the feature is compatible with models from the following manufacturers:

• Canon
• Contax
• Fujifilm
• Kodak
• Konica Minolta
• Leaf
• Leica
• Nikon
• Olympus
• Panasonic
• Pentax
• Sigma
• Sony

Select All

Synchronize...

DSC_0006.NEF

DSC_0012.NEF

Raw file editor, Camera Raw

Menu: File > Open, Bridge: File > Open in Camera Raw
Shortcut: Bridge: Ctrl/Cmd R   **See also:** Raw files
Version: CS, CS2

Photoshop CS was the first version of the program to have a full featured Raw editor built into the program. Called Camera Raw the feature was designed specifically to allow you to take the unprocessed Raw data directly from your camera's sensor and convert it into a usable image file format. Camera Raw also provides access to several image characteristics that would otherwise be locked into the file format.

Variables such as color depth, white balance mode, image sharpness and tonal compensation (contrast and brightness) can all be accessed, edited and enhanced as a part of the conversion process (3). Performing this type of editing on the full high-bit, Raw data provides a better and higher quality result than attempting these changes after the file has been processed and saved in a non-Raw format such as TIFF or JPEG.

When you open a Raw camera file in Photoshop you are presented with the Camera Raw editing dialog containing a full color, interpolated preview (1) of the data captured by the sensor. Using a variety of menu options, dialogs and image tools you will be able to interactively adjust image data factors such as tonal distribution and color saturation. Many of these changes can be made with familiar slider-controlled editing tools normally found in features like Levels and the Shadows/Highlights control (3). The results of your editing can be reviewed immediately via the live preview image and

associated histogram graphs (2). After these general image-editing steps have taken place you can apply some enhancement changes such as filtering for sharpness, removing color noise and applying smoothing (4).

The final phase of the process involves selecting the color depth, image size and image orientation (5). Clicking the OK button sets the program into action, applying your changes to the Raw file, whilst at the same time interpolating the picture (Bayer) data to create a full color image and then opening the processed file into the full Photoshop workspace.

Highlight clipping

Shadow clipping

The integrated Highlight and Shadow clipping warnings (6) in the Raw editor provide visual cues when dark pixel details are being converted to pure black (blue) or delicate highlights are being clipped to pure white (red). Make sure that these settings are on before starting to edit.

Raw file multi-processing

Menu: Bridge: File > Open with Camera Raw
Shortcut: Ctrl/Cmd R   **See also:** Camera Raw
Version: CS2

The new version of Camera Raw that is included in both Bridge and Photoshop CS2 is capable of processing multiple Raw files at the same time or even whilst continuing editing work in Photoshop.

Multiple thumbnails can be selected from the Bridge workspace and then the Open with Camera Raw option selected from the File menu. The feature will then display the pictures in film strip mode with the selected photos listed down the left side of the dialog (1). Conversion settings can be applied to each file in turn choosing to Save, apply (Done) or Open the pictures. Alternatively, with all the photos selected you can apply the changes to one picture and then Synchronize them to all files (2).

Unprocessed Raw file

After Raw processing

Camera Data
(f-stop, shutter speed, ISO, camera
exposure mode, focusing distance etc)

Image Data
(white balance, sharpening,
colour mode, tonal compensation)

Image
(full 16 or 12bit colour and tone)

Raw files

Menu: –	
Shortcut: –	See also: Camera Raw,
Version: CS, CS2	Raw file editor

More and more medium- to high-end cameras are being released with the added feature of being able to capture and save your pictures in Raw format.

Selecting the Raw format stops the camera from processing the color separated (primary) data from the sensor and reducing the image's bit depth, and saves the picture in this unprocessed file type.

This means that the full description of what the camera 'saw' is saved in the picture file and is available to you for use in the production of quality pictures.

Many photographers call this type of file a 'digital negative' as it has a broader dynamic range, extra colors and the ability to correct slightly inaccurate exposures.

So what is in a Raw file?

To help consolidate these ideas in your mind try thinking of a Raw file as having three distinct parts:

Camera Data, usually called the EXIF data. Including things such as camera model, shutter speed and aperture details, most of which cannot be changed.

Image Data which, though recorded by the camera, can be changed in a Raw editor and the settings chosen here directly affect how the picture will be processed. Changeable options include color mode, white balance, saturation, distribution of image tones and application of sharpness.

The **Image** itself. This is the data drawn directly from the sensor sites in your camera in a non-interpolated form (Bayer pattern form). For most Raw cameras, this image data is supplied with a 16-bit color depth (12-bit for some cameras) providing substantially more colors and tones to play with when editing and enhancing than found in a standard 8-bit JPEG or TIFF camera file.

Advantages of Shooting Raw

- You get to use the full tonal and color range that was captured by the camera.

- You can remove many of the file processing decisions from the camera to the desktop where more time and care can be taken in their execution. This includes

  – White balance changes
  – Tonal adjustments
  – Applying sharpness
  – Manipulating saturation
  – Color mode switches

- You create and save the most comprehensive digital picture file – 'digital negative' – currently available.

- You can make image data changes such as switching white balance settings without image loss. This is not possible with non-Raw formats as the white balance results are fixed in the processed file.

- You can 'upscale' using primary image data (straight from the sensor) rather than pre-processed information which arguably leads to better results.

Disadvantages

- Bigger file sizes to store on you camera's memory card.

- Having to process the images before use in Photoshop proper.

R

Read Watermark

Menu: Filter > Digimarc > Read Watermark	
Shortcut: –	See also: Watermarks
Version: 6.0, 7.0, CS, CS2	

To check to see if a picture you are editing is watermarked, select Filter > Digimarc > Read Watermark (1).

Marked pictures will then display a pop-up dialog (2) with author's details and a linked website where further details of use can be obtained.

Before

After

172

Reconstruct tool, Liquify filter

Menu: Filter > Liquify
Shortcut: –   **See also:** Liquify filter, Filters
Version: 6.0, 7.0, CS, CS2

Whilst working inside the Liquify filter dialog it is possible to selectively reverse any changes made to the photo by applying the Reconstruct tool.

When applied to the surface of the image the distorted picture parts are gradually altered back to their original state.

Like the other tool options in the filter, the size of the area affected by the tool is based on the Brush Size setting and the strength of the change is determined by the Brush Pressure value.

R

Rectangle Tool	U
Rounded Rectangle Tool	U
Ellipse Tool	U
Polygon Tool	U
Line Tool	U
Custom Shape Tool	U

Rectangle shape tool

Menu: –
Shortcut: U   **See also:** Shape tools
Version: 6.0, 7.0, CS, CS2

One of the vector-based shapes that you draw on the page.

The shape fills with the foreground color and can be resized to suit the job you're doing.

It appears on a new layer and has an adjustment icon where you can change its color. These can also be used to mask individual image layers.

Other shape tools include Rounded rectangle, Ellipse, Polygon, Line and Custom shape.

In the example a layer effect has been applied which then affects any shape that's added to the canvas.

Rectangular Marquee

Menu: –
Shortcut: M   **See also:** Elliptical Marquee
Version: 6.0, 7.0, CS, CS2

By clicking and dragging the Rectangular Marquee tool on the picture surface, it is possible to draw rectangle or box selections (1).

Holding down the Shift key whilst using this tool restricts the selection to square shapes (2), whereas using the Alt (Windows) or Options (Mac) keys will draw the selections from their centers.

Before   **NEW for CS2**

After

Spot Healing Brush Tool	J
Healing Brush Tool	J
Patch Tool	J
Red Eye Tool	J

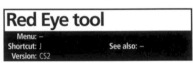

Red Eye tool

Menu: –
Shortcut: J   **See also:** –
Version: CS2

The new Red Eye tool is designed to quickly and easily rectify the problem of red eye by switching the red hue with a more natural black color.

The feature is very easy to use. Simply select the tool and adjust the Pupil Size and Darken Amount settings in the tool's option bar and then click in the center of the pupil. Photoshop automatically locates the red hue and changes for black.

Before

NEW for CS2

After

Mode: Nor

② Reflected Gradient

Adobe Photoshop

e Edit Image Layer Select Filter View Wir

Redo Type Tool   Ctrl+Z

Step Forward   Shift+Ctrl+Z

Step Backward   Alt+Ctrl+Z

Redo

Menu: Edit > Redo (Previous step)
Shortcut: Ctrl/Cmd Z   **See also:** Undo
Version: 6.0, 7.0, CS, CS2

The Redo command performs the action that was last reversed by the Undo command.

Located under the Edit menu, the actual Redo entry changes depending on the nature of the last action that was undone.

If the Undo command hasn't been used then the Redo option is unavailable (grayed out).

Reduce noise

Menu: Filter > Noise > Reduce Noise
Shortcut: –   **See also:** Dust & Scratches filter,
Version: CS2   JPEG artifact removal

To help combat the noisy (spotty) photos produced when using the high ISO setting on many cameras the Adobe engineers included a new Noise Reduction filter in Photoshop CS2.

The feature includes a preview window and in Basic mode a Strength slider (1), a Preserve Details control (2), a Reduce Color Noise slider (3) and a Sharpen Details slider (4). As is the case with the Dust & Scratches filter, you need to be careful when using this filter to ensure that you balance removing noise whilst also retaining detail.

The best way to guarantee this is to set your Strength setting first, ensuring that you check the results in highlights, midtone and shadow areas. Next gradually increase the Preserve Details value until you reach the point where the level of noise that is being reintroduced into the picture is noticeable and then back off the control slightly (make the setting a lower number). For photographs with a high level of color noise (random speckles of color in an area that should be a smooth flat tone) you will need to adjust this slider at the same time as you are playing with the Strength control.

In the advanced mode (5) Strength and Preserved Details controls can be applied per Red, Green and Blue channel with the dialog displaying grayscale previews of the grain in each channel.

The feature also contains a JPEG artifact removal setting (6) that smooths out the box-like patterning that can occur when photos are highly compressed.

Reflected Gradient tool

Menu: –
Shortcut: G   **See also:** Gradients
Version: 6.0, 7.0, CS, CS2

Photoshop has five different gradient types. All the options gradually change color and tone from one point in the picture to another.

The Reflected Gradient (1) changes color along a drawn line from the start to finish point and then reflects the same linear gradient on the opposite side of the starting point.

To create a gradient start by selecting the tool and the Reflected Gradient type (2). Then adjust the controls in the options palette. Choose the colors from the Gradient Picker and then click and drag the mouse pointer on the canvas surface to stretch out a line that marks the start and end points of the gradient. Release the button to fill the layer with the selected gradient.

Overall | Per Channel

Channel: Red
Strength: 8
Preserve Details: 9 %

① Strength: 10
② Preserve Details: 19 %
③ Reduce Color Noise: 83 %
④ Sharpen Details: 11 %
☐ Remove JPEG Artifact ⑥

Before

After

Before

After

174

R

Reflection tool, Liquify filter

Menu: Filter > Distort > Liquify
Shortcut: –   **See also:** Liquify filter
Version: 6.0, 7.0, CS, CS2

The Reflection tool paints mirrored pixels as it is dragged across the surface of the photo. The direction in which the tool is applied determines which pixels are mirrored.

When the brush head is moved downwards the pixels on the left are mirrored into the painted area. Moving the brush upwards mirrors the pixels on the right. Painting from right to left mirrors the top pixels and from left to right the bottom ones.

Like the other Liquify tools, the size of the area affected by the tool is based on the Brush Size setting and the strength of the change is determined by the Brush Pressure value.

Relative Colorimetric rendering intent

Menu: –
Shortcut: –   **See also:** Saturation rendering
Version: 6.0, 7.0, CS, CS2   intent

At various points in the digital photography process it is necessary to change or alter the spread of colors in a picture so that they fit the characteristics of an output device, such as a screen or printer, more fully. Relative Colorimetric is one of the four different approaches that Photoshop can use in this conversion process. The other choices are Perceptual, Saturation and Absolute Colorimetric.

Each approach produces different results and is based on a specific conversion or 'rendering intent'. The **Relative Colorimetric** setting squashes or stretches the range of colors in the original so that they fit the range of possible colors that the new device can display or print.

The **Saturation** option tries to maintain the strength of colors during the conversion process (even if color accuracy is the cost). The **Perceptual** setting puts conversion emphasis on ensuring that the adjusted picture, when viewed on the new output device, appears to the human eye to be very similar to the original photo. The **Absolute Colorimetric** option translates colors exactly from the original photo to the range of colors for the new device. Those colors that can't be displayed are clipped.

Specific Intents can be selected as part of the printing process via the color management controls in the Show More Options section of the Print Preview dialog (1).

Remove all color, Desaturate

Menu: Image > Adjustment > Desaturate
Shortcut: Shft Ctrl/Cmd U   **See also:** Hue/Saturation
Version: 6.0, 7.0, CS, CS2

The Desaturate feature erases all traces of color from the picture, just leaving the detail and tone.

The final result is a grayscale image which is still stored in an RGB Color mode. This is handy as it allows you to hand-color or tone the picture whereas color pictures that are converted to the grayscale mode need re-converting back to RGB Color before this type of enhancement can occur.

The feature produces the same result as dragging the Saturation slider in the Hue/Saturation control all the way to the left (1).

Rename a layer

Menu: –	
Shortcut: –	**See also:** Layers
Version: 6.0, 7.0, CS, CS2	

The title, or name, of a layer can be changed from the default assigned by the Photoshop program by double-clicking the layer's name in the Layers palette (1). The new layer name is typed directly into the Layers palette (2).

As your Photoshop compositions become more and more complex, careful naming of layers when they are created will make for easier navigation and editing of the many picture parts.

Background layers cannot be renamed unless they are converted to a standard image layer first.

New blank layers created via the Layer > New > Layer route can be named in the New Layer dialog as part of the creation process (3).

Rename, Batch

Menu: Bridge: Tools > Batch Rename	
Shortcut: Ctrl/Cmd Shft R	**See also:** –
Version: CS2	

The Batch Rename feature located in Bridge allows the user to rename a selected group files in a single action.

The files to be renamed need to be multi-selected first before choosing Batch Rename from the Tools menu (1). Next the Batch Rename dialog is displayed where the destination folder (2), file naming (3) and format compatibility options (4) are set. Then to start the renaming process press the OK button.

Replace Color

Menu: Image > Adjustments > Replace Color	
Shortcut: –	**See also:** Paint Bucket tool
Version: 6.0, 7.0, CS, CS2	

The Replace Color feature is designed to carefully select a specific color in a photo and replace it with another hue.

To select the color to be replaced choose the standard eyedropper (1) from the feature's dialog. Refine the selection by adding extra colors to the selection range with the 'plus eyedropper' or removing colors with the 'minus eyedropper'. The precision of the color selection is based on the Fuzziness control (2). Higher values encompass a more varied range of hues.

You can review the areas that are being included in the selection using the preview window (with the Selection option active). The preview image (3) works in a similar way to the layer mask with the light areas fully selected, the gray areas partially selected and the dark areas not chosen at all.

The Replacement section (4) of the dialog is used for choosing the color that will be used as the selected color.

With all the options now selected, proceed to replace the selected color by pressing the OK button.

Before

R

Resample Image

Menu: Image > Image Size
Shortcut: Ctrl/Cmd Alt/Opt I   **See also:** Interpolation
Version: 6.0, 7.0, CS, CS2

When the Resample Image option (1), located in the Image Size feature, is selected Photoshop interpolates the original picture information to create either more or less pixels.

This means that the program adds extra pixels to make the photo larger or combines pixels to make the image smaller. Photoshop uses one of five different interpolation algorithms to create the new picture (2). Select the method you wish to use from the drop-down list.

Deselecting the Resample option stops the program from altering the number of pixels in the picture. In this event, picture sizes are altered by changes in resolution (the spread of pixels over a printed inch).

After

Reselect

Menu: Select > Reselect
Shortcut: Ctrl/Cmd Shft D   **See also:** Save Selection,
Version: 6.0, 7.0, CS, CS2   Load Selection

The Reselect command re-establishes the latest selection made on the image.

After using a selection for making an editing change, most users will remove the selection by choosing Select > Deselect. If at a later time in the editing session you need to reselect the same areas simply choose Select > Reselect.

Keep in mind when using this feature that:

– it only restores the last selection created,

– changes to image or canvas size lose the selection and

– once a file has been closed and reopened the feature will not restore the original selection.

To permanently store a selection use the Select > Save Selection option.

Reset All Tools

Menu: –
Shortcut: –   **See also:** Reset Tool
Version: 6.0, 7.0, CS, CS2

The Reset All Tools feature returns all tools to their default settings. The option is located by clicking on the tool's icon in the tool's option bar and then displaying the pop-up menu via the side-arrow at the top of the presets dialog.

Reset All Warning Dialogs

Menu: Edit > Preferences > General
          Bridge: Edit > Preferences > General
Shortcut: Ctrl/Cmd K   **See also:** Preferences
Version: 6.0, 7.0, CS, CS2   Photoshop

The Reset All Warning Dialogs button located in the Preferences > General section of the Bridge and Photoshop workspaces restores all pop-up warning dialogs to their original shipped state. This action overrides the previous selection of the 'Don't Show Again' option in message dialogs throughout the program.

The option is positioned at the bottom of both the Bridge (1) and Photoshop (3) General preference dialogs. After pressing the Reset All Warning Dialogs button a confirmation dialog will be displayed (2).

How the image will be used	Resolution
Screen or web use only	72 pixels per inch
Draft quality inkjet prints	150 ppi
Large posters (that will be viewed from a distance)	150 ppi
Photographic quality inkjet printing	200–300 ppi
Magazine printing	300 ppi

Reset Tool

Menu: –
Shortcut: –   See also: Reset All Tools
Version: 6.0, 7.0, CS, CS2

The Reset Tool feature returns only the selected tool to its default settings. The option is located by clicking on the tool's icon in the tool's option bar and then displaying the pop-up menu via the side-arrow at the top of the presets dialog.

Resolution

Menu: –
Shortcut: –   See also: DPI, Pixel dimensions,
Version: 6.0, 7.0, CS, CS2   Resolution option,
                                  Image Size command

The resolution of a digital image is the measure of the number of pixels that are used to represent an inch of the picture. The units used to express this measure are pixels per inch or PPI.

Generally speaking, high PPI values mean that fine details in the photo are represented more clearly and the image appears to have continuous tone. When using low PPI settings the overall quality of the picture is less and, in extreme cases, individual pixels may be seen as colored blocks.

Different resolution settings are used for different outcomes and suggestions for these are tabled above. Changing the PPI means that a single image (with a fixed set of pixel dimensions) can be printed or displayed at a variety of different sizes.

The PPI value for a picture is altered via the Resolution setting in the Image Size dialog.

Resolution option

Menu: Image > Image > Size
Shortcut: Ctrl/Cmd Alt/Opt I   See also: Resolution, Image Size
Version: 6.0, 7.0, CS, CS2   command,
                                          Pixel dimensions

By altering the resolution of a file, an image with the same pixel dimensions can have several different document sizes based on the change of the spread of the pixels when the picture is printed (or displayed on screen).

In this way, you can adjust a high-resolution file to print the size of a postage stamp, postcard or a poster by only changing the PPI or resolution. This type of resizing has no detrimental quality effects on your pictures as the original pixel dimensions remain unchanged – no extra pixels have been added or taken away from the photo in the process.

To change resolution, open the Image Size dialog, select the Constrain Proportions item and uncheck the Resample Image option (1). Next, change either the resolution, width or height settings to suit your output. Changing any of these amounts will automatically adjust the other values to suit.

The default resolution used when creating new documents can be altered in the Units & Rulers preferences dialog (2).

Restore Preferences

Menu: –
Shortcut: Ctrl/Cmd Alt/Opt Shft   **See also:** Preferences
Version: 6.0, 7.0, CS, CS2   Photoshop

If Photoshop starts to exhibit unusual behavior the cause may be a damaged preferences file. The file stores all the preference settings allocated either by default or as a result of changes made by the user to the settings via the Edit > Preferences menu.

Use the following keystroke combination immediately after Photoshop begins launching to restore the program's preferences to their default settings:

Windows: Alt Ctrl Shft

Macintosh: Opt Cmd Shft

Click Yes (1) when asked, to delete the current settings.

Reticulation filter

Menu: Filter > Sketch > Reticulation
Shortcut: –   **See also:** Filters
Version: 6.0, 7.0, CS, CS2

The Reticulation filter, as one of the group of Sketch filters, simulates the look of film that has been reticulated. This traditional effect is created by immersing film in hot and then cold baths during processing. As a result of the massive change in temperature the surface of the film breaks into the small textured clumps that are recreated digitally with this filter.

The dialog contains three controls. The Density slider (1) determines the overall darkness of the effect. The Foreground Level control (2) is used to adjust how the texture is applied to shadow areas and the Background Level slider (3) performs the same task but for the lighter tones in the picture.

As the filter uses the current foreground and background colors in the creation of the effect, altering these hues can change the end results radically (4).

Reveal All

Menu: Image > Reveal All
Shortcut: –   **See also:** Trim
Version: 6.0, 7.0, CS, CS2

Often when combining or resizing several different picture layers in the one document it is not possible to see the full extent of the layer contents.

Rather than having to adjust the canvas size manually to provide a view of the content of all layers you can simply select the Reveal All command (1). This feature automatically resizes the canvas so that it fits the content of all layers.

In the process the extra space created in each layer is made transparent, except in the case of the background layer, where it is filled with the current background color.

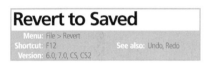

Reveal in Explorer

Menu: –		
Shortcut: –	**See also:** –	
Version: CS2		

Reveal in Explorer is one of the options that can be found in the right-click pop-up menu (1) of the Bridge workspace. Selecting this option automatically opens Windows Explorer and displays the folder (and all its contents) where the original photo is located (2).

Using this feature is a quick and easy way to locate the precise storage location of images that displayed in the Bridge workspace.

The feature is also included in the Photoshop File Browser of previous versions of the program.

Reverse, layer order

Menu: Layer > Arrange > Reverse		
Shortcut: –	**See also:** Bring To Front,	
Version: CS2	Send To Back	

As well as the Bring To and Send To options for moving selected layers within the stack, the Arrange menu provides another organizational selection – Reverse.

This command moves all selected layers and relocates them so that they are in the reverse order to their original position in the stack.

Revert to Saved

Menu: File > Revert		
Shortcut: F12	**See also:** Undo, Redo	
Version: 6.0, 7.0, CS, CS2		

The Revert feature restores the photo to the way that it looked the last time it was saved.

In the example, the photo was colored using the Hue/Saturation control and then filtered with the Posterize filter to produce the Before result. Next the File > Revert to Saved option was selected and the picture was restored to the way it was before the changes – the After image.

Pro's Tip The opening snapshot in the History palette does not always represent the last saved version.

For example, let's look at the following editing sequence:

1. Open image
2. Apply edits
3. Save
4. Apply more edits
5. Revert to Saved

In this instance, the image will look like step 3 after Reverting, but the snapshot in the History palette looks like step 1.

Combined
Red
Green
Blue

© www.abestock.com 2005

Before

Rotate 90° Left

Rotate Canvas

Menu: Image > Rotate Canvas
Shortcut: –   See also: Rotate Layer
Version: 6.0, 7.0, CS, CS2

The Image > Rotate Canvas menu contains
a list of options that can be used to rotate
your pictures (1). These orientation options
work with whole images irrespective of the
number of layers they contain.

To rotate just the selected layer use the Edit
> Transform > Rotate options instead.

. . . .

Rotate Layer

Menu: Edit > Transform
Shortcut: –   See also: Rotate Canvas
Version: 6.0, 7.0, CS, CS2

The Edit > Transform menu contains
a list of options (1) that can be used to
manipulate the content of individual
layers. Amongst these are several choices
for rotating a layer. Select the layer first
in the Layers palette before choosing the
Rotate option from the Transform menu.

RGB (Red, Green, Blue)

Menu: –
Shortcut: –   See also: Color modes
Version: 6.0, 7.0, CS, CS2

In all digital photos several primary colors
are mixed to form the many millions of
distinct colors we see on screen or in print.
These primary colors are often referred to
as color channels.

Most images that are created by digital
cameras are made up of Red, Green and
Blue colors or channels and so are said to
be RGB pictures.

In a standard 24-bit picture (8 bits per
color channel) each of the colors can have
a brightness value between 1 and 256. So
to represent a specific color you will have
three values that describe the mix of red,
green and blue used to create the hue.

You can see these values for any pixel in
your pictures by displaying the Info palette
(Window > Info) and then moving the
cursor over your photo. The RGB values
at any point are reflected in the Info
palette (1).

In contrast, those pictures that are
destined for printing are created with
Cyan, Magenta, Yellow and Black channels
(CMYK) to match the printing inks.

Sometimes the channels in an image
are also referred to as the picture's color
mode.

Rough Pastels filter

Menu: Filter > Artistic > Rough Pastels
Shortcut: –   See also: Filters
Version: 6.0, 7.0, CS, CS2

The Rough Pastels filter, as one of the group
of Artistic filters, recreates the photo so that
it looks like it has been drawn with colored
pastels on a roughly textured paper.

The filter dialog contains several controls
that adjust the look and feel of the effect.

The settings used for the Stroke sliders (1)
determine how strong the pastel stroke
effect will be. High values create a coarse
result where the pastel stroke is dominant.
Low settings retain more of the original
detail. The controls in the Texture section
(2) vary the strength and type of texture
that is added to the picture. Increasing the
values used for both Scaling and Relief
sliders will create a more textured result.

The Light option (3) controls the direction of
the light that is used to create the highlight
and shadow areas in the texture.

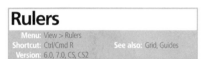

Rounded Rectangle tool

Menu: –
Shortcut: –
Version: 6.0, 7.0, CS, CS2
See also: Brush tool

The Rounded Rectangle tool (1) is one of the vector shape drawing tools available in Photoshop.

The feature draws rectangles with rounded corners (1) and is particularly good for creating buttons for websites and other interactive media. The example shows a simple button created with the tool and a preset layer style (2).

The size of the radius used for the rounded corners can be set in the tool's options bar (3).

Roundness

Menu: –
Shortcut: –
Version: 6.0, 7.0, CS, CS2
See also: Brush tool

The Roundness option is one of the Brush tool controls that is located in the Brushes palette > Brush Tip dialog.

When set at 100% the brush tip is in the shape of a circle; as the value is decreased the shape becomes an oval that becomes more and more squashed. In the example the brush tip is shown at values of 100% (1), 50% (2), 25% (3) and 5% (4).

A preview of the altered brush tip shape is displayed in the thumbnail when adjusting the Roundness value in the Brushes palette (5).

Rulers

Menu: View > Rulers
Shortcut: Ctrl/Cmd R
Version: 6.0, 7.0, CS, CS2
See also: Grid, Guides

The Rulers option displays both horizontal and vertical rulers around the edge of the image window.

Clicking and dragging from the top left-hand corner (where the rulers intersect) allows you to reposition the '0' points of each ruler. This is helpful when using the feature to measure various picture parts.

Double-clicking anywhere on a ruler displays the Units & Rulers preferences dialog, where a new unit of measure can be selected from the choices in the drop-down menu (1).

R

Sample All Layers

Menu: –
Shortcut: –   **See also:** Brush tool
Version: CS2

Previously called Use All Layers, this setting is found in the options bar of the Clone Stamp, Smudge, Blur, Sharpen, Paint Bucket and Healing Brush tools. It allows the user to select a sample area based on all visible layers not just the contents of the selected layer.

In CS2 the Sample All Layers replaces the Use All Layers name. This setting still resides on the options bar of the tools with which it can be used.

Sample Size, Eyedropper tool

Menu: –
Shortcut: –   **See also:** Info palette
Version: 6.0, 7.0, CS, CS2

The Eyedropper tool samples the color of an area in an open image or on the desktop. When the mouse button is clicked the color of the area under the pointer is stored as the new foreground color.

The size of the sample area can be set in the tool's options bar (1). The Point Sample copies the precise color of the pixel beneath the cursor whereas the 3 by 3 or 5 by 5 options store a color that is the average of the pixels contained in these sample areas.

After

Saturation +100

Saturation +50

Saturation -normal

Saturation -50

Saturation -100

Saturation

Menu: –	
Shortcut: –	See also: Hue/Saturation,
Version: 6.0, 7.0, CS, CS2	Remove all color – Desaturate

The saturation of a color photo is usually described as the color's strength or vibrancy.

Decreasing the saturation in a picture gradually removes the color from the image, creating more subtle or pastel shades. Continuing to lessen the saturation will eventually reach a point where no color remains and the photo is effectively a grayscale image.

Increasing the saturation makes the colors more vibrant. You have to be careful when adjusting the picture in this way though as overly saturated pictures often print as flat areas of color with no detail.

Saturation changes are made by moving the Saturation slider (1) in the Hue/Saturation feature. This feature is also available as an Adjustment layer so that you can apply non-destructive saturation changes.

Saturation blending mode

Menu: –	
Shortcut: –	See also: Blend modes
Version: 6.0, 7.0, CS, CS2	

The Saturation blending mode is one of the group of Hue modes that base their effects on combining the hue, saturation and luminosity of the two layers.

This option creates the result by combining the hue and luminance of the bottom layer with the saturation of the top layer.

There is no change if the top layer has no saturation (is filled with neutral grays).

183

S

NEW for CS2

Saturation rendering intent

Menu: –
Shortcut: – **See also:** Perceptual rendering intent
Version: 6.0, 7.0, CS, CS2

At various points in the digital photography process it is necessary to change or alter the spread of colors in a picture so that they fit the characteristics of an output device, such as a screen or printer, more fully. Saturation is one of the four different approaches that Photoshop can use in this conversion process. The other choices are Perceptual, Relative Colorimetric and Absolute Colorimetric.

Each approach produces different results and is based on a specific conversion or 'rendering intent'. The **Saturation** option tries to maintain the strength of colors during the conversion process. This occurs even at the expense of color accuracy.

The **Relative Colorimetric** setting squashes or stretches the range of colors in the original so that they fit the range of possible colors that the new device can display or print. The **Perceptual** setting puts conversion emphasis on ensuring that the adjusted picture, when viewed on the new output device, appears to the human eye to be very similar to the original photo. The **Absolute Colorimetric** option translates colors exactly from the original photo to the range of colors for the new device. Those colors that can't be displayed are clipped.

Specific Intents can be selected as part of the printing process via the color management controls in the More Options section of the Print Preview dialog (1).

Save

Menu: File > Save
Shortcut: Ctrl/Cmd S   **See also:** Save for Web, Save a Version, Save an Alternate
Version: 6.0, 7.0, CS, CS2

Saving images edited in the Photoshop workspace is a three-step process that starts by choosing File > Save from the menu bar.

With the Save dialog open, navigate through your hard drive to find the directory or folder you wish to save your images in. Next, type in the name for the file and select the file format you wish to use.

The Save feature is grayed out, or unavailable, if no changes have been made to the picture since the last Save action.

Save a Version

Menu: File > Save a Version
Shortcut: –   **See also:** Versions,
Version: CS2   Save an Alternate

In order to make it possible to use the Save a Version feature in Photoshop (or any other CS2 program) the folders or files that you are working with must be organized in a Version Cue project or workspace. In addition the Enable Version Cue options in the preferences of each of the CS2 programs also need to be selected. In Photoshop this setting is located in the File Handling Preferences dialog.

Now when a Version Cue protected file is opened and enhanced or edited in any way you have the Save a Version option available on the File menu (1). Following selecting the menu item a Save a Version dialog is displayed (2). The window contains all the details for the picture as well as a space for you to enter comments about the version you are saving. After clicking the Save button the latest version of the file is then saved and displayed in the standard thumbnail view in Bridge but when the workspace is switched to the Versions and Alternates View all the previous iterations of the design are also shown.

Alternatively you can also view the versions by setting the Status Bar display to Version Cue and then choosing the Versions option from the pop-up menu.

A separate window will be displayed showing all the Versions available for the file that is currently open.

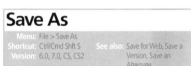

185

Save an Alternate

Menu: –
Shortcut: –
Version: CS2

See also: Versions,
Save a Version

With Version Cue installed and enabled in the File Handling preferences in Photoshop CS2 it is also possible to save an Alternate copy of the current document. Unlike versions which document a linear set of changes, Alternates provide exact copies of pictures allowing branching design changes arising from a common base.

An Alternate can be saved for any project file that is open in a CS2 program. Start by choosing File > Save As, then switch the Dialog box styles to the Adobe Dialog (1) by pressing the Use Adobe Dialog button at the bottom left of the standard OS Save As dialog.

In the Adobe Dialog select the Save as Alternate option (2) at the bottom of the dialog and then press the Save button.

You can view the Alternate copies of the document by switching the workspace to the Versions and Alternates View or by setting the Status Bar display to Version Cue and then choosing the Alternates option from the pop-up menu (3).

A separate window will be displayed showing all the Alternates available for the file that is currently open (4).

Save As

Menu: File > Save As
Shortcut: Ctrl/Cmd Shft S
Version: 6.0, 7.0, CS, CS2

See also: Save for Web, Save a Version, Save an Alternate

For most images you should use the Photoshop or PSD format.

This option gives you a file that maintains all of the specialized features available in Photoshop. However, if you want to share your images with others, either via the web or over a network, then you can choose to save your files in other formats, like JPEG or TIFF.

To save a file in a format other than the PSD file type, select the File > Save As option, selecting a different option from the drop-down format menu.

The options in the Save As dialog box allow you to change the name of the file, the location you are saving to, or the format you are saving in.

S

S

Save for Web

Menu: File > Save For Web
Shortcut: Shft Alt/Opt Ctrl/Cmd S   **See also:** Save As
Version: 6.0, 7.0, CS, CS2

When preparing photos for use on the Internet it is difficult to balance the good compression with acceptable image quality. So how much compression is too much? Well, Photoshop helps with this dilemma by including a special 'Save for Web' feature that previews how the image will appear before and after the compression has been applied.

Start the feature by selecting the Save for Web option from the File menu of the Photoshop workspace. You are presented with a dialog that shows side-by-side 'before' and 'after' versions of your picture. The settings used to compress the image can be changed in the top right-hand

(1) Original picture. (2) Compressed preview. (3) Compression settings. (4) Size settings. (5) Animation settings (GIF only). (6) File size information.

corner of the screen. Each time a value is altered, the image is recompressed using the new settings and the results redisplayed.

JPEG, GIF and PNG can all be selected and previewed in the Save for Web feature. By carefully checking the preview of the compressed image (at 100% magnification) and the file size readout at the bottom of the screen, it is possible to find a point where both the file size and image quality are acceptable. By clicking OK it is then possible to save a copy of the compressed file to your hard drive ready for attachment to an e-mail or use in a web page.

Save Selection

Menu: Select > Save Selection
Shortcut: –   **See also:** Load Selection
Version: 6.0, 7.0, CS, CS2

The Save Selection option allows the user to store complex, multi-step selections with the file that they were created for.

To save a selection choose the option after creating a selection and whilst it is still active. The selection is saved as part of the Photoshop file (PSD) and can be restored, using the Load Selection feature, next time the picture is opened. The Reselect option provides a similar function but only restores the last selection made during the current editing session.

TIFF, PDF and JPEG2000 file formats also support saved selections.

• •

Save Swatches

Menu: –
Shortcut: –   **See also:** Swatches palette
Version: 6.0, 7.0, CS, CS2

The Save Swatches feature allows you to store new, or edited, color swatches, or swatch libraries in a file that can be loaded again later.

To save swatches press the sideways arrow at the top of the palette and then select the Save Swatches item from the pop-up menu.

The feature opens a file browser dialog so that you can save the new swatch file (ACO) to a selected folder. Swatch files are generally stored in the Photoshop/Presets/Color Swatches folder.

Before

After

© www.adestock.com 2005

Scale

Menu:	Edit > Transform > Scale	
Shortcut:	–	See also: Image Size
Version:	6.0, 7.0, CS, CS2	command,
		Canvas Size

The Scale feature allows the resizing of the content of individual layers. After selecting Image > Resize > Scale, click and drag one of the corner handles of the bounding box that appears to resize the layer.

Holding down the Shift key whilst resizing constrains the proportions of the change to the picture so that they are the same as the original. Double-click inside the bounding box to confirm the scale change or click the commit button in the options bar. When using the feature with a background image the layer will be converted to a normal image layer first. The overall dimensions of the image do not change.

Scatter option, Brush tool

Menu:	–	
Shortcut:	–	See also: Roundness
Version:	6.0, 7.0, CS, CS2	

Scattering is one group of options that controls how the Brush tool behaves. The options can be found in the Scattering section of the Brushes palette.

Dragging a brush when the Scatter value is set at 0% creates a single line of brush strokes. Selecting higher values causes the brush strokes to deviate randomly from the drawn path. In the example a brush has been dragged across the canvas with scatter values of 0% (1), 50% (2) and 100% (3).

Count and Color Jitter controls are also included in this dialog.

Scratch disks

Menu:	Edit > Preferences > Plug-Ins & Scratch Disks	
Shortcut:	–	See also: Preferences
Version:	6.0, 7.0, CS, CS2	Photoshop

A scratch disk is really pseudo RAM or pretend memory. When Photoshop runs out of the RAM needed to perform an enhancement change, it can use part of your hard drive as a fake extension to the system's memory.

The section of hard drive nominated as the RAM extension is called a scratch disk and correctly allocating such a disk will improve the performance of Photoshop on even the most humble machines.

Scratch disks are allocated in the Plug-Ins & Scratch Disks Preference dialog (1), with the new settings taking effect after the program has been rebooted. As many as up to four different disks can be used by the feature. Your fastest and least used drive should be allocated first, with other drives with a little extra space being nominated next.

 In most cases, internal drives are faster than external, though there are some exceptions. **Pro's Tip** For instance, a RAID array of Firewire 800 drives works particularly well as an external storage option for a Photoshop scratch disk.

187

S

The Preferences settings for Photoshop are located under the Edit > Preferences menu. Here you will find a series of settings that allow you to adjust the default workings of the program. To change or allocate scratch disks select the Plug-Ins & Scratch Disks option from the menu.

The Plug-Ins & Scratch Disks dialog has settings to allocate up to four different locations for use as extra RAM. It is best not to use the same location for Windows virtual memory. It is also worth selecting your fastest drive first as the extra speed will also help increase performance.

With the scratch disks now allocated click OK to close the window and then quit Photoshop as the changes will not take effect until you restart the program. Next time you use Photoshop you will be able to work with bigger files and perform more complex operations than ever before.

Screen blending mode

Menu: –	
Shortcut: –	**See also:** Blend modes
Version: 6.0, 7.0, CS, CS2	

The Screen blending mode is one of the group of Lighten modes and as such always produces a result that is brighter than the original.

This mode produces its effect by multiplying the inverse of the colors from the top and bottom layers.

Blending with black produces no change. Blending with white produces a white result.

Scripts Event Manager

Menu: File > Scripts > Scripts Event Manager	
Shortcut: –	**See also:** Scripts
Version: CS2	

To provide yet another level of automation possibilities in Photoshop, Adobe has introduced a new feature called the Scripts Event Manager into CS2. The feature automates the running of scripts or actions when a specific event occurs in Photoshop. This means that it is possible do such things as automatically save copies of files in a different format whenever you click the save button or set up a specific workspace and document characteristics each time you select File > New.

The Scripts Event Manager dialog contains drop-down lists for selecting the triggering event (3) and the script (4) or action (5) that is to be run when this event occurs. Above this section is a preview space (2) that lists the events and associated actions/scripts that are currently defined and an Enable Events to Run option (1) that essentially turns the feature on and off.

Photoshop CS2 ships with several scripts, a range of default actions and some preinstalled events that can be used in conjunction with the feature. Customized as well as user generated scripts and actions can be added to extend the capabilities of the feature further and other events can be added (6) to the dialog as well so long as they are defined scripting events.

Scripts

Menu: File > Scripts	
Shortcut: –	**See also:** Scripts Event Manager
Version: CS, CS2	

Photoshop supports scripting as a way of automating events within the application as well as providing options to control other CS2 programs.

Windows users can produce scripts in VisualBasic and supporters of the Macintosh platform AppleScript. These languages allow the automation on a single platform whereas creating scripts using JavaScript allows cross platform use.

A good example of what is possible with scripting is the Image Processor (File > Scripts > Image Processor) produced by Adobe's very own Russell Brown (1).

Search Adobe Stock Photos

Menu: Bridge: Edit > Search Adobe Stock Photos	
Shortcut: –	**See also:** Bridge
Version: CS2	

One of the integrated features in the Bridge workspace is the ability to search for, locate, pay and download stock photos directly from inside the workspace. Adobe has joined forces with several of the world's leading providers of stock photos and illustrations to provide the feature.

As well as the standard menu option (Bridge: Edit > Search Adobe Stock Photo) the search workspace (2) also provides the ability to refine the search parameters via the advanced search dialog (1) which is displayed by pressing the button in the options bar.

Select All

Menu: Select > Select All
Shortcut: Ctrl/Cmd A   **See also:** Selections
Version: 6.0, 7.0, CS, CS2

The Select > All command automatically draws a selection marquee around the edges of the current document.

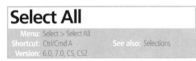

Select All Layers

Menu: Layer > Select All Layers
Shortcut: Ctrl/Cmd Alt/Opt A   **See also:** –
Version: CS2

The new Select All Layers option quickly multi-selects all non-background layers in the current document.

Select Similar Layers

Menu: Select > Similar Layers
Shortcut: –   **See also:** –
Version: CS2

The Select > Similar Layers option multi-selects all layers in the current document that are of the same content type as the current active layer.

This means that if an image layer is currently active then choosing the Select > Similar Layers would highlight all image layers in the document. In the example a text layer was made active and then the feature selected causing all text or type layers to be selected.

189

S

Before

After

Selections

Menu: –	
Shortcut: –	**See also:** Elliptical Marquee,
Version: 6.0,	Rectangular Marquee,
7.0, CS,	Magnetic Lasso tool, Lasso tools,
CS2	Polygonal Lasso tool,
	Magic Wand tool

When first starting most Photoshop users apply editing and enhancement changes to the whole photograph, but before too long it becomes obvious that sometimes it would be a benefit to restrict the alterations to a specific part of a picture. For this reason image-editing packages contain features that allow the user to isolate small sections of a photo, which can then be altered independently of the rest of the picture.

The process of isolating a picture part is called 'making a selection'. When a selection is created in Photoshop, the edges of the isolated area are indicated by a flashing dotted line, which is sometimes referred to as the 'marching ants'.

A selection restricts any changes made to the image to just the area isolated by the marching ants.

(1) Non-selected area.
(2) Area selected with the Rectangular Marquee tool.
(3) Marching ants signifying the boundaries of an active selection.

To remove the selection and resume full image-editing mode, the area has to be Deselected (Select > Deselect).

The selection tools in Photoshop can be divided into two groups:

Drawing selection tools, or those that are based on selecting pixels by drawing a line around the part of the image to be isolated. These include the Rectangular and Elliptical Marquee and Lasso tools.

Color selection tools, or those features that distinguish between image parts based on the color or tone of the pixels. An example of this type of tool is the Magic Wand.

 The marching ants of a feathered selection are located at the point where 50% or more of the image is selected.

Selective Color

Menu: Image > Adjustments > Selective Color	
Shortcut: –	**See also:** –
Version: 6.0, 7.0, CS, CS2	

The Image > Adjustment > Selective Color feature allows you to adjust a specific color in a picture without affecting any other hues.

The Selective Color dialog (1) provides options for adjusting cyans, yellows, magentas, blacks, whites, grays, reds, greens and blues independently.

NEW for CS2

Before

Before

After Send Backward

After Send to Back

Recycle Bin

Send Backward

Menu: Layer > Arrange > Send Backward
Shortcut: Ctrl/Cmd | **See also:** Send to Back
Version: 6.0, 7.0, CS, CS2

The Send Backward option moves the selected layer one layer lower in the stack.

In the example, the 'writer' layer was sent backwards, which means that its new position is below the 'Type' layer, causing it to become partially obscured.

Send to Back

Menu: Layer > Arrange > Send to Back
Shortcut: Shft Ctrl/Cmd | **See also:** Send Backward
Version: 6.0, 7.0, CS, CS2

The Layer > Arrange menu contains a list of options that can be used for moving the active layer up and down the layer stack. Moving the position of image layers that contain sections that are transparent or semi-transparent will alter the look of the combined picture. The Send to Back option transports the selected layer to the very bottom of the stack (but not below the background layer). In the example, the 'writer' type layer was sent back from its uppermost position to below the 'Picture' layer so that it is now hidden from view.

Send to Recycling Bin

Menu: Bridge: File > Send to Recycling Bin
Shortcut: Ctrl/Cmd Del   **See also:** –
Version: CS2

Files can be sent to the operating system's Recycling Bin (1) from inside the Bridge application by selecting the file's thumbnail and then choosing File > Send to the Recycling Bin. Alternatively, you can select the same option from the right-click pop-up menu (2).

Recycled files can be restored to their original location and position in Bridge by locating them in the Recycling Bin folder and then choosing the Restore option (3) from the right-click pop-up menu.

Recycled files cannot be restored if the bin has been emptied. Such an action permanently deletes the file from the system.

Before

After

Shadow/Highlight

Menu: Image > Adjustments > Shadow/Highlight
Shortcut: –   **See also:** Curves, Levels command,
Version: CS, CS2   Brightness/Contrast

A clever new feature first introduced in Photoshop CS that allows you to adjust the shadow and highlight areas of an image by correcting each pixel based on the luminance values of neighboring areas. Image contrast can be increased in the shadows or highlights or both without significantly sacrificing contrast in other regions.

As with many Photoshop adjustments you have several sliders to fine tune your corrections. The Shadows and Highlights sections each have an Amount, Tonal Width and Radius slider.

The **Amount** slider controls the steepness of a brightening or darkening curve. Larger values lighten shadows and darken highlights. A value of zero for both Shadows and Highlights produces a straight line and no modification of the pixel, while a value of 100 produces a very steep curve

with maximum modification. The default is a setting of 50 which is fine for most backlit subjects, but for severe backlighting with very dark subjects, you will need to increase this towards 100%, while images needing moderate correction can be set to smaller values of around 20%.

The **Tonal Width** slider adjusts how much modification you make to the shadows, midtones and highlights. When correcting shadows select a small value in the Tonal Width to place emphasis on the darker regions of the image. Larger values place emphasis on midtones and highlights as well.

The default is set to 50%. If you are trying to lighten a dark subject but the midtones or lighter regions are changing too much, move the Shadow Tone Width slider to the left so only the darkest regions are lightened. If you need to brighten up the midtones as well as the shadows, move the slider to the right.

The **Radius** averages out the luminance of neighboring pixels so that each pixel is modified according to its surrounding

data. A larger radius increases the extent that the neighborhood luminance is averaged out.

As you adjust the slider you can obtain a good balance between subject contrast and differential brightening or darkening of the subject compared with the background.

The bottom sliders let you adjust **Color Correction** and **Midtone Contrast**. The clip values entered here determine how much of the extremes are clipped when you adjust the slider. Set this too high and the adjustments will appear dramatic, with detail in highlights and shadows being lost or clipped.

Shape Blur filter

Menu: Filter > Blur > Shape Blur
Shortcut: – **See also:** Filters
Version: CS2

CS2 introduces a new flexible blur filter in the form of the Shape Blur feature.

The filter blurs images using a user selected shape as the basis for the blurring action. The dialog contains a preview (1), a radius slider (2) and thumbnail list (3) of currently loaded shapes.

To blur a picture choose a low radius to start with (high values can take considerable time to process a preview) and then choose the shape from those listed. Try a range of different shapes and when you are satisfied with the look of the blur then start to refine the strength of the effect using the radius slider.

Shape tools

Menu: –
Shortcut: U **See also:** Brush tool
Version: 6.0, 7.0, CS, CS2

Photoshop contains both painting and drawing tools. The shape tools are drawing tools that, in contrast to the Brush, Airbrush and Pencil tools, are vector or line based.

The objects drawn with these tools are defined mathematically as a specific shape, color and size. They exist independently of the pixel grid that makes up your image until it comes time to print when they are simplified (rasterized).

They produce sharp-edged graphics and are particularly good for creating logos and other flat colored artwork.

The shape tools include Rectangle tool (1), Rounded Rectangle tool (2), Ellipse tool (3), Polygon tool (4), Line tool (5), Custom Shape tool (6) and the Shape Selection tool (7).

Specific settings that control the way that each shape tool functions are available from the pop-up dialog in the tool's options bar (8).

Share Online

Menu: Bridge: Tools > Photoshop Services > Photo Sharing
Shortcut: – **See also:** Print Online
Version: CS2

Using the online resources of Kodak Easy Share Gallery, formerly ofoto.com, it is possible to share your photos with family and friends via the web.

After choosing a location and registering as a new user with the EasyShare Gallery, select the images to share from the Bridge workspace and then choose the Tools > Photoshop Services > Photo Sharing option.

Select the recipients and add a subject and message in the dialog that appears. Add new recipients if they are not already listed. After clicking Next the files will be uploaded and an e-mail message sent to the recipients, letting them know that there are pictures to be shared now online.

Original Unsharpened

After Sharpen More

After Sharpen

After Sharpen Edges

194

Sharpen filters

Menu: Filter > Sharpen
Shortcut: –   **See also:** Unsharp Mask filter,
Version: 6.0, 7.0, CS, CS2   Smart Sharpen filter

Photoshop provides a variety of sharpening filters designed to increase the clarity of digital photographs. The options are listed in the Filter > Sharpen menu and include the Sharpen, Sharpen Edges, Sharpen More, Unsharp Mask and the new Smart Sharpen filters. Here we will look at the first three options with the Unsharp Mask and Smart Sharpen filters being handled separately under their own headings.

Digital sharpening techniques are based on increasing the contrast between adjacent pixels in the image. When viewed from a distance, this change makes the picture appear sharper. These Sharpen and Sharpen More filters are designed to apply basic sharpening to the whole of the image and the only difference between the two is that Sharpen More increases the strength of the sharpening effect.

One of the problems with sharpening is that sometimes the effect is detrimental to the image, causing areas of subtle color or tonal change to become coarse and pixelated. These problems are most noticeable in image parts such as skin tones and smoothly graded skies. To help solve this issue, Adobe included another filter in Photoshop, Sharpen Edges, which concentrates the sharpening effects on the edges of objects only. Use this filter when you want to stop the effect being applied to smooth image parts.

For the ultimate control of your sharpening use the advanced features in the new Smart Sharpen filter or the Unsharp Mask filter.

After Sharpen tool

Sharpen tool

Menu: –
Shortcut: R   **See also:** Blur tool
Version: 6.0, 7.0, CS, CS2

In addition to using a filter to sharpen your image, it is also possible to make changes to specific areas of the picture (1) using the sharpening tool located in the Photoshop toolbox.

The size of the area sharpened is based on the current brush size. The intensity of the effect is controlled by the Strength value found in the options bar.

As with the Airbrush tool, the longer you keep the mouse button down the more pronounced the effect will be. Be careful not to overapply the tool as the effects can become very noticeable very quickly and impossible to reverse (2).

These features are particularly useful when you want to change only small parts of an image rather than the whole picture.

Shear filter

Menu: Filter > Distort > Shear
Shortcut: –   **See also:** Filters
Version: 6.0, 7.0, CS, CS2

The Shear filter, as one of the group of Distort filters, creates a twisted and push/pulled version of the original photo.

The filter dialog contains an interactive effect box (1) that contains a graph and a control line. Using the mouse the user can add control points to the line and push, pull and twist the line within the confines of the graph. The distortions are then reflected in the preview thumbnail at the bottom of the screen.

Also included are two options for controlling the way that the undefined areas (2), or gaps created by the distortions, are handled. Wrapping uses the picture parts on the opposite side of the frame to fill the space whereas the Repeat Edge Pixels option duplicates the color and brightness of the detail at the edge of the distortion.

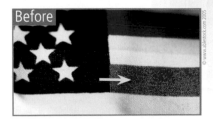

Shortcuts buttons, Bridge

Menu: –
Shortcut: –   See also: –
Version: CS2

A series of shortcuts buttons are located at the top right of the Bridge window.

These buttons provide quick access to filtering, create new folder, rotation, delete item and switch to compact mode options.

- -

Show options, Bridge

Menu: Bridge: View >
Shortcut: –   See also: –
Version: CS2

The View menu in Bridge contains several different Show options that provide another way to filter the images that are displayed in the workspace.

Show Thumbnail Only – Displays images with no text or metadata labels.

Show Hidden Files – The files shown also include those that are tagged with a Hidden property by the operating system.

Show Folders – Displays folders as well as pictures.

Show All Files – Shows graphic, Raw and vector files.

Show Graphic Files Only – Only displays graphic or picture files.

Show Camera Raw Files Only – Restricts the view to just Raw files.

Show Vector Files Only – Shows vector-based pictures only.

Similar, select

Menu: Enhance > Adjust Lighting > Levels
Shortcut: –   See also: Expand selection,
Version: 6.0, 7.0, CS, CS2   Contract selection

Listed under the Select menu is a range of options for adjusting selections after they have been created.

The Select > Similar is one of these options. The feature looks for, and selects, pixels throughout the whole picture with similar color and tonal characteristics to those already included in the selection.

The tolerance settings of the selection tool used to make the initial selection are used when creating the new 'similar' selection. If the tool you used doesn't have a tolerance setting, switch to the Magic Wand before proceeding.

The Select > Grow feature is similar except that it restricts its selection of new pixels to only those adjacent to those currently selected.

16-bit

Menu: –
Shortcut: 6.0, 7.0, CS, CS2   See also: Color depth
Version:

Or High Bit as it is sometimes called is a picture mode that supports many more colors (65,000 colors) per channel than the standard 8-bit file (256 colors).

Working in 16-bit mode helps to ensure better accuracy of capture and smoother enhancement and editing results. In addition you will find that much more exacting levels of control are possible when working with a 16-bit file instead of an 8-bit one.

- -

Skew

Menu: Edit > Transform > Skew
Shortcut: –   See also: Distorting a layer; Free
Version: 6.0, 7.0, CS, CS2   Transform command, Warp

The Skew feature is one of the distortion options available under the Edit > Transform menu.

Selecting the feature surrounds your layer with the standard bounding box complete with corner and middle-of-edge handles. Click-dragging of a handle creates a horizontal or vertical shift of the edge of the layer, producing a rhomboid or squashed box effect (1).

Double-click inside the bounding box to apply the changes.

195

S

Slice, image

Menu: –
Shortcut: –   **See also:** Slice tool
Version: 6.0, 7.0, CS, CS2

Slices are used in web optimized images to break a picture into smaller usable parts.

Photoshop contains a variety of features for creating and using image slices.

Each slice is stored as an individual filestogether with its own settings, effects, color palette and links.

Slideshow mode, Bridge

Menu: Bridge: View > Slideshow
Shortcut: Ctrl/Cmd L   **See also:** Compact mode
Version: CS2   – Bridge

Slideshow is one of the view modes available in the Bridge workspace.

Selecting this option creates an automatic self-running slideshow (1) containing the images in the current workspace or those multi-selected before choosing the feature.

Pressing the H key displays a list of commands (2) that can be used to navigate, edit and adjust the slideshow.

Smart Blur filter

Menu: Filter > Blur > Smart Blur
Shortcut: –   **See also:** Filters
Version: 6.0, 7.0, CS, CS2

The Smart Blur filter, as one of the group of Blur filters, selectively blurs your picture whilst retaining the sharpness of edge details. The filter dialog contains several controls to adjust the strength and location of the blur. The Radius setting (1) controls the strength of the effect. The Threshold slider (2) determines where the blurring will occur. High values include more of the picture in the blur action. The Quality drop-down menu (3) controls the image quality of the final result. When set to high the filter processing takes longer. The Mode option (4) is used to select other ways of applying the effect, including adding edge detection lines to the finished results.

Slice tool

Menu: –
Shortcut: K   **See also:** Slice – image
Version: 6.0, 7.0, CS, CS2

The Slice tool lets you cut a picture up into smaller segments to aid with speedy web display.

The overall picture containing the slices will still appear seamless but each slice has its own web code and can be adjusted so that it appears to change color, dim down, glow or whatever other effect you apply when the cursor goes over it.

Each area is designated with a number.

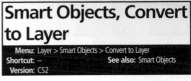

Smart Objects, Convert to Layer

Menu: Layer > Smart Objects > Convert to Layer
Shortcut: –   **See also:** Smart Objects
Version: CS2

Smart Objects layers can be converted to standard image layers by selecting the object layer and then choosing Layer > Smart Objects > Convert to Layer.

Smart Guides

Menu: View > Show > Smart Guides
Shortcut: –   **See also:** Rulers, Guides,
Version: CS2   Grid

New for CS2 is the Smart Guides feature that automatically aligns different layer contents with other elements in a Photoshop document. When moving layer content Photoshop will automatically snap contents to align with edges or centers of other picture parts (1).

To display the Smart Guides as you arrange picture parts select Smart Guides from the View > Show menu (2).

The color of the Smart Guide display lines can be altered via the Edit > Preferences > Guides, Grid & Slices dialog (3).

Smart Objects

Menu: –
Shortcut: –   **See also:** –
Version: CS2

Smart Objects is a new imaging technology available for the first time in Photoshop CS2. Using Smart objects it is possible to store vector and bitmap files within an open document and still maintain the integrity of these files throughout the editing and enhancing process.

To best understand the idea think of the technology as embedding one file within another. The embedded file is the smart object. It can be edited in its original form or non-destructively as part of the document it is embedded in.

For example, when placing an EPS vector art file in Photoshop CS2 it automatically becomes a Smart object and is represented in a single Smart Object layer (1). The object can then be transformed and edited just like any other picture part in the document. Unlike in previous versions of Photoshop the placed file retains its vector status rendering or rasterizing the picture details to form the composite image we see in the workspace.

Smart objects don't have to be completely separate files, a group of layers can be converted into a smart object.

Smart Objects, Edit Contents

Menu: Layer > Smart Objects > Edit Contents
Shortcut: –   **See also:** Smart Objects
Version: CS2

The contents of Smart Objects can be edited separately from the Photoshop document in which they are embedded.

When editing the source files for the objects they are opened into Photoshop if they contain Raster or Raw data and Illustrator if the object is based on EPS or PDF files.

Embedded files are edited by selecting the Smart Object layer first and then choosing the Edit Contents option from the Layer > Smart Objects menu (2). Alternatively you can double-click the Smart Objects thumbnail in the Layers palette (1).

NEW for CS2

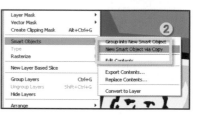

Smart Objects, Export Contents

Menu: Layer > Smart Object > Export Contents
Shortcut: –   **See also:** Smart Objects
Version: CS2

The contents of a Smart Object can be exported and saved as a separate file using the Export Contents option in the Layer > Smart Objects menu.

To export an object select the layer the object is stored in and then choose the Export Contents option.

Smart Objects that have been created from a group of layers are exported to a new document that contains all the documents intact.

Smart Objects, Group Into

Menu: Layer > Smart Object > Group Into New Smart Object
Shortcut: –   **See also:** Smart Objects
Version: CS2

As well as holding raster, Raw and vector content, the Smart Object format can also contain groups of layers.

To change several layers into a Smart Object multi-select the layers and then choose the Group Into New Smart Object option from the Layer > Smart Object menu.

Smart Objects, New Via Copy

Menu: Layer > Smart Object > Group Into New Smart Object
Shortcut: –   **See also:** Smart Objects
Version: CS2

As Smart Objects work on a 'file within a file' basis, the source file is always linked back to the document in which it is embedded. This remains the case even when duplicating the object's layer.

When copying Smart Object layers the user also has a choice about whether these copies are linked to each other as well as the source image.

Duplicate Smart Object layers that are linked will reflect changes made in any layer across all linked layers. Changes made to a non-linked Smart Object duplicate will only affect the individual layer that has been edited.

Consequently there are two different ways to duplicate a Smart Object layer in Photoshop CS2:

Copy with link (1) – To copy a Smart Object layer and continue to maintain the link to the source file you can

• Drag the layer to the New Layer button at the bottom of the Layers palette or

• Select the layer and then choose Layer > New > Layer Via Copy.

Both these methods will maintain the link so that any edits made to the copy will affect the original Smart Object and vice versa.

Copy breaking the link (2) – To duplicate the Smart Object but break the link with the original object select the layer and then choose the Layer > Smart Objects > New Smart Object Via Copy copy.

Smart Objects, Replace Contents

Menu: Layer > Smart Objects > Replace Contents
Shortcut: –   **See also:** Smart Objects
Version: CS2

The contents of a Smart Object can be replaced with another file. This command is particularly useful if you need to update multiple instances of the Smart Object within a document as replacing the contents once will permeate throughout the rest of the document.

To replace the contents of a Smart Object, select the Smart Object layer and then choose the Replace Contents (1) option from the Layer > Smart Object menu. Next navigate to and select the file (2) that is to be used as the replacement and press the Place button. The contents of the Smart Object will update automatically (3).

● ●

Smart Sharpen filter

Menu: Filter > Sharpen > Smart Sharpen
Shortcut: –   **See also:** Filters, Sharpen filters,
Version: CS2   Unsharp Mask filter

Until the release of CS2 the best way to take control of the sharpening in your photographs was to use the Unsharp Mask filter. But in this release of Photoshop Adobe has included a brand new sharpening tool that will easily steal this crown.

The Smart Sharpen filter provides all the control that we are familiar with in the Unsharp Mask dialog plus better edge detection abilities, which leads to less apparent sharpening halos and specific controls for shadow and highlight sharpening (in advanced mode).

The filter dialog contains a zoomable preview (1), Advanced and Basic controls (2), the ability to save and load favorite settings (3) and a settings section (4).

In Basic mode (4) the user can control the sharpening effect with the following settings:

Amount – Strength of sharpening effect.

Radius – Determines the extent of sharpening. Higher values equals more obvious edge effects.

Remove – Determines sharpening algorithm used. Gaussian Blur uses the same approach as the Unsharp Mask filter. Lens Blur concentrates on sharpening details and produces results with fewer halos. Motion Blur reduces the effects of blur caused by camera shake or subject movement.

Unsharpened

After Smart Sharpen

Angle – Sets motion blur direction.

More Accurate – Longer processing for better results.

In Advanced mode (5) the feature offers these additional controls for both highlight and shadow parts of the picture:

Fade Amount – Controls the amount of sharpening in these areas.

Tonal Width – Sets the range of tones included in shadow/highlight ranges. Low values restrict changes to just dark and light regions of the picture.

Radius – Sets the size of area around each pixel that is used to determine if the pixel is to be considered a shadow or highlight tone.

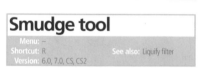

Smooth

Menu: Select > Modify > Smooth
Shortcut: –   **See also:** Expand selection,
Version: 6.0, 7.0, CS, CS2   Contract –
selection

The options in the Select > Modify menu are designed for adjusting selections after they have been created.

The Select > Modify > Smooth searches for unselected pixels within the nominated radius. If these areas are surrounded by selected pixels then they will be included in the selection; if the surrounding areas are not selected then they will not be included.

Smudge Stick filter

Menu: Filter > Artistic > Smudge Stick
Shortcut: –   **See also:** Filters
Version: 6.0, 7.0, CS, CS2

The Smudge Stick filter, as one of the group of Artistic filters, recreates the photo so that it looks like it has been drawn with coarse pastels or crayons.

The filter dialog contains several controls that adjust the look and feel of the effect.

The settings used for the Stroke Length (1) determine the strength of the effect. High values create a coarse result. The Highlight Area slider (2) sets the brightness of the middle and shadow areas. The Intensity option (3) controls how much of the original image detail is retained. Low values maintain much of the detail from the original photo.

Smudge tool

Menu: –
Shortcut: R   **See also:** Liquify filter
Version: 6.0, 7.0, CS, CS2

The Smudge tool is used to push and blur picture parts by click-dragging the mouse cursor.

The tool has been used to add speed lines to the running man in the example.

Similar effects can be created with the Liquify filter.

Before | NEW for CS2

After

History

1717h0011.jpg

Snapshot 1

Crop

Snap and Snap To

Menu: View > Snap, View > Snap To
Shortcut: Ctrl/Cmd Shft ; (Snap)   **See also:** Grid, Guides
Version: 6.0, 7.0, CS, CS2

Used in conjunction with Photoshop's grid and guides features, Snap (View > Snap) and Snap To (View > Snap To) automatically align drawn objects such as shapes and marquees with the nearest grid or guide line.

The Snap To settings control the elements that are used for alignment and the Snap option turns the feature on and off.

Snap to Layers

Menu: View > Snap To > Layers
Shortcut: –   **See also:** Snap and Snap To
Version: CS2

New for Photoshop CS2 is the ability to snap layer contents to the edges of other contents.

The Snap To > Layers option is one of several snap choices that aid the layout of various picture parts in a multi-layer document.

To activate the feature firstly select View > Snap To > Layers then turn on all selected snapping options – choose View > Snap. A small '✓' will be displayed when the feature is activated.

Now when you use the Move tool to arrange picture parts the edges of the layer will snap to the content of other layers in the document.

Snapshot

Menu: –
Shortcut: –   **See also:** History palette
Version: 6.0, 7.0, CS, CS2

Snapshot is a History palette feature that allows you to take an instant record of the state of the open document.

Unlike other history states snapshots can be labeled and are stored for the whole time that the document is open.

You can create a snapshot by pressing the Create a Snapshot button (2) at the bottom of the History palette. The new snapshot is then displayed at the top of the palette (1).

202

Soft Light blending mode

Menu: –	
Shortcut: –	See also: Blend modes
Version: 6.0, 7.0, CS, CS2	

The Soft Light blending mode is one of the group of Overlay modes that base their effects on combining the two layers depending on the tonal value of their contents.

This option is similar to the Overlay mode but produces a more subtle and sometimes less contrasty result. The content of the top layer is either Screened or Multiplied depending on its color and tonal value.

Blending with 50% gray produces no change.

Softening selection edges

Menu: Select > Feather	
Shortcut: Ctrl/Cmd Alt/Opt D	See also: Feather command
Version: 6.0, 7.0, CS, CS2	

The Select > Feather feature softens the edges of existing selections by gradually mixing the edge pixels with transparency (1).

A soft edge can be applied before creating the selection by inputting a Feather value in the selection tool's options bar (2).

Solarize filter

Menu: Filter > Stylize > Solarize	
Shortcut: –	See also: Filters
Version: 6.0, 7.0, CS, CS2	

The Solarize filter, as one of the group of Stylize filters, recreates the look of when a color photograph is exposed to light during its processing. This traditional photographic effect is called solarization.

The filter contains no controls to adjust the strength or look of the effect. The end result is based on inverting some of the hues of the unfiltered image and then adding them back to the picture in combination with the original colors.

NEW for CS2

Sort by ascending filenames

Sort by descending ratings

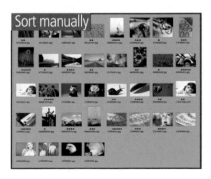

Sort manually

Solid Color fill layer

Menu: Layer > New Fill Layer > Solid Color
Shortcut: –   **See also:** Fill layers
Version: 6.0, 7.0, CS, CS2

The Solid Color fill layer option creates a new layer filled with a selected color (1). The layer's color can be altered at any time by double-clicking on the layer thumbnail (3) and selecting a new hue from the Color Picker palette.

Creating a new Solid Color fill layer is a three-step process. After selecting Layer > New Fill Layer > Solid Color input a name into the New Layer dialog and then choose a color from the Color Picker.

New fill layers can also be created via the option in the Layer menu or by pressing the Create New Adjustment and Fill Layer button (2) in the Layers palette.

Sort Files, Bridge

Menu: Enhance > Adjust Lighting > Levels
Shortcut: Ctrl/Cmd Alt/Opt Shft L   **See also:** Curves, Shadow/
Version: CS2   Highlight

The thumbnails that are displayed in the Bridge workspace can be sorted and displayed in a variety of different ways.

By default the pictures are displayed in ascending order based on their filenames but Bridge provides a variety of other options in the View > Sort menu (1).

Most of the settings listed here are self-explanatory.

In addition, the following related features can also give you control over how your files are displayed:

- The Show options in the View menu,

- Ratings and Labels features together with the filtering options contained in the drop-down menu at the top right of the Bridge workspace.

204

Spatter filter

Menu: Filter > Brush Strokes > Spatter
Shortcut: –   **See also:** Filters
Version: 6.0, 7.0, CS, CS2

The Spatter filter, as one of the group of Brush Strokes filters, repaints the colors and tones of the photo with a spattered spray paint effect.

The filter has two slider controls to adjust the way that the filtered result appears.

The Spray Radius slider (1) determines the strength of the effect and how much of the original photo detail is retained. Low values retain detail.

The Smoothness control (2) varies the way that the color is applied to the picture. High values create an almost watercolor-like effect, whereas low values produce a detailed spattered result.

Specular highlights

Menu: –
Shortcut: –   **See also:** Levels command,
Version: 6.0, 7.0, CS, CS2   Lens Flare filter

Specular highlights are the very bright glints or sparks of light that reflect off very shiny gloss or silvered surfaces.

These highlights contain no detail and are completely white with tonal values of 256 for each of the channels. It is important to recognize and not tone down these highlights when they occur in your pictures.

They need to remain at the pure white level and shouldn't be adjusted back into the white highlight detail area of the tonal range with tools such as Levels or Shadows/Highlights.

Spherize filter

Menu: Filter > Distort > Spherize
Shortcut: –   **See also:** Filters
Version: 6.0, 7.0, CS, CS2

The Spherize filter, as one of the group of Distort filters, shapes the picture onto either the ballooned outside of a ball or the concave inside surface.

The filter dialog contains several controls that adjust the look and feel of the effect. The Amount slider (1) determines the strength of the effect.

The wire frame thumbnail (2) provides an example of the distortion level associated with the amount setting.

The Mode choice (3) allows the user to select to spherize the picture either horizontally, vertically or in both directions. The filter is useful for correcting barrel distortion.

Scanning resolution (samples per inch)	Image size to be scanned	Output size (pixels)	Output size (inches for print @ 200 dpi)	File size (Mb)
4000	35 mm film frame (24 mm x 36 mm)	4000 x 6000	20 x 30	72.00
2900	35 mm	2900 x 4350	14.5 x 21.75	37.80
1200	35 mm	1200 x 1800	6 x 9	6.40
600	35 mm	600 x 900	3 x 4.5	1.62
400	5 x 4 inch print	2000 x 1600	10 x 8	9.60
1000	5 x 4 inch print	5000 x 4000	25 x 20	60.00
400	10 x 8 inch print	4000 x 3200	20 x 16	38.40

NEW for CS2

SPI, samples per inch

Menu: –
Shortcut: –   **See also:** Resolution
Version: 6.0, 7.0, CS, CS2

Scanning resolution, as opposed to image or printing resolution, is determined by the number of times per inch that the scanner samples your original image. The unit of measure for this is called samples per inch or SPI.

The number of pixels generated by a digital camera has an upper limit that is fixed by the number of sensors in the camera. This is not the case for scanner capture. By altering the number of samples taken for each inch of the original print or negative you can change the total number of pixels created in the digital file. This figure will affect both the 'enlargement' potential of the final scan and its file size. The general rule is the higher the resolution the bigger the file and the bigger the printed size possible (before seeing pixel blocks or digital grain).

Does this mean that we always scan at the highest resolution possible? The intelligent answer is NO! The best approach is to balance your scanning settings with your printing needs. If you are working on a design for a postage stamp you will need fewer pixels to play with than if you want your masterpiece in poster format. For this reason it is important to consciously set your scanning resolution keeping in mind your required output size.

Some scanning software will give you an indication of resolution, file size and print size as part of the dialog panel, but for those of you without this facility use the table above as a rough guide.

Before

© www.ablestock.com 2005

After

Sponge tool

Menu: –
Shortcut: O   **See also:** Burn tool,
Version: 6.0, 7.0, CS, CS2   Dodge tool

In addition to using the Hue/Saturation feature to adjust the vividness of color in your image, it is also possible to make changes to specific areas of the picture (1) using the Sponge tool located with the Dodging and Burning tools in the Photoshop toolbar.

The tool can be set to either Saturate (make the colors more vibrant) or Desaturate (decrease the color strength until only the gray tone remains). The size of the area altered is based on the current brush size. The intensity of the effect is controlled by the Flow value found in the options bar. Repeated strokes over the picture to be enhanced gradually builds up the effect.

Just like the dodging and burning tools this feature is very useful for emphasizing a point of focus, but in this case it is achieved by increasing the area's color strength.

Spot Healing brush

Menu: –
Shortcut: J   **See also:** Healing Brush,
Version: CS2   Patch tool

In recognition of just how tricky it can be to get seamless dust removal with the Clone Stamp tool, Adobe decided to include the Spot Healing Brush that originally started life in Photoshop Elements in Photoshop CS2.

After selecting the new tool you adjust the size of the brush tip using the options in the tool's option bar and then click on the dust spots and small marks in your pictures.

The Spot Healing Brush uses the texture that surrounds the mark as a guide to how the program should 'paint over' the area. In this way, Photoshop tries to match color, texture and tone whilst eliminating the dust mark.

The results are terrific and this tool should be the one that you reach for first when there is a piece of dust or a hair mark to remove from your photographs.

Dodge Tool
Burn Tool
Sponge Tool

Spotlight, Lighting Effects filter

Menu: –
Shortcut: –   **See also:** Filters
Version: 6.0, 7.0, CS, CS2

Spotlight is one of the lighting types featured in the Lighting Effects filter. The Spotlight style shines a focused disk of light onto the main subject.

This light type is great for highlighting a specific part of a scene whilst reducing the brightness of the rest of the picture.

Move the position of the light by click-dragging the light's center. You can decrease or increase the size of the spotlight light source by click-dragging one of the light handles.

Adjust the characteristics of the light source by changing its properties. The brightness of the light is determined by the Exposure and Intensity sliders.

Sprayed Strokes filter

Menu: Filter > Brush Strokes > Sprayed Strokes
Shortcut: –   **See also:** Filters
Version: 6.0, 7.0, CS, CS2

The Sprayed Strokes filter, as one of the group of Brush Strokes filters, combines the textured stroke appearance of filters like the Graphic Pen with the sprayed-on approach of the Spatter filter.

The filter dialog contains several controls that adjust the look and feel of the effect.

The Stroke Length slider (1) adjusts the look of the sprayed pattern from a dot, at low values, to a pen-like stroke at higher settings. The Spray Radius control (2) determines both the strength of the effect and the amount of original detail that is conserved. Low values retain more of the original photo and produce subtle results. The Stroke Direction option (3) controls the direction of the line that is used in a repeated pattern.

Stained Glass filter

Menu: Filter > Texture > Stained Glass
Shortcut: –   **See also:** Filters
Version: 6.0, 7.0, CS, CS2

The Stained Glass filter, as one of the group of Texture filters, simulates the look of a stylized stained glass window by breaking the picture into colored cells and surrounding them with a thick black border.

The Cell Size slider (1) determines how large each individual 'glass panel' is. Higher values create bigger cell sizes and retain less of the original picture detail.

The Border Thickness control (2) varies the size of the black edge that surrounds each colored cell. The Light Intensity slider (3) controls brightness of the center of the image.

After Spotlight Lighting Effects

Before

Stamp filter

Menu: Filter > Sketch > Stamp
Shortcut: –   **See also:** Filters
Version: 6.0, 7.0, CS, CS2

The Stamp filter, as one of the group of Sketch filters, converts the picture to just black and white areas and works like a sophisticated version of the Threshold filter.

The filter dialog contains two controls that adjust the look and feel of the effect.

The Light/Dark Balance control (1) determines the tones that are converted to white and those changed to black. High values convert more of the tones to black.

The Smoothness slider (2) varies the amount of edge detail retained in the picture. Lower values contain more detail.

Standard Screen mode

Menu: –
Shortcut: F   **See also:** –
Version: 6.0, 7.0, CS, CS2

Photoshop contains three different screen modes that alter the way in which the workspace appears.

When Photoshop first launches the workspace is set to the default or Standard screen mode. Altering the mode will change the way that the menu bar, title bar, toolbar and scroll bars are displayed. The following options are possible:

Standard Screen Mode – This is the default view with menu bars, scroll bars and palettes visible (1).

Full Screen Mode with Menu Bar – This option switches the document to maximize mode and removes the title bar from the program but keeps the menu bar visible (2).

Full Screen Mode – Shows the image against a black background and hides both the menu and title bars. Menu options can be selected from the side arrow at the top of the toolbar (3).

To change the present screen mode press the F key or click on a different mode button in the toolbar (4).

Changes in screen mode are often used in conjunction with the Tab key which hides the option and toolbars in order to display your picture with no distractions.

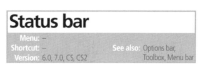

Status bar

Menu: –
Shortcut: –   **See also:** Options bar,
Version: 6.0, 7.0, CS, CS2   Toolbox, Menu bar

The status bar at the bottom of the document window displays a variety of information that includes:

Magnification (2) – The current zoom level.

Data section (1) – displays one of the following: Version Cue, Document Sizes, Document Profile, Document Dimensions, Scratch Sizes, Efficiency, Timing, Current Tool or 32-bit exposure.

To alter the display in the status bar press the sideways arrow and select the Show option before choosing the desired display from the pop-up menu (3).

S

Step Backward

Menu: Edit > Step Backward
Shortcut: Ctrl/Cmd Alt/Opt Z   **See also:** Undo, Redo
Version: 6.0, 7.0, CS, CS2

The Edit > Step Backward command is similar to the Edit > Undo option in that it returns the picture to its state before the last change.

Choosing the option repeatedly gradually steps back through all current history states

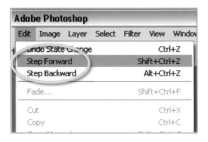

Step Forward

Menu: Edit > Step Forward
Shortcut: Ctrl/Cmd Shft Z   **See also:** Undo, Redo
Version: 6.0, 7.0, CS, CS2

The Edit > Step Forward command returns the picture to the next step in the History palette list.

The option is only available if you have first stepped backward.

Stock Photos, Bridge

Menu: –
Shortcut: –   **See also:** Bridge
Version: CS2

The Bridge application is not only a pivot point for the organization of your own digital media assets but the feature can also be used to search for, pay, download and managed stock images and illustrations.

Adobe has linked with Photodisc, Comstock Images, DigitalVision, Imageshop and Amana to provide Photoshop users with access to hundreds of thousands of stock photos.

The collection can be searched or browsed from inside of the Bridge workspace and candidate images can be downloaded in a low resolution comp form suitable for creating presentation visuals to clients. Full resolution versions of the photos can be paid for and downloaded all without leaving the Bridge application.

Straighten (and crop)

Menu: File > Automate > Crop and Straighten
Shortcut: –   **See also:** Crop tool
Version: 6.0, 7.0, CS, CS2

The Crop and Straighten Image option in Photoshop is designed for enhancing scanned images that have been captured a little askew.

The feature isolates the consistent neutral background in the original scan and automatically remove this white space as it straightens and crops the picture.

If the crop or straighten effect is not accurate Edit > Undo the results and use the Crop tool manually.

Stroke a selection

Menu: Edit > Stroke
Shortcut: –　　　　**See also:** Borders – printing
Version: 6.0, 7.0, CS, CS2

Photoshop has a function called Stroke which is often used to create simple line borders around photos. This command is used to draw a line that follows the edge of a selection.

So the process of creating a border requires the creation of a selection first and whilst it is still active, applying a Stroke to the marquee's edge.

In the example we simply select the whole image and stroke the selection with a line of a given color and pixel width.

Open a suitable image in Photoshop. Here we use a picture of a red Vespa. Make a selection of the whole photo using Select > All.

Now to draw a line that follows the selection. Using the Edit > Stroke feature we can trace the selection with a line that is the foreground color and a set number of pixels wide.

Be sure to select the color of the stroke and 'inside' for the stroke location.

Style settings

Menu: Layer > Layer Style
Shortcut: –　　　　**See also:** Layer Styles
Version: 6.0, 7.0, CS, CS2

Layer styles can be applied very effectively to type and image layers and provide a quick and easy way to enhance the look of these picture elements.

Everything from a simple drop shadow to complex surface and color treatments can be applied using this single-click feature.

Each style is applied using the default values that were set when it was first created but these attributes can be adjusted to suit the context in which you are using the effect.

The settings of individual styles and the effects that they are comprised of can be edited by double-clicking on the 'f' icon (1) in the text layer and adjusting one or more of the style settings in the dialog that appears (2).

The particular effects used for each style are listed below the layer in the Layers palette (3).

Styles palette

Menu: Window > Styles and Effects
Shortcut: –　　　　**See also:** Layer Styles
Version: 6.0, 7.0, CS, CS2

A collection of layer styles that are included in Photoshop can be found in the Styles palette.

A variety of different style groups are available from the drop-down list (1) accessed via the side arrows button in the top right of the palette. Small example images (2) of each style listed are provided as a preview of the effect.

Additional styles can be downloaded from websites specializing in resources for Photoshop users. These should be installed into the Adobe\Photoshop\Presets\Styles folder. The next time you start Photoshop, the new styles will appear in the Layer Styles palette.

Alternatively they can be loaded into the palette via the Load Style entry in the pop-up menu (3).

S

Sumi-e filter

Menu: Filter > Brush Strokes > Sumi-e
Shortcut: –   **See also:** Filters
Version: 6.0, 7.0, CS, CS2

The Sumi-e filter, as one of the group of Brush Strokes filters, recreates the photo with softer hues in broad areas of color that are defined with a dark outline and small strokes to indicate texture.

The filter dialog contains several controls that adjust the look and feel of the effect.

The Stroke Width slider (1) determines how fine the border and texture stroke will be. High values create pictures with strong edges and dark texture.

The Stroke Pressure control (2) varies the strength of the texture as well as what proportion of the image it covers.

The Contrast option (3) adjusts the overall contrast present in the filtered photo.

Surface Blur filter

Menu: Filter > Blur > Surface Blur
Shortcut: –   **See also:** Filters
Version: CS2

The Surface Blur filter is a new addition to the Blur filter line-up. The filter blurs whilst at the same time preserving edge detail.

Careful adjusting of the two slider controls in the filter allows precise placement of the blur effect making this feature useful for minimizing noise in an overly grainy picture.

The Radius slider (1) controls the strength of the effect and the Threshold setting (2) is used to adjust which pixels are blurred and which are considered edges and therefore preserved.

Swatches palette

Menu: Window > Swatches
Shortcut: –   **See also:** Palettes
Version: 6.0, 7.0, CS, CS2

The Swatches palette houses the color swatch groups and color tables that are available for use in Photoshop.

The palette is displayed by selecting Window > Swatches. Swatch groups that are already loaded into the palette can be displayed by selecting them from the side arrow drop-down menu (2).

Additional swatch groups can be loaded into the palette via the Load command in the pop-up menu accessed by pressing the side arrow button (1).

Customized swatch groups can be saved using the Save Swatches option also available in this menu.

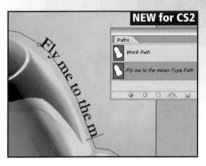

NEW for CS2

Text

Menu:	–
Shortcut:	–
Version:	6.0, 7.0, CS, CS2

See also: Type

'Text' is often used interchangeably with 'Type' to indicate the Photoshop tool used for combining letters, words, sentences and phrases with your photos and illustrations (2).

Blocks of text can be selected in other programs, such as Microsoft Word (1), copied and then pasted into a Photoshop picture as a new Type layer.

Text on a Path

Menu:	–
Shortcut:	–
Version:	CS2

See also: Type

Adding type to a path is a new feature for Photoshop but it is one that should be familiar to users of DTP or illustration packages.

Start by creating a path in the shape that you want the text to follow. Make sure that the path is active in Paths palette. Next select the Type tool from the Photoshop toolbar and position the tool's pointer so that it is over the path. The pointer (cursor) will change to the Type on a Path pointer. Click to set a starting point and then input your text.

If you have selected the Horizontal Type tool the letter shapes will be placed at right angles to the path. Using the Vertical Type tool will straddle the letter shapes along the path.

Grayscale Texture Fill file

Texturizer
Texture: Brick
Scaling 159 %
Relief 22
Light: Top

NEW for CS2

Image Layer Select Filter View Window
Mode ▸ Bitmap
  Grayscale
Adjustments ▸ Duotone
  Indexed Color
Duplicate... ✓ RGB Color
Apply Image... CMYK Color
Calculations... Lab Color
  Multichannel
Image Size... Alt+Ctrl+I
Canvas Size... Alt+Ctrl+C 8 Bits/Channel...
Pixel Aspect Ratio ▸ 16 Bits/Channel...
Rotate Canvas ▸ ✓ 32 Bits/Channel
Crop
Trim...

Texture Fill filter

Menu: Filter > Render > Texture Fill
Shortcut: –   **See also:** Filters
Version: 6.0, 7.0, CS, CS2

The Texture Fill filter, as one of the group of Render filters, fills a layer or picture by seamlessly repeating a selected grayscale picture.

The filter contains no controls for altering the strength or look and feel of the effect. After selecting the Texture Fill option a file browser window is displayed. It is here that you locate the picture to be used for the effect. Clicking OK fills the current picture with a repeating pattern of the selected texture picture.

To make a color photo suitable for use as a Texture Fill file you must first change its color mode to grayscale (Image > Mode > Grayscale) and then save the image in the PSD format (File > Save As).

Texturizer filter

Menu: Filter > Texture > Texturizer
Shortcut: –   **See also:** Filters
Version: 6.0, 7.0, CS, CS2

The Texturizer filter, as one of the group of Texture filters, recreates the picture to give the appearance that the photo has been printed onto the surface of a particular texture.

The Scaling (2) and Relief (3) sliders control the strength and visual dominance of the texture, whilst the Light direction (4) menu alters the position of the highlight and shadow areas. Different surface types are available from the Texture drop-down menu (1).

The filter also contains the option to add your own files and have these used as the texture that is applied by the filter to the image. Use the steps below to create your own texture for use with the filter.

32-bit files

Menu: Image > Mode > 32 bits/channel
Shortcut: –   **See also:** High Dynamic Range
Version: CS2

In Photoshop CS2 Adobe has introduced the ability to perform basic operations on 32 bits per channel files. Though the operations that you can perform on these documents are still limited the introduction of new high dynamic range technology will help photographers capture and manipulate the full tonal range that exists in high contrast scenes.

High dynamic range (HDR) images contain 32 bits per color channel which is substantially more information levels of tone per color channel than what is contained in a standard 8 bits per channel file and is more than capable of storing a contrast range of 100,000:1.

1 Open Recent ▸
Edit in ImageReady   Shift+Ctrl+M
Close   Ctrl+W
Close All   Alt+Ctrl+W
Close and Go To Bridge...   Shift+Ctrl+W
Save   Ctrl+S
Save As...   Shift+Ctrl+S
Save for Web...   Alt+Shift+Ctrl+S

Shoot, scan or design a texture image and save as a Photoshop file (.PSD).

Select the Texturizer filter from the Texture heading in the Filter menu.

2 Load Texture...
20
22

Pick the Load Texture item from the drop-down list in the Texture menu. Browse folders and files to locate texture files. Click filename and then open to select.

3 Texturizer
Texture: texture 18 filter
Scaling
Relief 34
Light: Top
Invert
Texturizer

Once back at the Texturizer dialog, move the Scaling slider to change the size of the texture. Adjust the Relief slider to control the dominance of the filter. Select a Light direction to adjust the highlights and shadow areas of the texture. Click OK to filter the photo.

Original photo

32-bit preview options

Menu: –	
Shortcut: –	**See also:** High Dynamic Range
Version: CS2	

As the brightness range stored in a high dynamic range (HDR) file is beyond the display abilities of current monitor technology, Photoshop CS2 includes an interactive feature that allows users to alter the way that these files are displayed.

When displayed the 32-bit Exposure option (1) is located at the bottom of the document window and contains a single slider that can be used to control the way the HDR preview image is displayed on screen.

To display the feature select the Show > 32-bit Exposure item from the pop-up menu (2) in the documents status bar.

3D Transform – Cube

3D Transform – Sphere

3D Transform – Cylinder

3D Transform filter

Menu: Filter > Render > 3D Transform	
Shortcut: –	**See also:** Filters
Version: 6.0, 7.0, CS, CS2	

The 3D Transform filter, as one of the group of Render filters, projects the photo onto either a cube, sphere or cylinder and then lets you move and rotate the object in three dimensions.

To the left of the filter's dialog there is a toolbar (1) containing features used for defining and manipulating the three-dimensional objects that the picture is projected upon.

The middle of the dialog is taken up with an interactive preview (2) that displays the original picture and the superimposed 3D object.

The filter tools can be used to place, size and rotate the object within the boundaries of the preview window. Clicking OK applies the transformation.

Since the CS version of Photoshop the 3D Transform filter has been included as an optional plug-in on the CD but is not automatically installed. To use this filter copy the plug-in to the Photoshop filters folder and then restart the program.

Before

After Tile

Threshold filter

Menu: Filter > Adjustments > Threshold
Shortcut: –   **See also:** Filters
Version: 6.0, 7.0, CS, CS2

The Threshold filter, as one of the group of Adjustment filters, converts the picture to pure black and white, removing any tonal detail in the process. Tones darker than a selected point in the tonal scale are converted to black and those lighter than the selected value are converted to white.

The filter dialog contains a single slider control that selects the precise tonal level, which marks the change point (1) between black and white. A histogram of the distribution of the pixels in the picture is also included.

TIFF

Menu: File > Save As
Shortcut: Ctrl/Cmd Shft S   **See also:** JPEG format,
Version: 6.0, 7.0, CS, CS2   GIF format,
                                                Photoshop format

TIFF or Tagged Image File Format is generally considered the industry standard for images destined for publishing (magazines and books, etc.). In its most basic form TIFF uses a 'lossless' compression (no loss of image data or quality) called 'LZW compression'. Although preserving the quality of the image, LZW compression is only capable of compressing images a small amount.

Photoshop as well as the most recent edition of Photoshop Elements have included the ability to save in an upgraded TIFF format that contains a host of new options. These include the ability to include layers, save with a compression system other than LZW and the chance to specify how the content for individual layers is compressed.

Care should be taken when saving TIFF files using these new options as not all non-Adobe programs are completely 'savvy' with the changes in the new format. If in doubt, stick to TIFF with LZW compression and no layers.

Tile

Menu: Window > Arrange > Tile
Shortcut: –   **See also:** Tile Horizontally,
Version: 6.0, 7.0, CS   Tile Vertically

The Tile mode is one of the many ways that open pictures can be viewed in Photoshop. Selecting this option from the Window > Arrange menu will adjust the size of the pictures currently open in the workspace so that they can all fit on screen (with no overlapping).

In Photoshop CS2 this option has been replaced with the more useful Tile Horizontally and Tile Vertically commands.

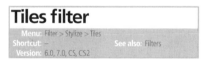

Tile Horizontally

Menu: Window > Arrange > Tile Horizontally	
Shortcut: –	**See also:** Tile Vertically,
Version: CS2	Tile

New to Photoshop is the Tile Horizontally option in the Window > Arrange menu.

Like the standard tile feature, this selection resizes the pictures that are currently open in the Photoshop workspace and arranges them so that all document windows are positioned edge to edge. But unlike the tile option, Tile Horizontally resizes the document windows so that they all form horizontal rectangles.

Tile Vertically

Menu: Window > Arrange > Tile Vertically	
Shortcut: –	**See also:** Tile Horizontally,
Version: CS2	Tile

An alternative to the Tile Horizontally option is the new Tile Vertically option that is also included in the Window > Arrange menu.

Like the standard tile feature, this selection resizes the pictures that are currently open in the Photoshop workspace and arranges them so that all document windows are positioned edge to edge. But unlike the tile option, Tile Vertically resizes the document windows so that they all form vertical rectangles.

Tiles filter

Menu: Filter > Stylize > Tiles	
Shortcut: –	**See also:** Filters
Version: 6.0, 7.0, CS, CS2	

The Tiles filter, as one of the group of Stylize filters, breaks the photo into a series of same-size tiles that are then randomly offset.

The filter dialog contains two main control areas. The number of tiles and maximum offset setting that is used in the filter are set in the first section of the dialog (1). Start with low values and then adjust if necessary.

The second area contains four options that determine what will be used to fill the vacant areas in the image that are created between the offset tiles (2).

Tolerance setting

Menu: –	
Shortcut: –	**See also:** Magic Wand tool, Paint
Version: 6.0, 7.0, CS,	Bucket tool, Color Replace-
CS2	ment tool, Magic Eraser tool,
	Background Eraser tool

The Tolerance setting (1) is found in the options bar of tools that make selections or picture changes based on the color and brightness of a group of pixels.

Essentially it is a setting that determines how identical a pixel has to be to the original to be included in the selection (2) or pixels that are changed. The higher the Tolerance value, the less alike the two pixels need to be, whereas a lower setting will require a more exact match before a pixel is added to the selection or pixel group to be changed.

Tools that have a Tolerance setting in their options bar include:

• Magic Wand
• Paint Bucket
• Color Replacement
• Magic Eraser
• Background Eraser
• Impressionist Brush and
• Replace Color (Fuzziness slider)

Tool Presets

Menu: Window > Tool Presets	
Shortcut: –	**See also:** Preset Manager
Version: 6.0, 7.0, CS, CS2	

Specific tool settings can be saved, edited and reused by adding them to the Tool Presets palette (1) (Window > Tool Presets) or the Tool Presets Picker in the options bar (2).

Storing your most used tools and their set-up here can speed up regular tasks.

Tolerance setting – 10

Tolerance setting – 50

Tolerance setting – 130

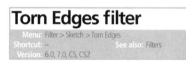

Toolbox

Menu: –	
Shortcut: –	**See also:** Menu bar
Version: 6.0, 7.0, CS, CS2	

Tools interact directly with the image and require the user to manipulate the mouse to define the area or extent of the tool's effect. The tools in Photoshop are all stored in a common toolbox (1 – see left), which is positioned on the left-hand side of the workspace.

Some tools contain extra options which can be viewed by clicking and holding the mouse key over the small triangle in the bottom right-hand corner of the tool button (2).

Alternatively the submenu may list a variety of tools related to the one currently selected. Selecting a new option from those listed will replace the current icon in the toolbox with your new choice. To switch back simply reselect the original tool.

The toolbox can be moved around the screen by click-dragging its title bar.

Tools, Bridge

Menu: Bridge: Tools > Photoshop	
Shortcut: –	**See also:** Bridge
Version: CS2	

Although no real editing or enhancement options are available in the Bridge feature it is possible to use the browser as a starting point for many of the operations normally carried out in Photoshop.

For instance, photos selected in the workspace can be batch renamed, printed online, used to create a Photomerge panorama, compiled into a contact sheet or combined into a PDF-based presentation all via options under the Tools menu.

Some of these choices will open Photoshop before completing the requested task whereas others are completed without leaving the Bridge workspace.

The precise options that are available in the Tools menu will depend on which components of Creative Suite 2 are installed on your machine.

Torn Edges filter

Menu: Filter > Sketch > Torn Edges	
Shortcut: –	**See also:** Filters
Version: 6.0, 7.0, CS, CS2	

The Torn Edges filter, as one of the group of Sketch filters, converts the picture to pure black and white shapes like the Threshold filter. Unlike this option though, the edges of the shapes are coarse and feathered and the dark and light tones contain a slight texture.

The filter dialog contains three sliders to alter the look of the end result.

The Image Balance slider (1) selects a tonal level to act as a turning point between black and white. High values create large dark areas as more tones are converted to black. The Smoothness option (2) adjusts how rough the edge areas are. High values produce a sharp demarcation between black and white, low values create a more textured, 'torn' look.

The Contrast control (3) adjusts the starkness of the final result. High values produce a more contrasty result.

T

A-Z

Before Transformation

After

Distort

Perspective

Skew / Warp

Trace Contour filter

Menu: Filter > Stylize > Trace Contour
Shortcut: –   See also: Filters
Version: 6.0, 7.0, CS, CS2

The Trace Contour filter, as one of the group of Stylize filters, locates picture parts where there is a big change in brightness and then outlines these with a thin colored line against a white background.

The Level slider (1) in the filter dialog sets the level of difference necessary to be outlined. The Lower and Upper options (2) nominate whether pixels with lighter values (upper) or darker values (lower) will be examined.

The end result is like a contour map of the contrast of the picture in a select tonal range.

Transform again

Menu: Edit > Transform > Transform Again
Shortcut: Ctrl/Cmd Shift T   See also: Transformations
Version: 6.0, 7.0, CS, CS2

Remembers the last transformation that you applied and repeats the action.

This is a useful option if you're creating a composite picture and are pasting in and adjusting several elements.

Transformations

Menu: Edit > Transform
Shortcut: –   See also: Free Transform command, Skew, Perspective changing, Warp
Version: 6.0, 7.0, CS, CS2

The Edit > Transform menu (1) contains four options that allow you to change the shape of your pictures from their standard rectangle format.

The **Scale** option is used for altering the size of the layer content.

Rotate provides a way to pivot the layer contents around a single point arbitrarily.

The **Skew** feature allows you to push and pull the sides of the rectangle to form diamond shapes.

The **Distort** allows you to move the corner handles of the picture totally independently.

You can correct or create converging verticals and other shape changes using the **Perspective** option.

Warp is a new addition to the transformations menu and provides a set of tools for twisting and distorting layer content in much the same way as the Warp Text feature and the Liquify filter.

After selecting the feature that you wish to use you may be prompted to change the background to a standard layer ready for transformation. Click Yes in this dialog.

When completed either double-click on the transformed layer or press the Enter/Return key to 'commit' the changes. To cancel press the Esc key.

The **Free Transform** (Edit > Free Transform) feature combines all the above (except Warp) and can be used to scale, rotate, distort, skew or even apply perspective changes to your picture.

Transparency option, GIF and PNG

Menu: File > Save for Web
Shortcut: Ctrl/Cmd Alt/Opt Shft S   **See also:** GIF format
Version: 6.0, 7.0, CS, CS2

The GIF (1) and PNG (2) formats are unique among file types that are suitable for web use in that they both contain an option for transparency.

To ensure that the transparent component in your picture is maintained when saved select the Transparency box in the Save for Web feature.

The Transparency option is good when you are working with graphics that are meant to sit upon a textured background and blend in seamlessly.

Trapping

Menu: Image > Trap (CMYK picture only)
Shortcut: –   **See also:** CMYK
Version: 6.0, 7.0, CS, CS2

A trap is a tiny overlap of picture parts that prevents small gaps appearing when printed using print technology based on several plates. Gaps occur if there's a slight misalignment or movement of the printing plates.

Photoshop can automatically apply trapping to CMYK-based pictures using the Image > Trap command.

Your printer will tell you when you need to use this feature and what values to enter in the Trap dialog box (1).

The Trap item (2) only appears on the Image menu when you are working with a picture that is in CMYK mode.

Trim

Menu: Image > Trim
Shortcut: –   **See also:** Reveal All
Version: 6.0, 7.0, CS, CS2

The Image > Trim command locates and removes unwanted background areas from a picture.

The feature can be set to base the trimmed area on the top left pixel, transparency or the bottom right pixel.

You can also choose which sides of the image you want trimmed.

Duotone Options

Type: Tritone

Ink 1: Black

Ink 2: PANTONE 216 CVC

Ink 3: PANTONE 409 CVC

OK
Cancel
Load...
Save...
☑ Preview

Duotone Curve

0:	0	%	60:		%
5:		%	70:		%
10:		%	80:	30	%
20:		%	90:		%
30:		%	95:		%
40:		%	100:	90	%
50:	0	%			

OK
Cancel
Load...
Save...

Tritones

Menu: Image > Mode > Duotone then Tritone
Shortcut: –   See also: Duotone
Version: 6.0, 7.0, CS, CS2

Just like their two color brothers, Duotones, the Tritone is a way of extending the tonal range of grayscale pictures by adding two other colors to the standard black ink.

Designed to help produce better black and white prints from offset printers Tritones are also frequently used to add subtle toning to black and white images.

You can Tritone preset by clicking on the Load button (1) and locating a suitable recipe in the Presets folder, or create your own color by clicking on the colored ink squares to call up the color wheel.

Before

Tritones – Red

Tritones – Brown

Tritones – Green

Tritones – Blue

Tritones – Sepia

T

Before

After Twirl

TWAIN

Menu: File > Import
Shortcut: –   **See also:** WIA support
Version: 6.0, 7.0, CS, CS2

The TWAIN interface provides a link between Photoshop and your camera and scanners. After installing a new camera or scanner, Photoshop must be restarted to register the device on the File > Import menu.

If more than one scanner or camera is installed then each device will be listed on this menu.

Selecting a TWAIN entry from the Import menu opens a separate driver window that either controls your scanner or provides download options for your camera. Input your scan settings and start the scanning process or select the picture to be downloaded from your camera. Once the download or scanning process is completed the image appears in Photoshop as a new document named Untitled.

It's wise to save this Untitled file straight away, because if the computer crashes you'll lose the file and will have to scan or download the photograph again.

In the Windows work environment many scanners and cameras are now connected using the WIA interface instead of the TWAIN technology detailed here.

Twirl filter

Menu: Filter > Distort > Twirl
Shortcut: –   **See also:** Filters
Version: 6.0, 7.0, CS, CS2

The Twirl filter, as one of the group of Distort filters, twists the picture around a central point, creating a spiral effect.

The filter dialog contains a single slider that controls the Angle of the effect (1). Movements to the right (positive values) create a clockwise rotation of the picture. Sliding the control to the left produces an anti-clockwise spiral (negative values).

The wire frame (2) and standard previews indicate the strength at the settings selected and predict the look and feel of the end results.

Twirl tool

Menu: Filter > Liquify
Shortcut: –   **See also:** Liquify filter, Bloat
Version: 6.0, 7.0, CS, CS2   tool, Pinch filter

The Twirl tools are two of the several tools in the Liquify filter that allow you to stretch, twist, push and pull your pictures. They spiral the pixels in a pivot around the center of the brush. The result is similar to that obtained with the Twirl filter.

To twirl your pictures, select either tool (Clockwise or Counter Clockwise) then adjust the brush size so that it is the same dimensions as the area to be changed and then hold down the mouse button until the picture has changed the required amount. You can drag the mouse across the canvas, twirling the pixels as you go.

To reverse the tool's effect either select the Revert button (top right) or paint over the surface with the Reconstruct tool.

Type

Menu: –
Shortcut: T   **See also:** Type editing,
Version: 6.0, 7.0, CS, CS2   Type Masks

Photoshop contains four different Type tools – two standard tools and two mask tools (1).

Of the standard Type tools (non-mask varieties), one is used for entering text that runs horizontally across the canvas and the other is for entering vertical type.

To place text onto your picture, select the Type tool from the toolbox. Next, click onto the canvas in the area where you want the text to appear.

Do not be too concerned if the letters are not positioned exactly, as the layer and text can be moved later. Once you have finished entering text you need to commit the type to a layer. Until this is done you will be unable to access most other Photoshop functions.

To exit the text editor, either click the 'tick' button in the options bar or press the Control + Enter keys in Windows or Command + Return for a Macintosh system.

Type editing

Menu: –
Shortcut: T   **See also:** Type, Type Masks
Version: 6.0, 7.0, CS, CS2

All the usual text change options that you would expect to find in word processors are available in Photoshop.

It is possible to alter the size, style, color and font of your type using the settings in the options bar (2).

You can either make the setting selections before you input your text or later by highlighting (clicking and dragging the mouse across the text) the portion of type that you want to change and then altering the settings (1).

In addition to these adjustments, you can also alter the justification or alignment of a line or paragraph of type.

After selecting the type to be aligned, click one of the justification buttons on the options bar. Your text will realign automatically on screen.

After making a few changes, you may wish to alter the position of the text; simply click and drag outside of the type area to move it around. If you have already committed the changes to a text layer then select the Move tool from the toolbox, making sure that the text layer is selected, then click and drag to move the whole layer (3).

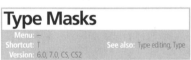

Type Masks

Menu: –
Shortcut: T   **See also:** Type editing, Type
Version: 6.0, 7.0, CS, CS2

The Type Mask tools are used to provide precise masks or selections in the shape and size of the text you input.

Rather than creating a new text layer containing solid colored text, the mask tools produce a selection outline. From this point on, the text mask can be used as you would use any other selection.

Adding text to Indexed Color or Bitmap mode files (which don't support layers) automatically creates Type Mask text.

223

Underline

Underlining type

Menu: –	
Shortcut: –	**See also:** Faux fonts
Version: 6.0, 7.0, CS, CS2	

The Type tool's Underline option draws a straight line below the group of letters it is applied to (1). The thickness and color of the line are determined by the current font size and color.

To add an underline to existing text, start by selecting the letters (click-drag the type cursor over the letter group) and then press the Underline button in the Character palette (Window > Character).

To create underline text from the very first letter you input, select the Type tool and then press the Underline option in the Character palette (2). Next click onto the canvas surface and add the text as normal.

Underpainting filter

Menu: Filter > Artistic > Underpainting	
Shortcut: –	**See also:** Filters
Version: 6.0, 7.0, CS, CS2	

The Underpainting filter, as one of the group of Artistic filters, adds both texture and brush stroke effects to the photo.

The dialog contains several controls that adjust the painting and texture effects. The top slider, Brush Size (1), alters the broadness of the brush stroke used to paint the picture. The Texture Coverage slider (2) controls how much of the picture the texture is applied to.

Texture options are provided in the bottom section of the dialog (3). The Texture and Light drop-down menus found here, along with the Scaling and Relief sliders, determine the type and strength of the underlying texture effect.

Before Undo ❷

After Undo ❶

© www.allstock.com 2005

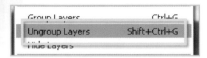

Group Layers	Ctrl+G
Ungroup Layers	Shift+Ctrl+G
Hide Layers	

Ungroup Layers

Menu: Layer > Ungroup Layers
Shortcut: Shft Ctrl/Cmd G   **See also:** Group
Version: 6.0, 7.0, CS, CS2

To ungroup all layers in a group (set) select the group heading in the Layers palette and then choose Layer > Ungroup Layers.

Unsharp Mask filter

Menu: Filter > Sharpen > Unsharp Mask
Shortcut: –   **See also:** Smart Sharpen filter
Version: 6.0, 7.0, CS, CS2

Of the various sharpen filters that Photoshop contains the Unsharp Mask and the Smart Sharpen filters provide the greatest control over the sharpening process by giving the user a range of sliders which when adjusted alter the way the effect is applied to pictures. Though a little confusing to start with, the Unsharp Mask filter is one of the best ways to make your scans or digital photographs clearer. However, to get the most out of the feature you must carefully control the three sliders.

The **Amount** slider (1) controls the strength of the sharpening effect. Larger numbers will produce more pronounced results whereas smaller values will create more subtle effects. Values of 50% to 100% are suitable for low-resolution pictures whereas settings between 150% and 200% can be used on images with a higher resolution.

The **Radius** slider (2) value determines the number of pixels around the edge that are affected by the sharpening. A low value only sharpens edge pixels. High settings can produce noticeable halo effects around your picture so start with a low value first. Typically values between 1 and 2 are used for high-resolution images, settings of 1 or less for screen images.

The **Threshold** slider (3) is used to determine how different the pixels must be before they are considered an edge and therefore sharpened. A value of 0 will sharpen all the pixels in an image whereas a setting of 10 will only apply the effect to those areas that are different by at least 10 levels or more from their surrounding pixels. To ensure that no sharpening occurs in sky or skin tone areas set this value to 8 or more.

File	Edit	Image	Layer	Select	Filter	View	Window
	Undo Hue/Saturation						Ctrl+Z
	Step Forward						Shift+Ctrl+Z
	Step Backward						Alt+Ctrl+Z

Undo

Menu: Edit > Undo (last action)
Shortcut: Ctrl/Cmd Z   **See also:** History palette, Redo
Version: 6.0, 7.0, CS, CS2

The Undo command reverses the changes made by the last action. In effect by selecting the Undo command you are converting the picture back to the state it was before the last action.

Located under the Edit menu, the actual Undo entry changes depending on the nature of the last action. In the example, the command reads 'Undo Adjust Hue/ Saturation' as the last change to the picture was made using the Hue/Saturation feature. Selecting Undo reverses the changes (2) and restores the picture to its state before the feature was applied (1).

Unlock

Menu: –
Shortcut: –   **See also:** Lock options
Version: 6.0, 7.0, CS, CS2

Photoshop contains four lock options located at the top of the Layers palette. These buttons enable the locking of layer transparency, pixels, position or all of these characteristics.

To apply a lock select a layer and click the appropriate lock button (1). To remove or unlock the layer press the button again (2).

224

U

Amount:	119	%	①
Radius:	1.4	pixels	②
Threshold:	0	levels	③

Amount – 100, Radius – 1.0, Threshold – 0

No sharpening

Before

A – 250, R – 1.0, T – 0

A – 500, R – 1.0, T – 20

After

Unwarp type

Menu: –
Shortcut: –
Version: 6.0, 7.0, CS, CS2
See also: Warp Text command

A – 500, R – 1.0, T – 0

A – 500, R – 20, T – 0

The Warp Text option creates twisted, stretched and distorted versions of text layers in Photoshop. The effect is applied by pressing the Warp Text button on the Type tool's options bar and then adjusting the settings in the Warp Text dialog. Once applied the layer thumbnail changes to indicate that the text has been warped (1). To unwarp the text, double-click the text layer, to switch to the Type tool and then press the Warp Text button on the tool's options bar. Next choose the None entry (2) from the Style menu in the Warp Text dialog. This action removes the warp effect from the text layer.

A – 500, R – 5.0, T – 0

A – 500, R – 10, T – 0

Updater

Menu: Help > Updates		
Shortcut: –	**See also:** –	
Version: CS2		

The Adobe Update Manager is a automatic utility that installs with Photoshop and is responsible for maintaining the currency of the program. The feature checks for the availability of new updates for Adobe software via an active web link at the time of starting the program.

The default settings for the feature can be altered in the Adobe Updater Preferences dialog (1). Which is displayed when Photoshop first opens or by selecting Help > Updates (2).

URL

Menu: –		
Shortcut: –	**See also:** –	
Version: 6.0, 7.0, CS, CS2		

Uniform Resource Locator, or URL, is the formal term that refers to the web address (1) of a specific website.

Clicking on the colored feathers icon (2) at the top of the toolbar is a shortcut to locating the official Photoshop website or URL. Pressing this button takes you directly to the site.

Use All Layers

Menu: –		
Shortcut: –	**See also:** –	
Version: 6.0, 7.0, CS, CS2		

The Use All Layers option (1) found in options bar of the Clone Stamp, Smudge, Blur, Sharpen, Paint Bucket and Healing Brush tools. It allows the user to select a sample area based on all visible layers not just the contents of the selected layer.

In CS2 the Use All Layers option has been replaced with the Sample All Layers feature (2). This setting still resides on the options bar of the tools with which it can be used.

Vanishing Point filter

Menu: Filter > Vanishing Point
Shortcut: Ctrl/Cmd Alt/Opt V   **See also:** –
Version: CS2

The Vanishing Point filter is a new addition to the specialist filter line-up that includes Extract, Lens Blur and Liquify. Like the others, the feature has its own dialog complete with preview image, toolbox and options bar. The filter allows the user to copy and paste and even Clone Stamp portions of a picture whilst maintaining the perspective of the original scene. Using the filter is a two-step process:

Define perspective planes

To start, you must define the perspective planes in the photo. This is achieved by selecting the Create Plane tool and marking each of the four corners of the rectangular-shaped feature that sits in perspective on the plane. A blue grid means that it is correct perspective, yellow that it is borderline, and red that it is mathematically impossible. In the example, the four corners of a window were used to define the plane of the building's front face. Next, a second plane that is linked to the first at an edge is dragged onto the surface of the left side wall.

Copy and Paste or Stamp

With the planes established the Marquee tool can be used to select image parts which can be copied, pasted and then dragged in perspective around an individual plane and even onto another linked plane. All the time the perspective of the copy will alter to suit the plane it is positioned on. The feature's Stamp tool operates like a standard Stamp tool except that the copied section is transformed to account for the perspective of the plane when it is applied to the base picture.

Usage summary:

1. Create a new layer above the image layer to be edited (Layer > New > Layer) and then choose the Vanishing Point filter from the Filter menu.

2. Select the Create Plane tool and click on the top left corner of a rectangle that sits on the plane you wish to define. Locate and click on the top right, bottom right and bottom left corners. If the plane has been defined correctly the corner selection box will change to a perspective plane grid. In the example, the front face of the building was defined first.

3. To create a second, linked, plane, Ctrl-click the middle handle of the existing

Before

After

228

plane and drag away from the edge. The left side of the building was defined using the second plane.

4. To copy the window from the building's front face, select the Marquee tool first, set a small feather value to soften the edges and then outline the window to be copied. Choose Edit > Copy then Edit > Paste menu options. This pastes a copy of the window in the same position as the original Marquee selection.

5. Click-drag the copy from the front face around to the side plane. The window (copied selection) will automatically snap to the new perspective plane and will reduce in size as it is moved further back in the plane. Position the window on the wall surface and choose Heal > Luminance from the Marquee options bar.

6. Press 'T' to enter the Transform mode and select Flip from the option bar to re-orientate the window so that the inside edge of the framework matches the other openings on the wall. Click OK to complete the process.

Vanishing Point tips:

Use the Edit Plane tool to click and drag the corners of the grid if grid lines do not match up with the edges of the picture parts that are sitting on the perspective plane.

In order to copy and paste in full perspective the source plane and destination plane must be joined by a series of linked perspective planes.

Use the Heal option to help match tones of the copied parts and their new locations.

Grids can be output as layers, are 16-bit capable, text can be pasted into a grid and grids are auto-saved as part of the PSD file format.

Vanishing Point tool

Menu: –
Shortcut: V (in Photomerge)   **See also:** Photomerge
Version: CS, CS2

When editing a panorama in Photomerge with the Perspective option selected, you can change the vanishing point from the default middle picture to any of the other source photos in the composition.

With a Photomerge composition open select the Perspective option from the settings on the right of the dialog (1). Next select the Vanishing Point tool (2) from the Photomerge toolbar on the left of the dialog and click onto the picture in the

composition to use as the new vanishing point. This photo will now be used as the basis for perspective in the panorama.

There can only be one vanishing point in any photomerge composition and the Vanishing Point tool only works with compositions that cover less than 120° of the view.

NEW for CS2

Variable Data Sets, apply

Menu: Image > Variables > Apply Data Set
Shortcut: –   **See also:** Variable Data Sets
Version: CS2   data sets

Once the base image has been created and the Data Sets compiled it is possible to apply any of the data sets and their picture, text and/or visibility settings to the base picture with the Apply Data Set feature.

After selecting the Apply Data Set option from the Image menu you can select the set and preview how the base template looks with the data applied. When you are happy with the set selected press the Apply button to permanently insert the data from the set in the base image.

As applying a data set changes the base image it is a good idea to save the changed image under a different filename.

Template — NEW for CS2

philip andrews

07 3444 8675
po box 341, coorparoo
phil@photos.com.au

Data set 2 — NEW for CS2

susan andrews

07 3444 8676
po box 347, coorparoo
susan@photos.com.au

Variables — NEW for CS2

Data set 1

bob andrews

07 3444 8675
po box 341, coorparoo
bob@photos.com.au

Data set 3

jill andrews

07 3444 8672
po box 348, coorparoo
jill@photos.com.au

Variable Data Sets, data driven graphics

Menu: –	
Shortcut: –	**See also:** Variable Data Sets data sets,
Version: CS2	Variable Data Sets define

Data Driven Graphics is a concept that makes it possible to quickly produce an array of versions of a picture or illustration containing different content but using the same basic template.

The feature is based on the idea of building a database of picture components whilst at the same time creating a template of the base graphic with image areas populated with variables rather than pictures. Next the different versions of the graphic are generated in a process where the database pictures replace the variables and then the completed design is exported as separate PSD files.

This feature was previously only available in ImageReady but it now makes an appearance in Photoshop for the first time in CS2.

Creating data-driven illustrations:

To create data driven illustrations start by making a base template with each of the data areas in the composition organized as separate layers in the composition. Next define the variables that will be used for each picture part. Now you can create the data set of images or text that will be substituted into the template. Next you preview the populated template before finally generating the final completed graphics.

Data options:

Photoshop can apply three different data types to a base image: images (pixel based), text and visibility.

Variable Data Sets, data sets

Menu: Image > Variables > Define/Data Sets	
Shortcut: –	**See also:** Variable Data Sets data driven
Version: CS2	graphics, Variable Data Sets define

A data set is a collection of pictures, text and/or visibility settings that is used to create different versions of a base template image.

After defining the variables to be included in a template picture you will need to create several different sets of data. Each data set stores a value (picture, text, visibility setting) for each of the variables in the set.

The data set is defined (each variable linked to a layer in the picture) and then the values added to new data sets via the Variables dialog (Image > Variables > Define/Data Sets).

Variable Data Sets, define

Menu: Image > Variables > Define	
Shortcut: –	**See also:** Variable Data Sets data driven
Version: CS2	graphics, Variable Data Sets data sets

Defining a data set is a process by which layers (1) in the base or template document are linked with a variable type (2) and name (3).

To define this relationship you must first create the base image making separate layers for each image/text part that will be replaced with a piece of data from the data sets. Next select Define from the Image > Variables menu to display the Variables dialog. Now select the name of the layer from the Layer drop-down menu and then pick the variable type (2). All the layers in the template document will be listed.

Depending on the layer you will have a different set of choices here. Text layers can be defined with either Text Replacement or Visibility variables whereas image layers can be associated with either Pixel Replacement or Visibility variables.

Finally, input a name for the variable or use the one suggested by Photoshop.

Once the variables are associated with the template picture then you can move on to creating data sets.

Variable Data Sets, generate

Menu: File > Export > Data Sets As Files
Shortcut: –   **See also:** Variable Data Sets data sets,
Version: CS2   Variable Data Sets define

Once you have created a template file, defined the variables and attached them to template layers and then made some data sets you can generate the data-driven graphics by selecting the Export Data Sets as Files option from the File > Export menu. With the dialog open Select a destination folder and which data set(s) to use in the process. Add some naming details and then press the OK button to generate the pictures.

• •

Variable Data Sets, import

Menu: Image > Variables > Data Sets
Shortcut: –   **See also:** Variable Data Sets data sets,
Version: CS2   Variable Data Sets define

As well as creating data sets inside Photoshop you can also import sets that have been created outside the program. After displaying the Variables dialog (Image > Variables > Data Sets) press the Import button and then set the import options in the dialog that is displayed.

External data sets can be created using a text editor or with a spread sheet program such as Microsoft Excel.

Variations

Menu: Image > Adjustments > Variations
Shortcut: –   **See also:** Color Balance
Version: 6.0, 7.0, CS, CS2

The Variations feature is often used for removing color casts in photographs. It is based on a color wheel, which is made up of the primary colors red, green and blue, and their complementary colors cyan, magenta and yellow.

Increasing the amount of one color in an image automatically decreases its complementary. Put simply, increasing red will decrease cyan, increasing green will reduce magenta and increasing blue will lessen yellow. You can target the color changes so that they only affect a selected group of tones by choosing highlights, midtones or shadows (1).

The strength of the changes is altered with the Fine/Coarse slider (2). In addition the dialog also contains options for adjusting saturation (4) and brightness (3) and previewing clipping (5).

Vector graphics

Menu: –
Shortcut: –   **See also:** Bitmap image
Version: 6.0, 7.0, CS, CS2

Unlike photographs which are constructed of pixels, vector graphics are created with a series of lines and curves that are mathematically designed. Such pictures can be resized and moved with no loss in quality and print with no jagged edges.

Typically pictures created in drawing packages such as Adobe Illustrator are vector based. However, some tools in Photoshop, which is primarily an editor of pixel-based photos, do create vector graphics. The Shape and Type tools use a vector approach in the graphics and layers they create.

Some editing techniques require the conversion of the vector drawings to a bitmap picture. This process is achieved by selecting the layer with vector content and then choosing Layer > Rasterize.

As computer screens display all picture content, both vector and bitmap, as pixelated images, enlarged versions of vector graphics will still show stepped or jagged edges that won't be evident when the picture is printed.

Vector Mask

Menu: Layer > Add Vector Masks
Shortcut: –   **See also:** Masks
Version: 6.0, 7.0, CS, CS2

A vector mask is a hard edged layer mask (1) that can be used like any other mask in Photoshop. Vector masks are often used to create a sharp edged transition when montaging several images together (3).

Unlike standard masks vector masks are not pixel based and so maintain their hard edge even when resized and adjusted. For this reason vector masks are edited using the Shape and Pen tools not pixel-based drawing or painting tools.

Layer styles and effects can be easily applied to layers containing vector masks (2).

Entire layer masks can be created using the Layer > Add Vector Mask > Reveal All and Layer > Add Vector Mask > Hide All commands. The mask can be edited by clicking onto the mask thumbnail in the Layers palette and then drawing on the canvas surface with the Shape or Pen tool.

Version Cue

Menu: –
Shortcut: –   **See also:** Versions
Version: 6.0, 7.0, CS, CS2

Version Cue is an Adobe Creative Suite component program which is designed to manage the design and photographic projects within a workgroup environment.

If you currently share images and design documents around a group of people with each person contributing his or her changes then Version Cue provides the management tools necessary to ensure that changes made in the design process are recorded and tracked.

Two Version Cue file management features that are very useful even for the non-workgrouped user are:

Versions – A feature designed to save and track different versions of the same file. All versions can be viewed in Bridge and any individual version can be promoted in the version stack at any time. This utility is great for managing sequential changes in a project.

Alternates – This option allows you to save a complete copy of the current project at any time. Each copy can then be changed and altered independent of each other providing alternative results from the same file. This feature is great for tracking branching non-sequential changes.

Version Cue is only included when you purchase 'Suite' versions of Adobe products.

Version Cue, project creation

Menu: Bridge: Tools > Version Cue > New Project
Shortcut: –   **See also:** Version Cue
Version: 6.0, 7.0, CS, CS2

The Version Cue program bases most of its features and management tools around a project structure. This means that the first step in employing Version Cue to manage your files is to create a project.

The easiest way to create a new project in Creative Suite 2 (CS2) is from inside Bridge. When Version Cue is installed alongside Bridge and other CS2 components extra Version Cue options become available in the Bridge menus.

To create a new Version Cue project select the New Project option from the Tools > Version Cue menu (1). This action will display the New Project dialog where you can input projects details such as Location, Name and comments as well as make the decision to share or not share access to the project and its associated resources (2).

Versions

Menu: File > Save a Version
Shortcut: – **See also:** Version Cue
Version: CS2

Versions are a very useful feature for dsigners and photographers who create multiple editions of the same image or design. The feature allows you to use the File > Save a Version option from inside Photoshop. Next a Save a Version dialog is displayed (3). The window contains all the details for the picture as well as a space for you to enter comments about the version you are saving. After clicking the Save button the latest version of the file is then saved and displayed in the standard thumbnail view in Bridge but when the workspace is switched to the Versions and Alternates View all the previous iterations of the design are also shown.

Alternatively, right clicking on the picture and selecting the Versions option (1) from the pop-up menu displays just the versions available for the selected image (2).

The version feature is only available when Version Cue is installed.

Vertical Type tool

Menu: –
Shortcut: T **See also:** Horizontal Type
Version: 6.0, 7.0, CS, CS2 tool

Along with the traditional Horizontal Type option, Photoshop also provides a Vertical Type tool that arranges the letters on top of each other rather than side by side.

Located in the same fly-out menu as the other Type tool options (1), the Vertical Type tool aligns the type according to the starting placement of the cursor (insert point) and the alignment option (2) selection in the options bar.

The top align option adds letter shapes above the insertion point, the bottom align below the insertion point and the center align places the text so that it straddles the insertion point.

Video filters

Menu: Filter > Video
Shortcut: – **See also:** Filters, De-interlace filter
Version: 6.0, 7.0, CS, CS2

Photoshop contains two specialist filters designed to alleviate common problems encountered when working with images that have been grabbed from video footage.

Listed under the Filter > Video menu the options are:

De-interlace – This filter is used to replace the missing picture detail that exists in captured video frames. It does this by either interpolating the pixels or duplicating the ones surrounding the area. Interpolation provides the smoothest results and Duplication the sharpest. The filter is not applied via the Filter Gallery dialog but rather has its own specific dialog that contains the Interpolation option.

NTSC Colors – The NTSC Colors filter ensures that the colors in the image will fit within the range of hues available for the NTSC television format. This sometimes means that the color gamut of the original image is compressed to ensure that no single hue is oversaturated when displayed via the television system.

Video Preview

Menu: Enhance > Adjust Lighting > Levels	
Shortcut: Ctrl/Cmd Alt/Opt Shft L	**See also:** Curves, Shadow/
Version: CS2	Highlight

The Video Preview option (1) is designed to export a preview image to an external video monitor. This option provides the chance for makers of video destined files to review their creations in a format that they were intended for.

After selecting the feature the Video Preview dialog appears (2). The options here allow you to choose and adjust settings for the external device (monitor) and Image.

View

Menu: View >	
Shortcut: –	**See also:** Curves, Shadow/
Version: 6.0, 7.0, CS, CS2	Highlight

The View menu in Photoshop contains a variety of options that control the way your image is displayed on screen. Also included in this menu are settings for the display of grids, guides, slices and proofing setups.

The Screen Mode settings (1) provide three different views of the workspace and can be coupled with the Tab shortcut option to hide palettes, tool and option bars to display the picture on a clear uncluttered background.

Vivid Light blending mode

Menu: –	
Shortcut: –	**See also:** Blend modes
Version: 6.0, 7.0, CS, CS2	

The Vivid Light blending mode is one of the group of Overlay modes that base their effects on the differences between the two pictures.

This option combines the effects of both Color Burn and Color Dodge modes in the one feature. The effect is created by increasing or decreasing the contrast depending on the brightness of the top layer. If the tones are lighter than 50% then the picture is lightened by decreasing the contrast. If the top layer tones are darker than 50% then the picture is darkened by increasing the contrast.

The overall result is more contrasty and there is no effect if the top layer is 50% gray.

Full Screen Mode plus Tab key

Standard Screen Mode

Full Screen Mode with Menu Bar

Full Screen Mode

After

Warp

Menu: Edit > Transform > Warp	
Shortcut: –	**See also:** Transform again
Version: CS2	

The Warp feature is a new image transformation option that makes its debut in CS2. Using this feature it is possible to distort an image layer in similar ways that the Warp Text option manipulates text layers.

Select the layer to warp and then choose the Warp type from the preset entries in the drop-down menu in the tool's options bar (1). Alternatively you can select the Custom option and then interactively push and pull the warp grid (2) to manipulate the picture yourself.

Warp Text command

Menu: –		
Shortcut: T		**See also:** Type
Version: 6.0, 7.0, CS, CS2		

One of the special features of the Photoshop type system is the 'Warping' option.

This tool forces text to distort to one of a range of shapes. An individual word, or even whole sentences, can be made to curve, bulge or even simulate the effect of a fish-eye lens.

The button (1) for the option is found on the options bar of the Type tool. The feature's dialog contains a drop-down menu list of styles (2) and a choice between vertical and horizontal warping (3). The strength and style of the effect can be controlled by manipulating the bend, horizontal and vertical distortion sliders (4).

This feature is particularly useful when creating graphic headings for posters or web pages.

Before

After

Warp tool, Liquify filter

Menu: Filter > Distort > Liquify
Shortcut: W (in Liquify) **See also:** Liquify filter
Version: 6.0, 7.0, CS, CS2

The Warp tool is one of the specialized tools in the Liquify filter. The Warp tool is used to push pixels as you move the cursor.

After selecting the tool from the top left of the dialog carefully drag the cursor over the canvas surface. Use the Reconstruct tool to repair areas where the warping effect is too great.

The example shows how easily an existing photo can be drastically changed by warping specific picture parts.

The area that is pushed is determined by the brush size on the right of the dialog. To make gradual rather than abrupt changes use a lower brush pressure. To warp along a straight edge click to start the line and then Shift-click to mark the end.

Water Paper filter

Menu: Filter > Sketch > Water Paper
Shortcut: – **See also:** Filters
Version: 6.0, 7.0, CS, CS2

The Water Paper filter, as one of the group of Sketch filters, simulates the look of the photo being painted on a very wet textured watercolor paper. The edges of the picture are very soft and with some details lost altogether. The colors and shapes blend into each other and, in contrast to these parts, occasionally the sharp texture of the paper shows through.

The dialog contains three controls that adjust the tone and texture effects. The top slider, Fiber Length (1), alters the sharpness and clarity of the painted image. Low values create a sharper picture with more of the original details preserved. The Brightness slider (2) works like a standard brightness control. High values produce a brighter picture, low values a darker one. The final setting, the Contrast slider (3), determines the overall contrast of the final result.

Watercolor filter

Menu: Filter > Artistic > Watercolor
Shortcut: – **See also:** Filters
Version: 6.0, 7.0, CS, CS2

The Watercolor filter, as one of the group of Artistic filters, adds both texture and brush stroke effects to the photo.

The dialog contains three controls that adjust the painting and texture effects. The top slider, Brush Detail (1), alters the look of the painted areas. The Shadow Intensity slider (2) controls how much of the picture is converted to darker tones. High values mean more of the picture is shadowed. The final setting, the Texture slider (3), determines how detailed the painted areas of the picture will be.

W

© www.ablestock.com 2005

Watermarks

Menu: Filter > Digimarc > Read Watermark
Shortcut: –   **See also:** –
Version: 6.0, 7.0, CS, CS2

Digital watermarks are slight, almost imperceptible, changes that are made to pictures to store copyright and author's details within the image.

Photoshop has the ability to embed (very basic versions), detect and read the digimarc.com style of watermarks. These are created and added to images either by the stand-alone software provided by the company or via filter plug-ins in programs like Photoshop or Photoshop Elements.

To check to see if a picture you are editing is watermarked, select Filter > Digimarc > Read Watermark (1). Marked pictures will then display a pop-up dialog with author's details and a linked website where further details of use can be obtained (2).

To embed a simple watermark select Filter > Digimarc > Embed Watermark and then select the options to include (3).

Note: The example pop-up dialog shown here is in demo mode. Registered users of the Digimarc system can mark their pictures with more extensive information including name, address, e-mail and URL personal details.

Wave filter

Menu: Filter > Distort > Wave
Shortcut: –   **See also:** Filters
Version: 6.0, 7.0, CS, CS2

The Wave filter, as one of the group of Distort filters, breaks up the picture by pushing and pulling the pixels in the form of a series of vertical and horizontal waves. The end results can be subtle or extreme depending on the settings used.

The dialog contains several controls that are used to adjust the wave-like pattern created on the picture surface. These include wavelength, amplitude, scale and number of wave generators (1). The effects of different settings for these controls can be previewed in the accompanying thumbnail (2).

Web Photo Gallery

Menu: File > Automate > Web Photo Gallery
   Bridge: Tools > Photoshop > Web Photo Gallery
Shortcut: –   **See also:** Automate
Version: 6.0, 7.0, CS, CS2

The Web Photo Gallery wizard is an automated feature that takes a group of pictures that have been multi-selected in Bridge and transforms them into a fully functioning website in a matter of a few minutes.

Folders of pictures or images currently open in the Photoshop workspace are used as the source photos when the feature is selected from within Photoshop.

Photoshop ships with a variety of gallery templates which can be selected and previewed from inside the dialog.

The text included in the gallery along with picture size and quality and site colors and security options are set via the controls included in the tabbed section of the dialog.

Most templates produce a gallery site that includes thumbnail and feature sized photos. Many contain a main or index page, a series of thumbnails (1) and a page for each image containing a larger gallery or feature picture (2).

237

Web Safe Colors

Menu: Window > Color Swatches
Shortcut: –   **See also:** GIF format
Version: 6.0, 7.0, CS, CS2

The Web Safe set of colors are a group of 216 colors that can be accurately displayed by both Macintosh and Windows systems.

Constructing your image of, or converting existing hues to, these colors will guarantee that they display predictably as part of a website on any computer system.

The Swatches palette (1) will display all the Web Safe Colors when the option is selected from the pop-up menu that is displayed when the side-arrow button (2) is pressed.

When choosing colors with the Color Picker a small cube icon indicates the selected hue is not a web safe color. Click the cube to get Photoshop to find a web safe color that is nearest your choice (3).

When converting photos to the GIF format using the Save for Web feature you can elect to use the Web Safe palette (Restrictive option) for the conversion (4).

Welcome Screen

Menu: Help > Welcome Screen
Shortcut: –   **See also:** –
Version: 6.0, 7.0, CS, CS2

When Photoshop is first opened, the user is presented with a Welcome Screen containing several options.

The selections are broken into two different sections. One detailing what is new in this version of the program and the second listing available tutorials.

To stop the screen displaying each time the program is opened deselect the Show this dialog at startup setting in the bottom left of the screen. The feature can be displayed at any time by selecting Help > Welcome Screen.

Below is a list of the Welcome Screen options for version CS2 of the program:

- New features at a glance
- New feature highlights
- See it in action (video clips)
- Learn the basics
- Advanced techniques
- Working with what's new

Wet edges

Menu: Window > Brushes
Shortcut: –   **See also:** Brushes palette
Version: 6.0, 7.0, CS, CS2

Wet Edges is one of the brush characteristics that can be customized in Photoshop. The effect simulates the look of accumulated paint (and therefore density of color and tone) that builds up at the edges of a wet pool of water color paint (4).

The dominance of the effect is determined by the hardness setting of the current brush tip. Low hardness settings such as 30% (1) produce a more pronounced result than those brush tips that are 100% hard (2).

The effect is activated by selecting the Wet Edges option in the Brushes palette (3).

W

White Balance, Raw

Menu: –
Shortcut: –   See also: Camera Raw
Version: 6.0, 7.0, CS, CS2

One of the real advantages of recording your photos in the Raw format is the ability to edit the white balance settings used for the pictures later on at the desktop. Though the setting used to capture the image is recorded as part of the EXIF data you can elect to fine tune this setting or even disregard it all together selecting a different setting to associate with the picture.

The White Balance option in the Camera Raw dialog (1) provides a series of preset options designed to match specific light sources. As well as these set options the Temperature and Tint sliders allow users to customise their white balance settings for a given image.

Controlling the white balance setting is one way to remove color casts in your photographs. Alternatively, intentionally choosing the wrong setting can be used to create dramatically different versions of your pictures as well.

WIA support

Menu: –
Shortcut: –   See also: Import command
Version: 6.0, 7.0, CS, CS2

The process of downloading pictures from your digital camera to the computer requires the installation of camera drivers before the transfer can begin.

Installing the software that came bundled with your camera usually also takes care of installing the drivers. Many cameras use a WIA or Windows Image Acquisition driver to connect to software that resides on the computer.

Both Photoshop and Windows XP make use of WIA drivers to communicate with a range of installed devices.

This feature has largely replaced the older TWAIN import option found on earlier versions of Photoshop.

Wind filter

Menu: Filter > Stylize > Wind
Shortcut: –   See also: Filters
Version: 6.0, 7.0, CS, CS2

The Wind filter, as one of the group of Stylize filters, simulates the look of wind blasting across the canvas surface by adding trailing lines from the edge details.

The dialog contains two controls, Method of type of wind (1) and Direction (2). A preview window is also supplied to help you judge the correct combination of settings for your photo.

Work Paths, converting selections to

Menu: –
Shortcut: –   See also: Paths, Selections
Version: 6.0, 7.0, CS, CS2

Many imaging workers steer away from creating paths because they feel that the tools needed to create and edit them (Pen and Direct Selection tools) are difficult and confusing to use. These same workers on the other hand often have no problem with using the various selection tools to create very sophisticated selections.

If you fall into this category and need to create a path quickly and easily then the best approach is to start by making a selection (1). Next display the Paths palette and then click on the Make Work Path from Selection button (3) at the bottom of the palette.

This automatically converts the selection to a path and places a thumbnail version of the path in the palette (2).

Workgroup

Menu: –
Shortcut: –   See also: Version Cue
Version: CS, CS2

As part of the process of creating a new project in Version Cue you have the option of allowing the project and its associated media assets with others in your network (1). Typically the group of users who collaboratively work on a common project is called a Workgroup.

Determining who has access and at what level this access is granted is managed via the Version Cue administration utility. Here the administrator of the project can add new users and alter their access settings (2).

> Version Cue is only avaiable to Creative Suite users.

Working spaces, ICC profile

Menu: –
Shortcut: –   See also: Color settings
Version: 6.0, 7.0, CS, CS2

Unlike print, monitor, camera or scanner profiles, a working profile or space is not linked to specific input or output characteristics. Instead a working space acts as an intermediate profile that provides a base for editing and enhancing picture colors and tones and also establishes a known reference point for these tones and colors when converting to other output specific spaces.

The ICC profile that you choose to use as your working space should reflect the requirements of the area that you work in the most. For instance, many photographers whose work is destined for the printed page choose to use the AdobeGB profile as their working space feeling that this space best suits their work environment. In contrast web designers often prefer to use sRGB as their working space as it reflects the characteristics of screen-based display more easily than other choices.

The options in the Edit > Color Settings dialog allows you to set the working spaces that will be used in Photoshop for RGB, CMYK, Gray and Spot (color) pictures. Also in this dialog are controls (Color Management Policies) that govern how Photoshop handles opening pictures that are not tagged or tagged with a profile that is different to the one nominated for the working space.

W

NEW for CS2

Workspace, Bridge

Menu: Bridge: Window > Workspace
Shortcut: Ctrl/Cmd F1 – F5   **See also:** Workspace customize,
Version: CS2   Workspace Photoshop

The way that your photos are displayed in Bridge can be altered via the options listed under the Window > Workspace menu (1). Here you can choose from four set workspace settings plus a reset setting or choose to save the current workspace as a custom setting.

File Navigator workspace

Filmstrip Focus workspace

Lightbox workspace

Metadata Focus workspace

W

Workspace, Customize

Menu: Window > Workspace > Save Workspace
       Bridge: Window > Workspace > Save Workspace
Shortcut: –   **See also:** Workspace Bridge, Workspace
Version: CS2   Photoshop

Both Photoshop and Bridge contain options to customize and save specific workspace setups. When a workspace is saved the custom setting is added to the list of available workspaces that is displayed in the Window> Workspace menu (1).

To create your own custom space in Photoshop or Bridge start by adjusting the size and position of interface components such as palettes and panels. Next select the Save Workspace option from the Window > Workspace menu and then enter the name and select the options to save in the Save Workspace dialog (2).

Photoshop CS2 has the additional benefit of being able to customize the keyboard shortcuts associated with the space and the appearance and contents of menus as well. This is achieved via the Keyboard Shortcuts & Menus dialog.

NEW for CS2

Workspace, Photoshop

Menu: Window > Workspace
Shortcut: –   **See also:** Workspace customize,
Version: CS2   Workspace Bridge

Photoshop ships with a range of preinstalled workspaces (1) which can be located listed under the Window > Workspace menu. Each of these settings controls the appearance and position of palettes, the allocation of keyboard shortcuts as well as the appearance of menu items.

Also listed in this menu are entries for resetting the workspace and saving customized workspace settings that suit your individual way of working.

Customized spaces are created by adjusting the settings in the Keyboard Shortcuts & Menus dialog (2) and arranging palettes before saving the setup via the Window > Workspace > Save Workspace option.

The newly created workspace then becomes a separated entry at the bottom of the Workspace menu.

XMP

Menu: –
Shortcut: –   **See also:** XMP sidecar files
Version: 6.0, 7.0, CS, CS2

XMP is short for Extensible Metadata Platform which is a metadata standard that Adobe built to house the information that relates to your picture files.

Information such as author, camera, resolution, color space and keywords are all stored in this format and for the most part the details are saved within the picture file itself, but when this is not possible the data is included in a separated sidecar file.

The presence of this information makes searching, sorting and managing of your pictures much easier as XMP is a key technology used in many features in Bridge and other applications in Adobe's Creative Suite 2.

The XMP detail that is linked to your files can be viewed in Photoshop via the File > File Info dialog (1) or by displaying the Metadata panel (2) in Bridge (View > Metadata Panel).

XMP is not the only metadata that can be stored with your files. Details may also be attached in EXIF, GPS and IPTC formats. When this occurs Adobe applications such as Photoshop and Bridge synchronize and describe this metadata in XMP in order to ensure better integration with applications features.

XMP sidecar files

Menu: –
Shortcut: –   **See also:** XMP
Version: 6.0, 7.0, CS, CS2

In some situations a portion of the XMP-based metadata that is stored with a picture is not saved in the file itself. Instead the information is stored in an XMP file that is saved with the original photograph (1). This extra file is called an XMP sidecar file (2).

One example of the use of sidecar files is the settings changes made when processing a file in the Camera Raw feature. The user can elect to save these changes settings in the original file or with the file in a sidecar format. Where the detail is stored can be set in the preferences for the feature which can be selected via the preferences entry in the pop-up menu displayed by pressing the side arrow next to the Settings menu in the Camera Raw dialog.

ZigZag filter

Menu: Filter > Distort > ZigZag
Shortcut: –   **See also:** Filters
Version: 6.0, 7.0, CS, CS2

The ZigZag filter, as one of the group of Distort filters, simulates up and down waves such as pond ripples.

The dialog contains controls that adjust the style and intensity of the effect. The Amount slider (1) alters the strength of the ripple effect, which basically translates to the depth and height of the resultant waves. Low values create shallower, more subtle effects, higher numbers produce more dramatic results.

The Ridges slider (2) increases or decreases the number of ridges used in the effect.

Three different types of ZigZag filtration are available from the drop-down Style menu (3) – Pond ripples, Out from the center and Around the center.

Also included is a simulated preview window, where the filter is applied to a wire frame representation of your picture (4).

Zoom In/Zoom Out

Menu: View > Zoom In/Zoom Out
Shortcut: Ctrl/Cmd =   **See also:** Zoom tool,
Ctrl/Cmd -   Navigator
Version: 6.0, 7.0, CS, CS2

The View > Zoom In/Zoom out menu options magnify and reduce the size of the onscreen image in a way that is similar to the Zoom tool.

Each selection of the menu item (or keystroke combination) changes the magnification of the image by set increments between a minimum of 1 pixel (usually less than 1%) and a maximum of 1600%.

Zoom tool

Menu: –
Shortcut: Z   **See also:** Match Zoom,
Version: 6.0, 7.0, CS, CS2   Navigator

The Zoom tool is used to adjust the magnification of your picture on screen.

After selecting the tool from the toolbar, choose a mode, Zoom In (1) or Zoom Out (2), from the settings in the options bar. Next click onto the picture part that you want to magnify, or make smaller. The onscreen image will increase, or decrease, in size and the magnification value will be displayed in the title bar of the document window (3).

Sections of a picture can be zoomed to fit the width of the program's workspace by click-dragging a zoom marquee around the area to be enlarged. Automatically the selected area is enlarged to fit the workspace.

Zoomed in view

Standard view

ZoomView files

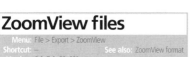

Menu: File > Export > ZoomView
Shortcut: –   **See also:** ZoomView format
Version: 6.0, 7.0, CS, CS2

The Export to ZoomView feature allows image makers to save their pictures in an innovative high resolution web deliverable format that allows both panning and zooming from within the browser window.

To convert your pictures to the viewpoint format open the file in Photoshop and then select File > Export > ZoomView (1). The Viewpoint ZoomView save dialog is then displayed (2). Choose to include instructions with the web page (3), select the location where the ZoomView files will be saved, input the base filename, allocate a tile size and level of quality and the dimensions that the picture window will be when displayed in a browser and click OK.

The feature creates two folders and two associated files including the main page or html file (4).

ZoomView format

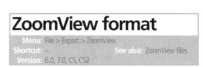

Menu: File > Export > ZoomView
Shortcut: –   **See also:** ZoomView files
Version: 6.0, 7.0, CS, CS2

The ZoomView file format is designed for delivering high resolution images over the internet.

Photoshop users can convert their pictures into this format by selecting the File > Export > ZoomView feature.

Pictures in this format can only be displayed when the free Viewpoint media player (www.viewpoint Media) is installed (1). Once installed the user can then zoom and pan high resolution photographs that have been saved in the ZoomView format.

Default Keyboard Shortcuts

Command	Shortcut
File	
New...	Ctrl/Cmd+N
Open...	Ctrl/Cmd+O
Browse...	Alt/Opt+Ctrl/Cmd+O
	Shift+Ctrl/Cmd+O
Open As...	Alt/Opt+Shift+Ctrl/Cmd+O
Edit in ImageReady	Shift+Ctrl/Cmd+M
Close	Ctrl/Cmd+W
Close All	Alt/Opt+Ctrl/Cmd+W
Close and Go To Bridge...	Shift+Ctrl/Cmd+W
Save	Ctrl/Cmd+S
Save As...	Shift+Ctrl/Cmd+S
	Alt/Opt+Ctrl/Cmd+S
Save for Web...	Alt/Opt+Shift+Ctrl/Cmd+S
Revert	F12
File Info...	Alt/Opt+Shift+Ctrl/Cmd+I
Page Setup...	Shift+Ctrl/Cmd+P
Print with Preview...	Alt/Opt+Ctrl/Cmd+P
Print...	Ctrl/Cmd+P
Print One Copy	Alt/Opt+Shift+Ctrl/Cmd+P
Exit	Ctrl/Cmd+Q
Edit	
Undo/Redo	Ctrl/Cmd+Z
Step Forward	Shift+Ctrl/Cmd+Z
Step Backward	Alt/Opt+Ctrl/Cmd+Z
Fade...	Shift+Ctrl/Cmd+F
Cut	Ctrl/Cmd+X
	F2
Copy	Ctrl/Cmd+C
	F3
Copy Merged	Shift+Ctrl/Cmd+C
Paste	Ctrl/Cmd+V
	F4
Paste Into	Shift+Ctrl/Cmd+V
Fill...	Shift+F5
Free Transform	Ctrl/Cmd+T
Transform>	
Again	Shift+Ctrl/Cmd+T
Color Settings...	Shift+Ctrl/Cmd+K
Keyboard Shortcuts...	Alt/Opt+Shift+Ctrl/Cmd+K
Menus...	Alt/Opt+Shift+Ctrl/Cmd+M
General...	Ctrl/Cmd+K

Image

Adjustments>

Levels...	Ctrl/Cmd+L
Auto Levels	Shift+Ctrl/Cmd+L
Auto Contrast	Alt/Opt+Shift+Ctrl/Cmd+L
Auto Color	Shift+Ctrl/Cmd+B
Curves...	Ctrl/Cmd+M
Color Balance...	Ctrl/Cmd+B
Hue/Saturation...	Ctrl/Cmd+U
Desaturate	Shift+Ctrl/Cmd+U
Invert	Ctrl/Cmd+I
Image Size...	Alt/Opt+Ctrl/Cmd+I
Canvas Size...	Alt/Opt+Ctrl/Cmd+C

Layer

New>

Layer...	Shift+Ctrl/Cmd+N
Layer via Copy	Ctrl/Cmd+J
Layer via Cut	Shift+Ctrl/Cmd+J
Create/Release Clipping Mask	Alt/Opt+Ctrl/Cmd+G
Group Layers	Ctrl/Cmd+G
Ungroup Layers	Shift+Ctrl/Cmd+G

Arrange>

Bring to Front	Shift+Ctrl/Cmd+]
Bring Forward	Ctrl/Cmd+]
Send Backward	Ctrl/Cmd+[
Send to Back	Shift+Ctrl/Cmd+[
Merge Layers	Ctrl/Cmd+E
Merge Visible	Shift+Ctrl/Cmd+E

Select

All	Ctrl/Cmd+A
Deselect	Ctrl/Cmd+D
Reselect	Shift+Ctrl/Cmd+D
Inverse	Shift+Ctrl/Cmd+I
	Shift+F7
All Layers	Alt/Opt+Ctrl/Cmd+A
Feather...	Alt/Opt+Ctrl/Cmd+D

Filter

Last Filter	Ctrl/Cmd+F
Extract...	Alt/Opt+Ctrl/Cmd+X
Liquify...	Shift+Ctrl/Cmd+X
Pattern Maker...	Alt/Opt+Shift+Ctrl/Cmd+X
Vanishing Point...	Alt/Opt+Ctrl/Cmd+V

View

Proof Colors	Ctrl/Cmd+Y
Gamut Warning	Shift+Ctrl/Cmd+Y
Zoom In	Ctrl/Cmd++
	Ctrl/Cmd+=
Zoom Out	Ctrl/Cmd+-
Fit on Screen	Ctrl/Cmd+0
Actual Pixels	Alt/Opt+Ctrl/Cmd+0
Extras	Ctrl/Cmd+H

Show>

Target Path	Shift+Ctrl/Cmd+H
Grid	Ctrl/Cmd+'
Guides	Ctrl/Cmd+;
Rulers	Ctrl/Cmd+R
Snap	Shift+Ctrl/Cmd+;
Lock Guides	Alt/Opt+Ctrl/Cmd+;
Actions	Alt/Opt+F9
	F9
Brushes	F5
Color	F6
Info	F8
Layers	F7

Help

Photoshop Help	F1

History

Step Forward	Shift+Ctrl/Cmd+Z
Step Backward	Alt/Opt+Ctrl/Cmd+Z

Layers

New Layer...	Shift+Ctrl/Cmd+N
Create/Release Clipping Mask	Alt/Opt+Ctrl/Cmd+G
Merge Layers	Ctrl/Cmd+E
Merge Visible	Shift+Ctrl/Cmd+E

Tool Presets

Tools	Shortcut	Tools	Shortcut
Rectangular Marquee Tool	M	Vertical Type Mask Tool	T
Elliptical Marquee Tool	M	Pen Tool	P
Move Tool	V	Freeform Pen Tool	P
Lasso Tool	L	Rectangle Tool	U
Polygonal Lasso Tool	L	Rounded Rectangle Tool	U
Magnetic Lasso Tool	L	Ellipse Tool	U
Magic Wand Tool	W	Polygon Tool	U
Crop Tool	C	Line Tool	U
Slice Tool	K	Custom Shape Tool	U
Slice Select Tool	K	Notes Tool	N
Spot Healing Brush Tool	J	Audio Annotation Tool	N
Healing Brush Tool	J	Eyedropper Tool	I
Patch Tool	J	Color Sampler Tool	I
Red Eye Tool	J	Measure Tool	I
Brush Tool	B	Hand Tool	H
Pencil Tool	B	Zoom Tool	Z
Color Replacement Tool	B	Default Foreground/ Background Colors	D
Clone Stamp Tool	S	Switch Foreground/ Background Colors	X
Pattern Stamp Tool	S		
History Brush Tool	Y	Toggle Standard/Quick Mask Modes	Q
Art History Brush	Y		
Eraser Tool	E	Toggle Screen Modes	F
Background Eraser Tool	E	Toggle Preserve Transparency	/
Magic Eraser Tool	E	Decrease Brush Size	[
Gradient Tool	G	Increase Brush Size	]
Paint Bucket Tool	G	Decrease Brush Hardness	{
Blur Tool	R	Increase Brush Hardness	}
Sharpen Tool	R	Previous Brush	,
Smudge Tool	R	Next Brush	.
Dodge Tool	O	First Brush	<
Burn Tool	O	Last Brush	>
Sponge Tool	O		
Path Selection Tool	A		
Direct Selection Tool	A		
Horizontal Type Tool	T		
Vertical Type Tool	T		
Horizontal Type Mask Tool	T		

More great titles by Philip Andrews...

Do you need more information on Photoshop, Photoshop Elements or general photography? Do you crave for extra tips and techniques? Do you want all these things but presented in a no nonsense understandable format?

Well Philip Andrews is one of the world's most published photography and imaging authors and with the following titles he can extend your skills and understanding even further.

Photoshop® CS2: Essential Skills

"...excellent coverage of Photoshop as a digital darkroom tool as well as covering a truly amazing amount of background information." Mark Lewis, Director of Technology Training, Mount Saint Mary College, USA

- Put theoretical knowledge into a creative context with this comprehensive text packed with original student assignments and a supporting CD-ROM
- Discover the fundamental skills vital for quality image manipulation and benefit from the highly structured learning approach!
- CD-ROM and dedicated website – *www.photoshopessentialskills.com*

ISBN: 0 240 52000 9 – $32.95 / £21.99 – Paperback – 384pp

Langford's Starting Photography
A guide to better pictures for film and digital camera users

"...full of information to help beginners become more familiar with their cameras and improve their technique." What Digital Camera magazine, UK

- Practical and user-friendly guide to get you started fast whether using film or digital photography for your image making
- Lavishly illustrated each step of the way with beautiful color images to show what you can achieve and to inspire your imagination

ISBN: 0 240 51967 1 – $31.95 / £15.99 – Paperback – 304pp

Adobe® Photoshop® Elements 3.0
A visual introduction to digital imaging

"...an unrivalled introduction to the budget imaging package, and an excellent overview of digital imaging." What Digital Camera magazine, UK

- Save valuable time with this successful, jargon-free introduction to digital imaging
- Real-life examples
- Fully updated to cover all the new Elements 3.0 features
- Clearly shows you how to put each technique into practice
- Full color, high quality illustrations visualize what can be achieved with this successful package
- Dedicated website full of resources and video tutorials – *www.guide2elements.com*

ISBN: 0 240 51958 2 – $29.95 / £18.99 – Paperback – 352pp

Adobe® Photoshop® Elements 3.0 A–Z
Tools and features illustrated ready reference

"...with Adobe Photoshop Elements A–Z at your side you will be up to speed in no time." Don Day, Photoshop Elements QE, Adobe Systems Inc.

- Discover and master the tools and features in Photoshop Elements 3.0 with this comprehensive, beautifully illustrated full color guide
- Save valuable time when trying to understand a function or tool – simply dip in and find the listing in this easy-to-use A–Z format
- Learn tool and feature tips and best practice from a professional photographer and Elements guru!
- Dedicated website full of resources and video tutorials – *www.elementsa-z.com*

ISBN: 0 240 51989 2 – $24.95 / £15.99 – Paperback – 192pp

Advanced Photoshop® Elements for Digital Photographers

"...a beautifully rendered and compellingly written exploration of the advanced features and techniques that can be accomplished with Photoshop Elements." Mike Leavy, Engineering Manager for Photoshop Elements, Adobe Systems, Inc.

- Provides tips from a pro to advance your Elements skills beyond the basics
- Step-by-step, color illustrated tutorials show you what can be achieved
- Full workflow coverage, includes digital cameras and web work
- Dedicated website full of resources and video tutorials – *www.adv-elements.com*

ISBN: 0 240 51940 X – $29.95 / £19.99 – Paperback – 288pp